No More Nice Girls

N☼ MORE

Countercultural
Essays

Ellen Willis

NICE GIRLS

Wesleyan University Press

Published by University Press of New England

Hanover and London

WESLEYAN UNIVERSITY PRESS

Published by University Press of New England,

Hanover, NH 03755

©1992 by Ellen Willis

All rights reserved

Permissions appear on page 275

Printed in the United States of America 5 4 3 2

CIP data appear at the end of the book

For Stanley

Contents

Acknowledgments

Thanks to:

Stanley Aronowitz, critic, sounding-board, and intellectual companion par excellence;

Karen Durbin, who edited some of the pieces in this book and inspired others;

my abortion rights zap group No More Nice Girls, the infamous Barnard Conference Planning Committee, and other advocates of feminist sexual revolution whose ideas about sex, gender, and feminism have influenced and challenged my own, with special appreciation to Ann Snitow, C. Carr, Carole Vance, and Alice Echols;

Janet Gallagher and Lynn Paltrow, whose research on fetal rights law informs "From Forced Pregnancy to Forced Surgery";

Jim Miller, who asked me to write an essay on "excess" for *Salmagundi*'s special issue on the '60s, an idea with my name on it but one I hadn't thought of;

Charlotte Sheedy and Regula Noetzli, my agents, who take an expansive view of their job.

Introduction: Identity Crisis

Last year I attended a feminist conference in Dubrovnik, Yugoslavia, amid preliminary rumblings of the civil war that would break up the country and mutilate the city in the name of nationalism. The conference, which brought women from all over Eastern Europe and the United States, was the first gathering of its kind in the East, a historic event. We introduced ourselves by name and place. For the women of what was still officially Yugoslavia, this was no casual moment; their various self-identifications were deliberate and pointed: "Yugoslavia"; "Croatia"; "Ljubljana"; "Europe." Most of the rest spoke as unproblematic Poles, Bulgarians, Americans and so on. But when it was my turn I said, "New York."

I recalled this scene months later, as I sat reading the *New York Times Book Review*. Ensconced in morning torpidity, dosing it with coffee, I came upon Morton Kondracke's review of two books by conservative sociologist Paul Hollander about the reactions of the American left to the fall of Communism. I woke up right away. In the first paragraph Kondracke lays out his (and presumably Hollander's) basic assumption: that finding systemic flaws in American society (racism and sexism are mentioned specifically) is equivalent to hating America and defending Communist dictatorships—in other words, any and every form of radical social dissidence is, for Americans, both self-hating and totalitarian. Now that the Cold War is won, Kondracke's tone as much as his words suggests, it's time for a mopping-up operation against the domestic collaborators, in the form of "a political and intellectual reckoning" with unrepentant Communist sympathizers "and their soul mates" (!) still spewing their poison—where else?—"on college campuses, from pulpits, and in books and magazines." "No one should be lined up against a wall," he ominously assures the reader, in a maneuver known to psychotherapists as the gratuitous denial. And a few lines later, "The First Amendment protects their right to rant, but the rest of us have a right to question their premises."

Since liberal, let alone radical, premises have already been the target of a decade-long jihad, it is hardly paranoid to wonder what beyond intellectual wrist-slapping Kondracke might have in mind (perhaps those colleges, churches, and publishers should stop giving aid and comfort?). But the real giveaway is his rhetoric of us and them. There I was, reading the mainstream book review of record, like thousands of other people of varying political persuasions, yet I was not part of its audience as this writer conceived it—I was at best an eavesdropper on a conversation in which "the rest of us" were engaged at my expense, just as if the *NYTBR* were, say, the *Conservative Digest*. In this peculiar role I nonetheless kept reading, till I got to Kondracke's parting shot: "And, one should note, for all their raving against America, few America-haters ever leave." That was when I thought of Dubrovnik. "Some of us left years ago," I muttered. "We live in New York."

For my generation, formed equally by the liberating exuberance of rock and roll and the imperial brutality of Vietnam, the question of where we stood on America was inescapable. Was this nation (it!) the enemy, tyrannical abroad, hopelessly racist at home, and in the process of choking to death on a glut of consumer goods? Or were we (we!), however corrupted by various forms of power, still the source of a vital democratic impulse that fed cultural dissidence and subverted authoritarian values all over the world? I took the latter position, and through the '60s and '70s, exploring its paradoxes was a central concern of my writing. The essays in this book are different. While all of them are, in one way or another, about American cultural politics, the question of what it means to be American, as a cultural and political identity, rarely arises—and when it does, it's in the context of loss. There is, for instance, my obituary of Andy Warhol, which is also, in a sense, an obituary for an American moment; or my comment on the Challenger disaster, another resonant death. And then there is "Escape from New York," a piece about a transcontinental bus trip I took in the pre-Reagan summer of 1980.

I didn't make up the title, but the editor who thought of it must have been aware of its irony. My trip had been a counterphobic move to combat my impulses toward isolation and connect with some larger community; after many ambivalent encounters I had escaped to New York, relieved to be back yet uneasy, knowing that while isolation could be an act of will, connection was a more complicated matter. Through my account of meetings and failed meetings with friends and strangers runs the contrapuntal theme of my tentative and wary involvement with a new lover back home. I see the piece as a parable about the end of the '70s, the exhaustion of the counterculture and its utopian version of the American dream, the beginning of a relentlessly privatized age. Granted that this interpretation comes long after the fact—at the time I wasn't sure what this odd mess of material amounted to—I think my unconscious knew what it was doing.

The New York versus America subtext also proved prophetic. My sense of national identity had depended on a conviction that America as a real and imagined collectivity had room for people like me, that indeed we affirmed and expanded its promise—a notion that seemed increasingly quixotic, perhaps even delusional, as the '80s wore on. Though as far back as the 1975 fiscal crisis I had begun to think of New York as a colony ("We are being governed by a junta of bankers," I wrote at one point), as late as the summer of my bus trip I was arguing that polls or no polls, Ronald Reagan would not win the election because "The American people aren't ready for this guy." To stretch my metaphor a bit further, it turned out that as far as the American trip was concerned, I was off the bus. After Reagan's 1984 landslide, my friend Ann Snitow noted in *The Village Voice* that she knew very few people who had voted for him. "What does this say about me?" she mused. I knew no one at all who had voted for him, and I had a pretty good idea of what that said about me.

Even now that the Morning-in-America a/k/a New-World-Order coach is wandering aimlessly, getting lower and lower on gas while the passengers yell and throw spitballs at the driver (when they can find him), my sense of dislocation remains. The rich have been robbing us blind for twelve years, and where does America's anger go? Toward punishing House members who overdrew their checking accounts and propelling into presidential contention a billionaire man-on-a-white-horse manque. (Of course, there are also the rioters in Los Angeles, but they aren't on the bus either.) Meanwhile, the cultural right has redefined the American project as closing the frontier. Frustrated that their political power has not translated into cultural hegemony, conservatives are methodically attacking cultural institutions—particularly the universities and the arts—ostensibly for being subverted by radicals, but actually for their persistent liberalism, especially that mushy pluralistic habit of allowing cultural dissidents on the premises. The right, very simply, wants us out of America's public life: the First Amendment may protect our right to rant, but only if we can do it without money and without space. These essays, then, come from New York: the real and imagined city where feminist sexual liberationists, rootless cosmopolitan Jews, not-nice girls/boys/others, loudmouth exiles of all colors are an integral and conspicuous part of the landscape; the pariah community Dan Quayle lambasted as a failed welfare state shortly before making his inspired leap from Murphy Brown's baby to L.A. lawlessness; the refuge of my polymorphous heroine Ruby Tuesday, the nation's Last Unmarried Person.

If this counter-American identity defines the sensibility of my book, the question of identity as an organizing principle of politics is a defining theme. This issue has gotten steadily more urgent as the decline of Marxism, with its universal class subject, has—depending on one's point of view—liberated or unleashed a politics of particularist identities in both East and West. In the former Communist countries—most dramatically in the devastated fragments of erstwhile Yugoslavia—ethnically-based nationalism threatens to drive governments from socialist to fascist dictatorship with at best a pit-stop at democracy. Here, identity politics has mostly come from left social movements; neoconservatives and centrist liberals have celebrated American nationalism as universal—on the grounds that it is defined not by ethnicity but by democratic ideals—and therefore the legitimate basis of a "common culture," as opposed to the divided and contentious society implied in the notion of "multiculturalism." For Kondracke and his, ah, soul mates, it's above all the refusal of that universal claim that puts radicals beyond the American pale. In reaction to this brand of false universalism, as well as the Marxist variety, the social movements have regarded with suspicion—when not rejecting outright—the very idea of universal principles. Yet it's increasingly clear that particularism has not delivered what it seemed to promise.

In the American context the term "identity politics" is often used loosely—I've used it this way myself—as a collective rubric for the liberation movements of women, blacks, gays and other subordinate or marginal groups. But in fact the phrase means, or is more usefully taken to mean, something more specific: the idea that one's experience as a member of such a group determines the authenticity and moral legitimacy of one's politics. This idea, first laid out by black power advocates and greatly elaborated by feminists, has pervaded '60s-and-after social activism; yet within the black, feminist, and gay movements there have also been bitter fights about its meaning, its consequences, its limits, and its dangers.

Identity politics arises from a radical insight—that domination is structured into the relations between groups, in part because members of dominant groups, however well-intentioned, tend to perceive the world—and to act on their perceptions—in ways that reinforce their status. Black radicals and women's liberationists saw that white liberal dominance in civil rights organizations and male dominance in the new left recreated the oppressive relations of the larger society; it followed that they had to take control of their own movements. The problem, as I put it in the first of these essays, is that "the further this principle is extended, the sharper are its contradictions. Though self-definition is the necessary starting point for any liberation movement, it can take us only so far."

The most obvious drawback of identity politics is its logic of fragmentation into ever smaller and more particularist groups: the fracturing of the radical feminist movement along class and gay-straight lines (the racial divide having kept most black women out of the movement to begin with) is the sobering paradigm. What's at stake here, however, is not only the pragmatic question (crucial as it is) of how to avoid being divided and conquered, but our understanding of what it means to be a principled radical. Most of us, after all, have complicated, mixed identities, partaking of both dominant and subordinate groups (indeed, from a global perspective we are all privileged Westerners). If our experience by definition makes whole areas of our political judgment suspect, on what moral basis can we act? Do we simply defer to the authority of whoever is more oppressed, relinquishing our own moral autonomy (and what if the more oppressed change their minds, or disagree with each other, as they have the inconvenient habit of doing)? Do we refuse to make certain kinds of political choices (and isn't such refusal in itself a luxury of the privileged)? For late-'60s and early-'70s activists grappling with the fallout of black nationalism, an increasingly atomized feminism, and gay liberation, such dilemmas were by no means abstract. Various agonized and predictably futile efforts to storm the ramparts of our own white, middle-class and/or male psyches soon gave way to widespread hysteria, depression, immobilization, and retreat.

As the left collapsed and the conservative backlash gained momentum, identity politics evolved in two directions. In the academy, feminists, neo-Marxists, and other cultural leftists turned their attention to analyzing the interrelations of difference, power, and subjectivity, in terms that came to be heavily influenced by French poststructuralist theory. While this line of inquiry has produced a rich body of scholarship and criticism, one of its more dubious results was the emergence, in the '80s, of a cultural politics that redefined fragmentation as postmodern pluralism, not a problem to be resolved but on the contrary, a condition of freedom and power. Meanwhile, in what was left of the social movements, disappointed hopes for equality were increasingly displaced onto affirmation of group identity as an end in itself, a form of community and a ritual moral protest. Identity politics congealed—at worst into racial and sexual orthodoxies built on the notion of intrinsic (and morally superior) black or female values; more commonly into a stale, pious rhetoric of comparative victimhood. None of this, of course, is either radical or new. While the moralists indulge in the American left's longstanding habit of substituting righteousness for thought, the pluralists, in their fear that universal claims or "totalizing" theories of any sort are inherently repressive, replicate the aversion to "ideology" that has always made liberals incapable of understanding the social system as a whole—or organizing an effective opposition to the frankly ideological right.

Almost from the beginning, second wave feminism was a study in the limits of the identity politics it did so much to promote. As I try to show in "Radical Feminism and Feminist Radicalism," the attempt of working-class feminists to create their own identity politics foundered on their lack of a class analysis or strategy that transcended the women's movement, while lesbian feminists—having largely rejected the identity of an oppressed erotic minority in favor of the claim that lesbianism meant female bonding and was therefore the purest form of feminism—in effect redefined the movement as a countercultural enclave. Black feminists, in contrast, were faced with defining their relationship to two forms of identity politics, neither of which truly represented them; they were the invisible term in the cultural equation of "black" with male and "female" with white.

The painful and explosive character of black women's dilemma erupted in public in 1978, when Michele Wallace's *Black Macho and the Myth of the Superwoman* forthrightly criticized black men's—and the black movement's—sexism: the book was championed by *Ms.*, well-received by white radical feminists, and reviled by most black critics, male and female alike. Despite the rage directed at Wallace, the ultimate result was a much freer debate. When I wrote "Sisters Under the Skin?" in the early '80s, the question political black women were asking was no longer whether or why they should be feminists, but what feminism meant in light of their dual identity and white women's racism. The dominant view among black feminists was that racial concerns had to take precedence because black people, male or female, were worse off than white women; others—lesbians, especially—refused to make such a choice, stressing black femaleness as an identity in its own right. (Ironically, my piece fails to take note of black lesbian feminist politics, betraying my own unconscious identification of lesbianism with whiteness.) Both groups were heavily invested in the idea of the black woman as ultimate victim, an idea that, as I've suggested, offered moral prestige as a substitute for elusive social change. But among black feminist intellectuals, yet another current was emerging: an effort to analyze the social and psychic space where race and gender converge.

Exploring the "racial-sexual nexus," as I call it in my article, was a compelling alternative both to victim politics as usual and to the kind of pluralism that had led the authors of one of the books I wrote about to talk evenhandedly of "Black" and "White" feminisms. At the time, my interest in this project was mostly centered on its potential for reconstructing "woman" as a political identity, and feminism as a movement for "women," along lines that were genuinely inclusive. But during the past decade, in which a burgeoning literature on feminism and multiculturalism has greatly expanded the discussion, my attention has increasingly shifted away from identity questions, toward the issue—only hinted at in my piece—of how the racial-sexual nexus shapes the overall politics of culture. "Like sexuality," I wrote, forays into this territory "radiate danger and taboo." I might have added that this was hardly surprising, given the volatile cultural association of blackness and femaleness with sexual desire, terror, and anarchy.

Nor is it a coincidence that concern with racial-sexual politics intensified around the same time as the feminist sex wars that occupy several of my essays. As with race, cultural and religious differences centering on sexual morality and "family values" had posed a particularly embarrassing public rebuke to feminists' visions of universal sisterhood. Many women refused to identify with feminism— or were vociferously anti-feminist—on these grounds, even when they did not embrace male dominance per se. By the beginning of the '80s, it was clear that feminists themselves were sharply divided on these questions. Even on abortion, where feminist consensus across political and demographic lines had been remarkable, there was a spectrum—from militant advocates of women's personal and sexual freedom, to defenders of "choice" (content cautiously unspecified) and "reproductive rights" (shorthand for making an end run around those sticky moral questions by tacking abortion on the social-welfare laundry list), to those who allowed that abortion was indeed a terrible thing, if not quite terrible enough to be outlawed, to a small group of "pro-life feminists" who saw abortion as encouraging male irresponsibility. Liberal and culturally-conservative feminists distanced themselves from radical critiques of the family, melding rhetorical approval of monogamy, motherhood, and "long-term relationships" (as opposed, in their view, to hedonism, careerism, and individualism) with the argument that feminists are the family's true champions because they espouse social and economic reforms that "help families." And the anti-pornography movement, whose sexual conservatism had been proclaimed and widely accepted as *the* feminist view, found itself challenged by feminist sexual radicals. Such conflict, on the most central issues of male-female relations, did not merely fragment female identity but threatened to rob the concept of all political meaning. It was the perception of that threat, as much as anything else, that reduced anti-pornography activists to vituperative hysteria when confronted with what they saw as betrayal of feminism from within. Pro-family feminists, on the other hand, were in a position to make common cause with non-feminist women and brand recalcitrants as isolated extremists (read man-hating, child-hating dykes).

The anti-heterosexual ideologues of the anti-porn movement were hardly in the pro-family camp—if anything they were targets of the latter's caricatures. But in terms of the larger culture these tendencies cohered: both strengthened the right. On the family, debate is now virtually nonexistent, at least in the mass media; the idea that the problems besetting contemporary families might have something to do with the structure of the institution itself—that domestic life may need to be transformed, rather than shored up with one or another palliative—has dropped from public view, a mind-boggling feat of collective repression. While feminist sexual radicals remain critical of the family and actively defend the right to lead unconventional personal lives, in recent years most have not made a major issue of family relations as such. Rather, they have focused on sex itself as a separate question.

My own view, argued in "Toward a Feminist Sexual Revolution," is that this separation doesn't hold up, that sexuality cannot be understood apart from familialism and its discontents. Ironically, I'm more in tune with the right on this point than with my closest political allies. The feminist sex debate has taken a different turn; following the contours of identity politics, it has to a large extent unfolded as an argument between moralism and pluralism. The first highly publicized clash between the two sides took place at Barnard College in 1982, at a controversial conference on sexuality organized by feminist sexual libertarians—myself included—and picketed by anti-porn activists (who also prompted the Barnard administration to confiscate conference literature). Opposing the anti-porners' attempts to prescribe, in the most judgmental of terms, a "feminist sexuality," the conference planners argued that sexual orthodoxy in the name of feminism was indistinguishable from the patriarchal kind. As feminists sensitized to the politics of difference, we rejected the idea of a unitary female sexuality, and emphasized the complex construction of erotic identities; we proposed to examine the varieties of female desire and sexual imagery from a standpoint that, as Gayle Rubin had once put it, presumed sex innocent until proven guilty, rather than the other way around. At the conference, and at a speakout planned to coincide with the event, lesbian sadomasochists and other practitioners of "politically incorrect" sex brandished the erotic-minority banner abandoned by mainstream lesbian feminists.

This confrontation set the tone of the debate that followed, and in crucial ways defined its terms. Within those terms, the libertarian argument has been able to expose the profoundly anti-sexual and sexist assumptions of the anti-porn movement, as well as its vulgar literalism in conflating images, fantasies, and acts. As genuinely radical feminism has always done, "pro-sex" feminism affirms women's right to be sexual without shame. But its pluralist framework does not encourage a systemic analysis of sex. What is the relationship of sexual morality to the larger social structure? Why do fear of sex, and contempt for it, have such a strong grip on people that these attitudes constantly reappear in covert forms? Why is sex in this culture so closely associated with violence? Unless radicals engage such questions, they can't effectively refute the conservative answer—that lust is fundamentally destructive, the enemy of civilization—or its anti-porn feminist variant—that sexual liberation is a male-supremacist plot.

What I'm suggesting is that the left has taken identity politics as far as it can go (not to mention some places we would have done better to avoid), and that this suggestion comes not from any presumption of objectivity but from the logic of my own particular standpoint in the world. (That is, I speak as a woman who does not represent "women"—and as a Jew convinced that the fundamental bond among Jews is neither Zionism nor the 613 commandments but our historic commitment to the ever-unpopular position that the Messiah is yet to come.) I also see members of other groups moving toward the same conclusion: that radicals need to recreate a politics that emphasizes our common humanity, to base our social theory and practice on principles that apply to us all. This doesn't mean rewriting history. We know too much to attempt to dissociate the political from the personal, or discount the fateful clashes of world views shaped by difference and disparity of power—the "you just don't get it" factor. Nor can we ignore the lessons of the Communist debacle: while systemic social theory and absolutist ideology are not synonymous (as the pluralists would have it), slipping from one to the other is far too easy for comfort. Yet finally, if we really hope to change our condition, there's no escape from the admittedly risky, admittedly arrogant project of reimagining the world.

The chief principle I invoke in these essays is democracy, in the most radical sense of that word: a commitment to individual freedom and egalitarian self-government in every area of social, economic, and cultural life. Democracy, as I envision it, assumes that the purpose of community is to foster individual happiness and self-development; that the meaning of life lies in our capacity to experience and enjoy it fully; that freedom and eros are fundamentally intertwined; and that a genuine sense of responsibility to other human beings flows from the desire for connection, not subordination to family, Caesar, or God.

This is a universalist philosophy—one that has often been criticized, from the standpoint of identity politics, as parochially "Western" or "upper-middle-class." The premise of that charge, I argue in my piece on Salman Rushdie, is the self-contradictory idea that while no group has a right to impose its values on another, each group has the right to dominate its own members. Similarly, I reject the relativism implicit in current attempts to proscribe racist and sexist speech; I find it a galling and dangerous irony that the right, with its attack on "political correctness," has staked out the moral high ground on the issue of free expression. It's tempting to be distracted by the brazen bad faith of the p.c. campaign, with its attempt to stifle all leftist dissidence in the name of combatting a new totalitarianism—this from the same characters who have tried to ban flag-burning, promoted censorship of "obscene" art, denied grants to artists and scholars on political grounds, forbidden federally-funded clinics to mention abortion, and generally shown as much respect for the First Amendment as for teenage welfare mothers. But the campaign has hit a nerve because it gets at something real. Coercion and guilt-mongering—the symbiotic weapons of authoritarian culture—inevitably provoke resistance; when the left uses these tactics it merely encourages people to confuse their most oppressive impulses with their need to be themselves, offensively honest instead of hypocritically nice. Perversely, racism and sexism become badges of freedom rather than stigmata of repression, while the roots of domination in people's rage and misery remain untouched.

My vision of democracy depends on the belief that it is, in fact, human unhappiness and not original sin that is our heart of darkness. Unhappiness is not the same as suffering or adversity; it is chronic estrangement from our capacity for pleasure. And so pleasure—its attainment, its blockage, its meaning—is another preoccupation of this book. My final essay, "Coming Down Again," is part manifesto, part elegy on the subject. When this piece was first published in 1989 it had a subtitle, "After the Age of Excess." I was referring to the '60s, of course, but not long afterward there was a media wave of upper middle class breast-beating about "the excesses of the '80s." For the times, an all too typical irony: a word that for me meant embracing—for better or worse—the quest for an ecstatic existence had been recast to refer to compulsive money-making. These days ecstasy is indeed out of fashion; it's become conventional to trivialize, when not simply condemning out of hand, the romance of sex and drugs that carried so much of my generation's transcendental baggage. Yet the power of the ecstatic moment—*this is what freedom is like, this is what love could be, this is what happens when the boundaries are gone*— is precisely the power to reimagine the world, to reclaim a human identity that's neither victim nor oppressor, to affirm difference not as separation but as variation on a theme. We can't live in such moments, and it's usually disastrous to try. But we need them to make sense of our politics and our lives—to be our compass—as we camp out on the border where New York and America meet, along with so much else.

1.

No More Nice Girls

Lust Horizons: Is the Women's Movement Pro-Sex?

My nominations for the questions most likely to get a group of people, all of whom like each other and hate Ronald Reagan, into a nasty argument: Is there any objective criterion for healthy or satisfying sex, and if so what is it? Is a good sex life important? *How* important? Is abstinence bad for you? Does sex have any intrinsic relation to love? Is monogamy too restrictive? Are male and female sexuality inherently different? Are we all basically bisexual? Do vaginal orgasms exist? Does size matter? You get the idea. Despite the endless public discussion of sex, despite the statistics of "experts" and the outpourings of personal testimony about our sexual desires, fantasies, and habits, we have achieved precious little clarity—let alone agreement—about what it all means. At the same time there is no subject on which people are more passionately, blindly, stubbornly opinionated.

What is especially disconcerting, to those of us who believe that an understanding of sexuality is crucial to a feminist analysis, is that feminists are as confused, divided, and dogmatic about sex as everyone else. This sense of an intractably resistant, perennially sore subject pervades two recent anthologies that in other ways could hardly be more disparate. *Women—Sex and Sexuality*, a collection of articles from the feminist academic journal *Signs*, is a sober mix of theoretical essays, reviews, reports on research, and historical documents. The theory section is the most consistently interesting: most of the essays, including some I violently disagree with, raise provocative questions or make points worth mulling. (I particularly recommend Judith Walkowitz on the politics of prostitution, Rosalind Petchesky on reproductive freedom, Ann Barr Snitow on sex in women's novels, Alix Kates Shulman on the genesis of radical feminist ideas about sex—I should add that the last two and I belong to the same women's group.) Otherwise the book is uneven, with valuable information and insights weighed down by reviews that are little more than summaries and research that borders on the trivial. Stilted academic prose is an intermittent problem, though less so than in most scholarly collections.

The sex issue of *Heresies*—a journal that was started by feminist artists and has put out 12 issues, each devoted to a single theme and edited by a different collective—is more fun to read. It is lively, raunchy, irreverent; it intersperses theoretical articles ("Pornography and Pleasure," "A Herstorical Look at Some Aspects of Black Sexuality," "Narcissism, Feminism, and Video Art") with stories, poems, satire, cartoons, and witty graphics. The *Signs* anthology defines its subject in the most inclusive terms; *Heresies* sticks to the aspect of sex feminists have had the most trouble discussing—desire ("Where do our desires come from? How do they manifest themselves in their infinite variations? And what, if anything, do they tell us about what it means to be a woman?"). The editors of *Women—Sex and Sexuality* see the movement's lack of any coherent sexual theory as healthy eclecticism: "Since female sexuality exists within specific contexts, within matrices of the body and the world, no single perspective, no single discipline, can do justice to it." The *Heresies* collective simply admits it couldn't agree on much; divergent editorials by individual (but anonymous) editors are scattered throughout the issue.

The failure of feminists to get a grip, so to speak, on this all-important subject is particularly disappointing, given our (naive?) hopes at the beginning. In "Sex and Power: Sexual Bases of Radical Feminism," her contribution to the *Signs* collection, Alix Kates Shulman explains the premise of radical feminist consciousness raising: "The so-called experts on women had traditionally been men who, as part of the male-supremacist power structure, benefited from perpetuating certain ideas. . . . We wanted to get at the truth about how women felt. . . . Not how we were *supposed* to feel but how we really did feel." As it turned out this was easier said than done, especially when the feelings in question were sexual. To challenge male "expertise" on what good sex is or ought to be, what women feel or ought to feel, is only a prerequisite to understanding "how we really feel." Women's sexual experience is diverse and often contradictory. Women's sexual feelings have been stifled and distorted not only by men and men's ideas but by our own desperate strategies for living in and with a sexist, sexually repressive culture. Our most passionate convictions about sex do not necessarily reflect our real desires; they are as likely to be aimed at repressing the pain of desires we long ago decided were too dangerous to acknowledge, even to ourselves. If feminist theory is to be truly based in the reality of women's lives, feminists must examine their professed beliefs and feelings with as much skepticism as they apply to male pronouncements. Otherwise we risk simply replacing male prejudices and rationalizations with our own. But what criteria do we apply to such an examination? How do we distinguish between real and inauthentic feelings?

An influential strain in early radical feminist thought assumed that women had a kind of collective wisdom, drawn from their experience, that would spontaneously emerge as the existence of a movement encouraged women to believe change was possible and to admit the truth of their situation, instead of fatalistically acquiescing (or pretending to acquiesce) in male supremacist lies. In practice, what this tended to mean was a faith in authenticity by consensus—particularly when the consensus of a feminist group seemed to dovetail with the traditional complaints and demands (the "individual struggles") of "apolitical" women. Not coincidentally, the consensus among proponents of this view was that women really want marriage and monogamy, albeit on equal terms that do not now exist. (To the extent that lesbianism was discussed, it was assumed either that lesbians were exceptions or that lesbianism was a response to male oppressiveness, rather than a positive choice.) The "free love" ideology of male leftists and bohemians was, they argued, nothing but a means of exploiting women sexually while avoiding commitment and responsibility; the "sexual revolution" had not benefited women, but merely robbed us of the right to say no. If some women nonetheless preferred "free love," it was only because marriage under present conditions was also oppressive. The opposite possibility was not considered: that women really want free love—on equal terms that do not now exist—and prefer to let the state police their sexual relationships only because the present male-defined and dominated "sexual revolution" has so little to do with either genuine love or genuine freedom.

For another faction in the movement—which also surfaced right at the beginning—the standard of authenticity became one's degree of antagonism toward men and male attitudes, particularly sexual attitudes. By this standard, marriage and "free love" are equally repugnant. Heterosexual relations are by definition a violation of women's true feelings; the only authentic choices are lesbianism or celibacy. Here there was some confusion, for separatists tended to talk as if lesbianism and celibacy were at once freely chosen alternatives and necessary responses to men's oppressive behavior. But this contradiction was resolved by an implicit biological determinism: men are inherently violent and predatory; women are inherently loving and nurturing; and the essence of men's oppressiveness is their insistence on imposing their maleness—especially their male sexuality—on unwilling women. (Adrienne Rich's article in *Women—Sex and Sexuality*, "Compulsory Heterosexuality and Lesbian Existence," is a classic example of this line of reasoning. Her premise is that both men and women desire women; this has impelled men to erect the whole structure of patriarchal relations for the specific purpose of ensuring their access to women's vaginas. Where homosexual men fit into this analysis is unclear.) This wing of the movement has been primarily responsible for putting a feminist imprimatur on certain familiar ideas—that men are too genitally oriented, that women are more interested in nongenital forms of eroticism, that the supposedly irrepressible sex drive is a male problem (or a male myth), that women can take sex or leave it.

These apparently opposed perspectives meet on the common ground of sexual conservatism. The monogamists uphold the traditional wife's "official" values: emotional commitment is inseparable from a legal/moral obligation to permanence and fidelity; men are always trying to escape these duties; it's in our interest to make them shape up. The separatists tap into the underside of traditional femininity—the bitter, self-righteous fury that propels the indictment of men as lustful beasts ravaging their chaste victims. These are the two faces of feminine ideology in a patriarchal culture: they induce women to accept a spurious moral superiority as a substitute for sexual pleasure, and curbs on men's sexual freedom as a substitute for real power.

In one form or another, sexual conservatism still permeates the movement. In their introduction the editors of *Women—Sex and Sexuality*, Catharine Stimpson and Ethel Spector Person, approach the issue of sexual freedom with cautious equivocation, but quickly betray an underlying conservatism. They ask, "Is female sexuality like male sexuality, or does it obey laws of its own?" then note that researchers with an "egalitarian bias," who prefer "to see the sexualities as essentially identical," have found support in recent scientific studies. But "such a belief can be only apparently feminist. Too often, egalitarians masculinize the model of sexuality. They believe that male sexuality most accurately embodies a human sexuality that neither cultural nor psychological constraints have corrupted." Perhaps. On the other hand, some egalitarians, including me, are inclined to believe that while "uncorrupted" male and female sexuality would be pretty much alike, cultural and psychological constraints have corrupted the sexuality of both sexes in different ways. But in the next sentence we see what all this has been leading up to: "They also tend to esteem a pure and unfettered sexuality as an invariant key to self-validation and autonomy." Translation: to be "egalitarian" is to legitimize unfettered male lust—for both sexes, yet. It's safer if female sexuality is different—maybe we don't want to be unfettered.

Person, a psychoanalyst, elaborates on this theme in an article called "Sexuality as the Mainstay of Identity: Psychoanalytic Perspectives." First, she reminds us that Freud's libido theory—the concept of sexual excitation as energy that presses for release and if not satisfied directly (in orgasm) will seek indirect or disguised outlets—is unproven. True, but it hasn't been disproven either. On the contrary, it remains the most plausible explanation for a whole range of phenomena, from the way sexual excitement feels, to the obvious correlation between sexual inhibition and certain neurotic symptoms or character traits, to the centrality of sexual restrictions in patriarchal morality. Anyway, one would think that whatever their hostility to other aspects of Freud's thought, feminists would welcome the libido theory, since it supports the claim that men's suppression of women's genital sexuality is an intolerable denial of our needs. But the assumption that women have genital needs is precisely what's unacceptable from Person's point of view. She argues that sexual activity and orgasm are indispensable to men's mental health, but not to women's; specifically, men need sex to feel like men, while in women "gender identity and self-worth can be consolidated by other means."

This argument reinforces a social stereotype while completely ignoring social reality. In this culture, where women are still supposed to be less sexual than men, sexual inhibition is as integral to the "normal" woman's identity as sexual aggression is to a man's; it is "excessive" genital desires that often make women feel "unfeminine" and unworthy. In rejecting the idea that an active, autonomous sexuality is a necessary aspect of female autonomy in general, Person also rejects the possibility that the systematic social inhibition of female sexuality is a way of inhibiting our self-assertion in other areas—that this indeed may be the chief social function of our antisexual training. She notes the "evidence in the clinical literature that masturbation in adolescent girls is related to high self-esteem and to the subsequent pursuit of career goals," but quickly dismisses the obvious inference: ". . . it is unlikely that masturbation itself is so beneficial; more likely some general assertiveness plays a role in the exploration of both sexuality and role experimentation."

From her dubious hypothesis Person reaches the following conclusions: "Many women have the capacity to abstain from sex without negative psychological consequences. (The problem for women is that they are often denied the legal right of sexual refusal.)" "One ought not dictate a tyranny of active sexuality as critical to female liberation." "Given a current liberal climate of thinking about sexuality there is a danger, not so much in an antierotic attitude, but in too much insistence on the expression of sexuality as the sine qua non of mental health and self-actualization." I hope that in the current conservative climate Person is having second thoughts, but I'm not counting on it. She goes on to say that a "neutral" discussion of sexuality must weigh not only the advantages of sexual activity but "the adaptive advantages of the capacity for abstinence, repression, or suppression." No doubt about it—when one must endure abstinence, repression, or suppression, the capacity to adapt does come in handy. But somehow I always imagined that feminism was about rebelling, not adapting.

It has been years since feminist sexual conservatism (a contradiction in terms, really) has had to face any sustained or organized opposition, but that is beginning to change. Both of these collections—particularly *Heresies*—reflect the early, tentative stirrings of a revived feminist debate on sexuality, which is in turn a response to the right-wing backlash. The right does have a coherent perspective on sex, one that unites a repressive sexual morality with the subordination of women. Since feminists are at best ambivalent about sexual freedom, they have not been able to make an effective counterattack. Indeed, the movement's attacks on sexual exploitation and violence, male irresponsibility, pornography, and so on, have often reinforced right-wing propaganda by giving the impression that feminists consider the loosening of controls over sexual behavior a worse threat to women than repression. While liberals appeared to be safely in power, feminists could perhaps afford the luxury of defining Larry Flynt or Roman Polanski as Enemy Number One. Now that we have to cope with Jerry Falwell and Jesse Helms, a rethinking of priorities seems in order.

Which is why I'm grateful for *Heresies'* sex issue. Both the content of individual pieces and an overall feistiness of style and tone assume that the purpose of women's liberation is to liberate women, not defend our superior capacity for abstinence. (The issue does include an article by a woman extolling the joys of celibacy, but even she admits to masturbating. This may technically be celibacy, but abstinence it ain't.) As one of the anonymous editorials puts it, "The work in this magazine encourages us to reflect on our individual and collective relationship to our desires for and of the flesh. . . . In a system where Women make love but do not fuck, where Women request but do not demand, women who actively strategize for their own pleasure are confused. . . . If we are not Women as we have been designed, then who are we? Many of us fear for our feminine identity . . . . As we proceed in this project of creating a feminist understanding of our sexual choices, our changing desires and our erotic possibilities, we prepare the way for a sexual politics that has pleasure as its goal." In "Pornography and Pleasure," Paula Webster argues that the antipornography movement "has chosen to organize and theorize around our victimization, our Otherness, not our subjectivity and self-definition. In focusing on what male pornography has done to us, rather than on our own sexual desires, we tend to embrace our sexually deprived condition and begin to police the borders of the double standard. . . . Indeed, I am convinced that pornography, even in its present form, contains important messages for women. As Angela Carter suggests, it does not tie women's sexuality to reproduction or to a domesticated couple or exclusively to men. It is true that this depiction is created by men, but perhaps it can encourage us to think of what our own images and imaginings might be like."

In short, *Heresies* #12 is, among other things, a forum for dissidents in the sex debate, and it tacitly acknowledges that role by publicizing a recent intramovement skirmish. Last year NOW, on the advice of its lesbian caucus, passed a resolution specifically excluding from its definition of lesbian rights certain forms of sexual expression that had been "mistakenly correlated with Lesbian/Gay rights by some gay organizations and by opponents of Lesbian/Gay rights seeking to confuse the issue": pederasty, pornography, sadomasochism (all of which were alleged to be issues of violence or exploitation, not of sexual preference), and public sex ("an issue of violation of the privacy rights of nonparticipants"). While the impetus for the resolution seems to have been opposition to the "boy love" movement, its effect is to endorse the moralistic rhetoric and the conventionally feminine sexual politics of the antiporn campaign; it also has disturbing overtones of a homophobic and/or self-hating insistence that "lesbians are respectable too."

The resolution inspired a letter of protest that has been circulating as a petition in feminist, lesbian, and gay circles and has collected about 150 signatures. My women's group (a hotbed of sexual dissidence) had a somewhat different point of view, so we wrote our own letter. All three documents are reprinted in *Heresies* under the headline, "News Flash: People Organize to Protest Recent NOW Resolution on Lesbian and Gay Rights."

Lesbians have been conspicuous on both sides of the clash between sexually conservative and libertarian feminists. On the one hand, it is lesbian separatists who have most militantly embraced a saccharinely romantic, nice-girl's view of female sexuality as the proper feminist outlook, while disparaging sexual attitudes deemed too aggressive or too bluntly lustful as "male-identified" (movementese for "unfeminine"). Other lesbians—impelled in part by the recognition that it's hardly in lesbians' interest to encourage moralistic attacks on unconventional sexual behavior—retort that feminists have no business setting up standards of politically correct sexuality and that women who do so are, like all bigots, fearfully condemning what they don't understand.

A recent focus of this argument within the lesbian feminist community has been the issue of sadomasochism (i.e., consensual sexual practices involving dominance and submission rituals and the infliction of pain or humiliation). The prevailing lesbian feminist line has been that S-M, like pornography, is a male trip, a form of violence rather than sex, a recreation of oppressive patriarchal, heterosexual patterns; lesbians don't have S-M relationships, and if they do it's because they are victims of heterosexist brainwashing. Dissenters have argued that lesbians do indeed have such relationships, that S-M is as legitimate a sexual taste as any other, and that its despised practitioners are an oppressed sexual minority.

Pat Califia carries on this debate in *Heresies*. In "Feminism and Sadomasochism," she argues that S-M is not a form of sexual assault but a fantasy—"a drama or ritual"—enacted by mutual consent: "The participants are enhancing their sexual pleasure, not damaging or imprisoning one another. A sadomasochist is well aware that a role adopted during a scene is not appropriate during other interactions and that a fantasy role is not the sum total of her being."

What then is the function and meaning of the drama? Why the desire to act out in bed roles that in other contexts would be distasteful? Califia's explanations are less than satisfying. She suggests that S-M involves a quest for "intense sensations" and "pleasure from the forbidden," that a sadist may encourage a masochist "to lose his inhibitions and perform an act he may be afraid of, or simply acknowledge shame and guilt and use it to enhance the sex act rather than prevent it." But she doesn't pursue these observations further, and in the end we learn little more than that S-M turns her on. For Califia this is enough; commenting on the term "vanilla"—S-M jargon for non-S-M people—she says, "I believe sexual preferences are more like flavor preferences than like moral/political alliances." To the question of whether sadomasochism will survive the revolution, she replies, "My fantasy is that kinkiness and sexual variation will multiply, not disappear, if terrible penalties are no longer meted out for being sexually adventurous."

Can it possibly be that simple? Here is Califia's list of the activities she enjoys: "leathersex, bondage, various forms of erotic torture, flagellation (whipping), verbal humiliation, fist-fucking, and watersports (playing with enemas and piss)." "There are many different ways to express affection or interest," she asserts. "Vanilla people send flowers, poetry, or candy, or they exchange rings. S-M people do all that, and may also lick boots, wear a locked collar, or build their loved one a rack in the basement."

Does the need to act out fantasies of debasing oneself or someone else really require no further explanation? Does it have nothing to do with buried emotions of rage or self-hatred? Nothing to do with living in a hierarchical society where one is "superior" to some people and "inferior" to others, where men rule and women serve? Can the need to connect sexual pleasure with pain and humiliation be unrelated to the fact that our sexual organs and their function are still widely regarded as bad, contemptible, and embarrassing, a reproach to our higher spiritual natures? Is it irrelevant that our first erotic objects were our all-powerful parents, who too often hurt and humiliated us by condemning our childish sexuality?

Puritanism is not the only obstacle to a feminist understanding of sex. If self-proclaimed arbiters of feminist morals stifle honest discussion with their dogmatic, guilt-mongering judgments, sexual libertarians often evade honest discussion by refusing to make judgments at all. I think that to read women out of the movement because of their sexual habits is outrageous, and that to label any woman's behavior as "male" is a sexist absurdity. I also think it's dangerous to assume that certain kinds of behavior will disappear "after the revolution" (as dangerous as assuming that "the revolution" is a discrete event, which will someday be over once and for all). But I don't believe our sexual desires are ever just arbitrary tastes. Rather, I see sadomasochism as one way of coping with this culture's sexual double binds, which make it painfully difficult for people to reconcile their sexual needs with dignity and equality. To be sure, the same can be said of many more conventional sexual practices: what, after all, is the ritual of male pursuit and female ambivalence (or, increasingly these days, the opposite) but a disguised and therefore respectable form of sadomasochistic theater? Probably none of us is free of sado-masochistic feelings; no doubt the hostility sadomasochists inspire is in large part horror at being directly confronted with fantasies most of us choose to repress, or to express only indirectly. The issue is whether such fantasies, expressed or denied, are themselves the product of thwarted desire. The very idea that "the forbidden" offers special pleasures suggests that the answer is yes.

Another source of controversy among feminists, lesbians, and gays is the claim of "man-boy love" advocates that theirs is yet another unconventional sexual taste, entirely consensual and beneficial to all concerned, that is unfairly maligned by puritanical homophobes as child molesting. This one is much stickier, for the question is not only whether sexual attraction between adults and children (most adult-child sex takes place between men and girls) is comparable to a yen for chocolate, but whether, given the vulnerability of children to the power of adults, such relationships can ever be truly consensual. I don't think they can. Adults can too easily manipulate children's needs for affection, protection, and approval; children are too inex-perienced to understand all the implications of what they're agreeing to (or even, in some cases, initiating). And it seems to me that what attracts adults to children is precisely their "innocence"—which is to say their relative powerlessness. There is the question, though, of where to draw lines. At what age does a child become a young per-son, and when does protecting children from exploitation become a denial of young people's sexual autonomy? Some 15-year-olds are more mature than many adults will ever be. And I agree that the pub-lic's readiness to equate all adult-child sex with child molesting comes in part from a need to deny that kids have active sexual desires. Still, in this instance I would rather err on the side of restrictiveness, for if children cannot rely absolutely on adult protection, they have no ground under their feet.

The "I'm O.K., you're O.K." brand of sexual libertarianism is a logical extension of the feminist and gay liberationist demand for the right to self-definition. But the further this principle is extended, the sharper are its contradictions. Though self-definition is the necessary starting point for any liberation movement, it can take us only so far. To me it is axiomatic that consenting partners have a right to their sexual proclivities, and that authoritarian moralism has no place in a movement for social change. But a truly radical movement must look (to borrow a phrase from Rosalind Petchesky) beyond the right to choose, and keep focusing on the fundamental questions. Why do we choose what we choose? What would we choose if we had a real choice?

June 1981

Nature's Revenge

Who would have predicted that just now, when the far right has launched an all-out attack on women's basic civil rights, the issue eliciting the most passionate public outrage from feminists should be not abortion, not "pro-family" fundamentalism, but pornography? The fervor with which some feminist activists have rallied against smut is more than a little ironic, for opposition to pornography is also a conspicuous feature of the new right's program. Furthermore, in certain respects the arguments of the two groups are uncomfortably similar. If anti-porn feminists see pornography as a brutal exercise of predatory male sexuality, a form of (and an incitement to) violence against women, the right also associates pornography with violence and with rampant male lust broken loose from the saving constraints of God and Family. Nor have conservatives hesitated to borrow feminist rhetoric about the exploitation of women's bodies.

This peculiar confluence raises the question of whether the current feminist preoccupation with pornography is really an attempt to extend the movement's critique of sexism—or whether, on the contrary, it is evidence that feminists have been affected by the conservative climate and are unconsciously moving with the cultural tide. Two very different new books suggest that it is both.

In *Pornography and Silence*, Susan Griffin argues that pornography is rooted in the fear of nature, in the futile desire to deny our vulnerable, mortal bodies. In a patriarchal society men identify themselves with culture and women with nature and the body; accordingly, men seek to control women and suppress the "female" in themselves. Women, identifying themselves with the despised body, become self-hating and self-punishing. The result, for both sexes, is an erotic fantasy life that is essentially sadomasochistic. The pornographic image, which objectifies and degrades the (usually female) body, represents a ritual in which the (usually male) pornographer or user, playing both killer and victim, re-enacts the murder of his bodily self; since the murder can never be truly accomplished, it must be compulsively repeated. Pornography, the author concludes, expresses not a yearning for sexual liberation but its opposite, "a desire to silence eros." Real sexual liberation requires a reconciliation with nature, a healing of the illusory split between body and spirit.

In affirming the fundamental goodness and wholeness of the erotic impulse, and connecting sexual repression with the subjection of women, Griffin boldly allies her feminism with the cultural revolutionary tradition of William Blake, Emma Goldman, Wilhelm Reich. Her book tackles questions of critical importance, for sadomasochism is indeed deeply embedded in our sexuality. Yet a fatal oversimplification derails her argument. In this society men (and women, too) identify femaleness not only with nature but, paradoxically, with conventional morality, while maleness represents not only culture but the aggressive natural drives that, for good or ill, defy convention. Thus pornography is in part a revolt of "male" libido against "female" morals. If it is "culture's revenge against nature," it is equally nature's revenge against culture—the return of the repressed in distorted, solipsistic, sometimes frightening form. By separating sexual acts and organs from their larger human context, pornography degrades them and at the same time exalts them as the only reality. It denies the body, yet denies with equal insistence (and futility) the shame, guilt and inhibition that denial of the body produces.

To flatly equate pornography with sadism, as Griffin does, is to miss the contradiction at the core of the pornographic experience. Indeed, the passages she devotes to condemning pornography, rather than analyzing it, are reductive and heavy-handed in a way the rest of the book is not. "Pornography," the author says, "endangers our lives." She defends this melodramatic assertion by arguing that all cultural images influence behavior. True, but only because they articulate and legitimize feelings that already exist. Pornography that offers concrete images of how to act out hatred of women may invite imitation and reinforce an atmosphere of complacency toward sexual violence, but the hatred and complacency that produce violence are built into the culture. In short, pornography is a symptom, not a root cause. And in fact *Pornography and Silence* is most convincing when it speculates on root causes: In tracing the sadomasochistic mentality to the intolerable choices—between "masculinity" and "femininity," bodily pleasure and power in the world—that parents force on their children, the author implicitly makes the radical claim that a sexist, sexually repressive family structure endangers our lives. Yet she chooses to focus her anger on the symptom.

Like most feminist opponents of pornography, Susan Griffin presumes an objective distinction between "pornographic images," which are sadistic by definition, and "simple, explicit depictions of sexuality." The fallacy here is that the range of potentially pornographic images—that is, images primarily used for the purpose of sexual arousal—is limited only by the user's imagination. Even if one wants to argue that the use of an image for sexual gratification requires a sadistic fantasy, the image itself may be "objectively" innocuous. And what about cryptopornography like Gothic novels? The appeal of Gothics is also rooted in sadomasochism, and just as *Hustler* magazine shows men how to act like rapists, Gothics show women how to act like victims. The crucial difference is that Gothics purvey a repressed, romanticized sexuality, while hard-core pornography is explicitly lustful and genital. In singling out the latter for condemnation, Griffin betrays an unwitting conservative bias.

Despite its flawed logic, *Pornography and Silence* is a serious effort to apply feminist insights to sexual psychology. Andrea Dworkin's *Pornography*, in contrast, is less a theoretical work than a book-length sermon, preached with a rhetorical flourish and a singleminded intensity that meet somewhere between poetry and rant. In Dworkin's moral universe the battle of the sexes is a Manichaean clash between absolute power and absolute powerlessness, absolute villains and absolute victims. The foundation of male power, "the prime component of male identity," is violence, physical and psychic. Men are predators, women their chief prey. To men, sex means rape; the penis is an instrument of power and terror. Pornography expresses, enforces, *is* male power:

The woman's sex is appropriated, her body is possessed, she is used and she is despised: the pornography does it and the pornography proves it.

The power of men in pornography is imperial power, the power of the sovereigns who are cruel and arrogant, who keep taking and conquering for the pleasure of power and the power of pleasure.

If Susan Griffin misses contradictions, Andrea Dworkin scorns the very idea of contradiction: Ambiguity is for the fainthearted, dialectics are the self-serving invention of male philosophers. "Male culture," she proclaims, "thrives on argument and prides itself on distinctions." She scoffs at the distinction women are "commanded" to make between pornographic fantasy and real life. In a chapter on the Marquis de Sade she conflates his life with his work, reduces his antinomian nihilism to a straightforward celebration of male power and dismisses Angela Carter's *The Sadeian Woman*—an illuminating study of how de Sade's writing, and by extension all pornography, unites reactionary and radical impulses—as a "pseudofeminist literay essay."

The misogyny Dworkin decries is real enough—it is just not all of reality. Between women and men (often the same women and men) there is love as well as war. This may be an impossible contradiction, but it happens to be the contradiction on which our social order rests. A world view that defines male sexuality as pornography as rape leaves no room for mutual heterosexual desire, let alone love; yet a feminism that does not take heterosexuality seriously can neither comprehend the average woman's life nor spark a movement that might change it. If relations with men offer nothing but violence and exploitation, most women's apparent desire for such relations must mean that either men are so diabolically powerful as to have crushed even passive resistance or women have been so brutalized that we have lost the will to resist. Where in this scenario is the possibility of struggle?

Without contradiction there can be no change, only impotent moralizing. And in the end moralizing always works against women: The Andrea Dworkins rail against male vice; the George Gilders come forward to offer God and Family as the remedy. Which is why I find *Pornography*'s relentless outrage less inspiring than numbing, less a call to arms than a counsel of despair.

July 1981

Toward a Feminist

Sexual Revolution

I t's perhaps some indication of the complex, refractory nature of my
subject that this is the third version of my preface to the article that
follows—itself the third revision of what began as a talk at a feminist
conference in 1981. At that time, feminists were just beginning to
engage in a passionate, explosive debate—or rather, a series of overlapping, intertwined debates—about sex. The arguments crystallized
around specific issues: pornography; the causes of sexual violence and
how best to oppose it; the definition of sexual consent; the nature of
women's sexuality and whether it is intrinsically different from men's;
the meaning of heterosexuality for women; the political significance
of "fringe" sexualities like sadomasochism and, more generally, the
relation of sexual fantasy to action, sexual behavior to political practice (in the early '80s, when feminists used the term "political correctness" it was to refer sarcastically to the anti-pornography movement's
efforts to define a "feminist sexuality"). Each of these issues, in turn,
became a focus of deeply felt disagreement over the place of sexuality and sexual morality in a feminist analysis and program. In one
way or another, they raise the question of whether sexual freedom, as
such, is a feminist value, or whether feminism ought rather to aim at
replacing male-defined social controls over sex with female-defined
controls.

While there has always been tension among feminists with differing sexual attitudes, it was only with the eruption of these debates
that the differences came to the surface and defined political factions,
creating a serious intramovement split. In my view, the reason for
this development (or at least its catalyst) was the rise of the new right.
The women's liberation movement had emerged in a liberal political and social climate; like the rest of the left it had devoted much

of its energy to making a radical critique of liberalism. So long as sexual liberalism appeared to be firmly entrenched as the dominant cultural ideology, feminists put a high priority on criticizing the hypocrisies and abuses of the male-dominated "sexual revolution." But as liberalism fell apart, so did the apparent feminist consensus on sex. Confronted with a right-wing backlash bent on reversing social acceptance of non-marital, non-procreative sex, feminists like me, who saw sexual liberalism as deeply flawed by sexism but nonetheless a source of crucial gains for women, found themselves at odds with feminists who dismissed the sexual revolution as monolithically sexist and shared many of the attitudes of conservative moralists.

Since the mid-'80s, the intensity of the sex debates has waned, not because the issues are any closer to being resolved, but because the two sides are so far apart they have nothing more to say to each other. "Pro-sex" feminists (as we came to be labeled) can claim some victories: we succeeded in countering the prevailing public assumption that the anti-pornography movement's sexual conservatism was *the* feminist position and the porn debate a conflict between "feminists" and "First Amendment absolutists"; we were instrumental in defeating ordinances that defined pornography as a form of sex discrimination, enshrining feminist sexual conservatism as public policy; and we largely won the battle for the hearts and minds of feminist academics, journalists, and other intellectuals. Yet on the level of the unexamined, semi-conscious attitudes that permeate popular culture and politics, the equation of sexual liberalism with sexism and violence against women is, if anything, more widespread than it was ten years ago. This, of course, reflects the accelerating intensity of the anti-sexual backlash during the Reagan-Bush years. But it also points up a fundamental failure on the part of the "pro-sex" camp: the failure to put forward a convincing alternative analysis of sexual violence, exploitation, and alienation.

These issues were of vital concern to an earlier wave of sexual liberationists. From the 1930s through the 1960s, sexual radicalism was anchored in a radical psychoanalytic tradition whose paradigmatic figure is Wilhelm Reich and whose basic assumptions derive from Freud's libido theory. For radical Freudians the sexual impulse is a biologically-given energy, a dynamic force that pushes toward gratification; sexual desire blocked from expression or awareness does not disappear but takes indirect forms, leaving its imprint both on individuals' feelings, fantasies, and behavior, and on social institutions. From this premise, sexual radicals argued that the patriarchal family's suppression and manipulation of children's sexual desires produced adults whose sexuality was distorted by unconscious rage; that the need to repress and control this rage led people to perpetuate and defend the very system that produced it; and that nonetheless it continually leaked out in all manner of antisocial and sadistic behavior.

With the advent of radical feminism, radical Freudianism came into political disrepute; the sexual politics of both feminist and gay liberation movements were informed by a deep (and well-founded) distrust of any kind of biologically-based theory, as well as anger at the sexist and homophobic history of psychoanalysis. This anti-Freudianism, combined with the impact on social theory of structuralist and post-structuralist discourse—in particular the influence of Jacques Lacan, Michel Foucault, and structural anthropology—gave rise to a major shift in the way most contemporary sexual radicals understand and talk about sex. At the heart of this shift is a sweeping, social constructivist rejection of any concept of a "natural" sexual drive, and of the idea that the biological dimension of sexuality, if it can be said to exist at all, in any way determines or shapes our actual experience.

I do not share this view. On the contrary, I believe we can't understand sex as an emotional, moral, or social issue, let alone formulate a politics of sexual liberation, without some recourse to the idea of sexual satisfaction as a biological need. While I'm convinced that a radical Freudian understanding of sex is "truer"—that is, has more explanatory power—than a social constructivist position, my essay does not attempt to make that argument. Rather, it explores the possibility that a version of the Reichian paradigm might resolve the seeming contradiction between a sexual liberationist politics and a feminist critique of male sexual aggression. Constructivist libertarians concur in the assumption on which this project rests: that sexual freedom is a basic human value and cannot be ceded or compromised. Yet to abstract sex from biology—from our bodily species-life—calls this premise into question. The idea that sex is wholly a social construction removes it from the realm of necessity and makes our sexual choices a matter of ethics and taste. But if libidinal gratification is not a need, on the same bedrock level as the need for self-preservation, why is a sexually free society necessarily preferable to a sexually restrictive one, particularly if sexual freedom appears to conflict with other social goods? At this historical moment, the greatest threat to the very idea of sexual liberation as a possibility is AIDS: those of us who still reject the imposition of a repressive sexual morality stand accused of pushing death. But that argument loses its force if sexual repression is itself deeply inimical to human well-being and even survival; if indeed repression fosters, rather than curbs, sexual and social irresponsibility and violence.

The radical Freudian analysis of sex is embedded in its psychosocial analysis of the family—specifically, of how children are inducted into the established social order, a crucial issue for feminists. In contemporary feminist discourse, however, these are two quite separate discussions. For the most part, feminists who look to psychoanalysis for an explanation of masculine and feminine character formation have adopted the perspective of object relations theory, in which sexual desire, per se, is not a central category. At the same time, feminist sexual liberationists have examined the varieties of desire—particularly "deviant," which is to say dissident, desire—and their representation, exploring their complex relation to (among other things) gender, race, class, heterosexual dominance, and erotophobia, but displaying little interest in their origins. Again, this lacuna is understandable: for both women and homosexuals, inquiry into the process of sexual development has always been linked with assumptions of pathology. Yet only by analyzing that process can we understand how sexual morality in a patriarchal culture becomes a primary instrument of social control. This question, finally, is the central concern of my essay, which I offer not only as an entry in the debate between feminist sexual radicals and conservatives, but as an invitation to further discussion of what sexual radicalism means.

I

The traditional patriarchal family maintains sexual law and order on two fronts. It regulates the relations between the sexes, enforcing male dominance, female subordination, and the segregation of "masculine" and "feminine" spheres. It also regulates sexuality per se, defining as illicit any sexual activity unrelated to reproduction or outside the bounds of heterosexual, monogamous marriage. Accordingly, the new right's militant defense of traditional family values has a dual thrust: it is at once a male-supremacist backlash against feminism and a reaction by cultural conservatives of both sexes against the "sexual revolution" of the '60s and '70s.

There is, of course, an integral connection between sexism and sexual repression. The suppression of women's sexual desire and pleasure, the denial of reproductive freedom, and the enforcement of female abstinence outside marriage have been primary underpinnings of male supremacy. Conversely, a restrictive sexual morality inevitably constrains women more than men, even in religious subcultures that profess a single standard. Not only is unwanted pregnancy a built-in punishment for female participation in sex (assuming the prohibition of birth control and abortion on the one hand, and lesbianism on the other) and therefore a powerful inhibitor; it is visible evidence of sexual "delinquency," which subjects women who break the rules to social sanctions their male partners never have to face. Still, it is important to recognize that the right's opposition to sexual permissiveness—as expressed in its attacks on abortion, homosexuality, "pornography" (defined as any sexually explicit material), sex education, and adolescents' access to contraception and abortion without parental consent—has consequences for both sexes. Gays and teenagers are obvious targets. But the success of the "pro-family" agenda would also impinge on the lives of adult heterosexual men, who would have to contend with the unwanted pregnancies of their wives and lovers, women's increased sexual fears and inhibitions, restrictions on frank discussion and public legitimation of sex and sexual fantasy, and a general chilling of the sexual atmosphere. While some men are willing to accept such constraints on their own freedom in order to reassert certain traditional controls over women, many are not.

The dual focus of right-wing sexual politics, on feminism and on sex itself, has serious implications for feminist theory and strategy. It means that feminists cannot define their opposition solely in terms of defending female autonomy against male power, nor can they ignore the fact that conflict over sexual morality cuts across gender lines. If the women's movement is to organize effectively against the right, it will have to develop a political theory of sexuality and in particular an analysis of the relation between feminism and sexual freedom. Such an analysis would help feminists to identify and avoid responses to sexual issues that unwittingly undercut feminist aims. It would clarify many disagreements among women who regard themselves as feminists. It would also enable feminists to seek alliances with male opponents of the right's sexual politics—alliances that are undoubtedly necessary if the battle is to be won—on the basis of a clear understanding of mutual interests, differences that need to be resolved to achieve a working coalition, and issues on which it is possible to agree to disagree. The intensity of debate on sex among feminists and gay activists reflects a visceral comprehension—if not always an articulate understanding—of how much is at stake.

At present, the right has its feminist opponents at an enormous disadvantage: it has a coherent ideology and program whose anti-feminist and anti-sexual aspects reinforce each other. In contrast, feminists are ambivalent, confused, and divided in their views on sexual freedom. While there have been feminist sexual libertarians in both the 19th century and contemporary movements, for the most part women's liberation and sexual liberation have developed as separate, often antagonistic causes. The sexual libertarian movement that began in the 1950s was conspicuously male-dominated and male-supremacist. Though it advocated a single standard of freedom from sexual guilt and conventional moral restrictions, it displayed no insight into the social reasons for women's greater inhibition and conformity to moral norms. On the contrary, women were blamed—often in virulently misogynist terms—for adhering to the sexual prohibitions men and a patriarchal society had forced on them. At the same time male libertarians intensified women's sexual anxieties by equating repression with the desire for love and commitment, and exalting sex without emotion or attachment as the ideal. From this perspective liberation for men meant rebelling against the demands of women, while liberation for women meant the opportunity (read obligation) to shuck their "hangups" about casual sex.

The question that remained unasked was whether men had sexual hangups of their own. Was the rejection of any link between sexual desire and emotional involvement really an expression of freedom—or merely another form of repression? To what extent did men's demand for "pure" sex represent a predatory disregard of women as people—an attitude that could only reinforce the conventionally feminine sexual reluctance, passivity, and unresponsiveness that men found so frustrating? There was also the touchy issue of whether sex as conventionally initiated and orchestrated by men was pleasurable for women. In theory there was much concern with female orgasm and the need for men to satisfy women; in practice that concern often translated into a demand that women corroborate men's ideas about female sexuality and protect men's egos by acting satisfied whether they were or not. A conservative popular Freudianism neatly coopted the idea that women had a right to sexual fulfillment by preaching that such fulfillment could be achieved only through "mature" acceptance of the feminine role. In effect women were told that to actively assert their sexual needs would make satisfaction of those needs impossible; if they were submissive and yet unsatisfied it meant they weren't submissive in their hearts. For women trapped in this logic, the theoretical right to orgasm became a new source of pain, inadequacy, and self-blame. Finally, the sexual revolution did not seriously challenge the taboo on lesbianism (or homosexuality in general).

At its inception, the women's liberation movement was dominated by young women who had grown up during or since the emergence of sexual libertarian ideology; many radical feminists came out of the left and the counterculture, where that ideology was particularly strong. Unsurprisingly, one of the first issues to surface in the movement was women's pent-up rage at men's one-sided, exploitative view of sexual freedom. From our consciousness-raising sessions we concluded that women couldn't win no matter how they behaved. We were still oppressed by a sexual double standard that while less rigid was by no means obsolete: women who took too literally their supposed right to sexual freedom and pleasure were regularly put down as "easy," "aggressive," or "promiscuous." Heterosexual women still lived in fear of unwanted pregnancy; in 1968 abortion was illegal—except in the most dire circumstances—in every state. Yet at the same time men were demanding that women have sex on their terms, unmindful of the possible consequences, and without reference to our own feelings and needs. In addition to suffering sexual frustration from the inhibitions instilled by repressive parents, fear of pregnancy, and men's sexual judgments and exploitative behavior, we had to swallow the same men's humiliating complaints about how neurotic, frigid, and unliberated we were. Unfortunately, the movement's efforts to make political sense of this double bind led to confusions in feminist thinking about sex that are still unresolved.

At least in theory, organized feminism from the '60s to the present has been united in endorsing sexual freedom for women, including the right to express our sexual needs freely, to engage in sexual activity for our own pleasure, to have sex and bear children outside marriage, to control our fertility, to refuse sex with any particular man or all men, to be lesbians. Almost as universally, feminists have regarded male sexuality with suspicion if not outright hostility. From the beginning radical feminists argued that freedom as men defined it was against women's interests; if anything men already had too much freedom, at women's expense. One faction in the movement strongly defended women's traditional demands for marriage and monogamy against the anti-nuclear family, sexual liberationist rhetoric of the counterculture. Proponents of this view held that the sexual revolution simply legitimized the age-old tendency of men in a male-supremacist society to coerce, cajole, or fool women into giving them sex without getting anything—love, respect, responsibility for the children, or even erotic pleasure—in return.[1] At the other extreme were feminists who argued that under present conditions, any kind of sexual contact with men, in marriage or out, was oppressive, and that the issue for women was how to resist the relentless social pressure to be with a man.[2] Later, lesbian separatists elaborated this argument, claiming that only women were capable of understanding and satisfying women's sexual needs.

The idea that in the interest of equality women's sexual freedom must be expanded and men's restricted has a surface common-sense logic. Yet in practice it is full of contradictions. For one thing, the same social changes that allow greater freedom for women inevitably mean greater freedom for men. Historically, a woman's main protection from sexual exploitation has been to be a "good girl" and demand marriage as the price of sex—in other words, relinquish her sexual spontaneity to preserve her bargaining power. Furthermore, this traditional strategy will not work for individual women if most women "scab" by abandoning it, which implies the need for some form of social or moral pressure to keep women in line. (If one assumes that women will voluntarily decline to take advantage of their increased freedom, then demanding it makes no sense in the first place.) In practice, relaxing social condemnation of female "unchastity" and permitting women access to birth control and abortion allays social concern about men's "ruining" or impregnating respectable women, and so invariably reduces the pressure on men— both from women and from other men—to restrain their demands for casual sex. Thus the feminist critique of male sexuality tends to bolster the familiar conservative argument that a morality restricting sex to marriage is in women's interest—indeed, that its purpose is to protect women from selfish male lust.

Another difficulty is that judgments of men's heterosexual behavior necessarily imply judgments about what women want. Dissenters within feminist groups immediately challenged the prevailing judgments, arguing with monogamists that they wanted to sleep with more than one man, or that they didn't want the state messing into their sex lives, and arguing with separatists that they enjoyed sex with men. As a result, assumptions about what women want were soon amended to authoritative pronouncements on what women *really* want/ought to want/would want if they were not intimidated/ bought off/brainwashed by men. The ironic consequence has been the development of feminist sexual orthodoxies that curtail women's freedom by setting up the movement as yet another source of guilt-provoking rules about what women should do and feel.

That irony is compounded by another: the orthodoxies in question dovetail all too well with traditional patriarchal ideology. This is most obviously true of polemics in favor of heterosexual monogamy, but it is no less true of lesbian separatism, which in recent years has had far more impact on feminist thinking. There have been two overlapping but distinct tendencies in lesbian feminist politics: the first has emphasized lesbianism as a forbidden erotic choice and lesbians as an oppressed sexual minority; the other—aligning itself with the separatist faction that surfaced in the radical feminist movement before lesbianism as such became an issue—has defined lesbianism primarily as a political commitment to separate from men and bond with women.[3] The latter tendency has generated a sexual ideology best described as neo-Victorian. It regards heterosexual relations as more or less synonymous with rape, on the grounds that male sexuality is by definition predatory and sadistic: men are exclusively "genitally-oriented" (a phrase that is always used pejoratively) and uninterested in loving relationships. Female sexuality, in contrast, is defined as tender, nonviolent, and not necessarily focused on the genitals; intimacy and physical warmth are more important to us than orgasm. The early pre-lesbian separatists argued that celibacy was a reasonable alternative to sleeping with men, and some suggested that the whole idea of a compelling sexual drive was a male invention designed to keep women in their place; women didn't need sex, and men's lust was less for pleasure than for power.[4] In short, to the neo-Victorians men are beasts who are only after one thing, while women are nice girls who would just as soon skip it. The inescapable implication is that women who profess to enjoy sex with men, especially penile-vaginal intercourse itself, are liars or masochists; in either case victims of, or collaborators with, oppression. Nor are lesbians automatically exempt from criticism; gay women whose sexual proclivities do not conform to the approved feminine stereotype are assumed to be corrupted by heterosexism.

Though neo-Victorianism has been most militantly promoted by lesbian separatists, in modified form—i.e., allowing that men (some men at least) can change their ways and be good lovers—it has also had wide appeal for heterosexual feminists. (Conversely, lesbians have been among its loudest critics; this is not a gay-straight split.) Its most popular current expression is the anti-pornography movement, which has seized on pornography as an all-purpose symbol of sex that is genitally-oriented, hence male, hence sadistic and violent, while invoking the concept of "erotica" as code for sex that is gentle, romantic, relationship-oriented—in a word, feminine. Clearly, this conventional view of female as opposed to male sexuality is consistent with many women's subjective experience. Indeed, there are probably few women who don't identify with it to some degree. But to take that experience at face value is to ignore its context: a patriarchal society that has systematically inhibited female sexuality and defined direct, active physical desire as a male prerogative. Feminist neo-Victorians have made the same mistake—only with the sexes reversed—as male libertarians who criticize female sexual behavior while adopting stereotypical male sexuality as the standard for judging sexual health and happiness. In the process they have actively reinforced the larger society's taboos on women's genital sexuality. From a conservative perspective, a woman who has assertive genital desires and acts on them is "bad" and "unwomanly"; from the neo-Victorian perspective she is "brainwashed" and "male-identified."

Overtly or implicitly, many feminists have argued that sexual coercion is a more important problem for women than sexual repression. In the last few years, the women's movement has increasingly emphasized violence against women as a primary—if not *the* primary—concern. While sexual violence, coercion, and harassment have always been feminist issues, earlier feminist analyses tended to regard physical force as one of several ways that men insure women's compliance to a sexist system, and in particular to their subordinate wife-and-mother role. The main function of sexual coercion, in this view, is to curb women's freedom, including their sexual freedom. Rape and the tacit social tolerance of it convey the message that, simply by being sexual, women are "provocative" and deserve punishment, especially if they step out of their place (the home) or transgress society's definition of the "good" (inhibited) woman. Similarly, sexual harassment on the street or on the job, and exploitative sexual demands by male "sexual revolutionaries," punish women for asserting themselves, sexually and otherwise, in the world.

The current feminist preoccupation with male violence has a very different focus. Rape and pornography, redefined as a form of rape, are regarded not as aspects of a larger sexist system but as the foundation and essence of sexism, while sexual victimization is seen as the central fact of women's oppression. Just as male violence against women is equated with male supremacy, freedom from violence is equated with women's liberation.[5] From this standpoint the positive aspect of freedom—freedom for women to *act*—is at best a secondary concern, and freedom for women to assert an active genital sexuality is, by the logic of neo-Victorianism, a contradiction in terms.

Whatever its intent, the effect of feminists' emphasis on controlling male sexuality—particularly when that emphasis is combined with a neo-Victorian view of women's nature and the conviction that securing women's safety from male aggression should be the chief priority of the women's movement—is to undercut feminist opposition to the right. It provides powerful reinforcement for conservative efforts to manipulate women's fear of untrammeled male sexuality, intimidating women into stifling their own impulses toward freedom so as to cling to what little protection the traditional roles still offer. The convergence of neo-Victorian and pro-family ideology is most striking in the recent attempts by so-called "feminists for life" to argue that abortion is "violence against women" and a way for men to escape responsibility for their sexual behavior. While this argument did not come from within the feminist movement but from anti-abortion pacifists seeking to justify their position to feminists, it is perfectly consistent with neo-Victorian logic. No tendency in organized feminism has yet advocated outlawing abortion, but one does occasionally hear the argument that feminists should spend less energy defending abortion and more on educating women to understand that the real solution to unwanted pregnancy is to stop sleeping with men.[6]

Neo-Victorians have also undermined feminist opposition to the right by equating feminism with their own sexual attitudes, in effect reading out of the movement any woman who disagrees with them. Since their notion of proper feminist sexuality echoes conventional moral judgments and the anti-sexual propaganda presently coming from the right, their guilt-mongering has been quite effective. Many feminists who are aware that their sexual feelings contradict the neo-Victorian ideal have lapsed into confused and apologetic silence. No doubt there are also thousands of women who have quietly concluded that if this ideal is feminism, then feminism has nothing to do with them.

I I

In short, feminists are at a theoretical impasse. If a feminist politics that advocates restrictions on male sexuality leads inexorably to the sexual repression of women and the strengthening of anti-feminist forces, such a politics is obviously untenable. But how can women support sexual freedom for both sexes without legitimizing the most oppressive aspects of male sexual behavior? I believe our hope for resolving this dilemma lies in reexamining certain widely shared assumptions about sex, male versus female sexuality, and the meaning of sexual liberation.

The philosophy of the "sexual revolution" as we know it is an extension of liberalism: it defines sexual freedom as the simple absence of external restrictions—laws and overt social taboos—on sexual information and activity. Since most people accept this definition, there is widespread agreement that we are already a sexually emancipated society. The easy availability of casual sex, the virtual lack of restrictions (at least for adults) on sexual information and sexually explicit material, the accessibility (for adults again) of contraception, legal abortion, the proliferation of massage parlors and sex clubs, the ubiquity of sexual images and references in the mass media, the relaxation of taboos against "deviant" sexual practices—all are regularly cited as evidence that this culture has largely overcome its anti-sexual history. At the same time, sexual liberalism has clearly not brought nirvana. Noting that "liberated" sexuality is often depressingly shallow, exploitative, and joyless, many men as well as women have concluded that sexual liberation has been tried and found wanting, that it is irrelevant or even inimical to a serious program for social change.

This is a superficial view. In the first place, this society is far from endorsing, even in principle, people's right to consensual sexual relations, of whatever sort they prefer, as a basic liberty. (Skeptics are invited to imagine public reaction to a proposed constitutional amendment guaranteeing freedom of sexual association.) There is strong and stubborn resistance to legalizing—let alone accepting as socially and morally legitimate—all sexual acts between consenting adults; children have no recognized sexual rights at all, and adolescents virtually none.[7] But a more basic problem with this premature disillusionment is that it focuses on the quantity and variety of sexual activity, rather than the quality of sexual experience. Ultimately, the premise of sexual libertarian movements is that a gratifying sexual life is a human need whose denial causes unnecessary and unjustified suffering. Certainly, establishing people's right to pursue sexual happiness with a consenting partner is a condition for ending that suffering. Yet as most of us have had occasion to discover, it is entirely possible to "freely" participate in a sexual act and feel frustrated, indifferent, or even repelled. From a radical standpoint, then, sexual liberation involves not only the abolition of restrictions but the positive presence of social and psychological conditions that foster satisfying sexual relations. And from that standpoint, this culture is still deeply repressive. Most obviously, sexual inequality and the resulting antagonism between men and women are a devastating barrier to sexual happiness. I will argue in addition that sexual liberalism notwithstanding, most children's upbringing produces adults with profoundly negative attitudes toward sex. Under these conditions, the relaxation of sexual restrictions leads people to try desperately to overcome the obstacles to satisfaction through compulsive sexual activity and preoccupation with sex. The emphasis on sex that currently permeates our public life—especially the enormous demand for sexual advice and therapy—attests not to our sexual freedom but to our continuing sexual frustration. People who are not hungry are not obsessed with food.

It is in this context that we need to examine the male sexual pattern feminists have protested—the emphasis on conquest and dominance, the tendency to abstract sex from love and social responsibility. Sexual liberalism has allowed many men to assert these patterns in ways that were once socially taboo, and to impose them on reluctant women. But to conclude from this fact that male sexual freedom is inherently oppressive is to make the uncritical assumption that men find predatory, solipsistic sexual relations satisfying and inherently preferable to sex with affection and mutuality. As I have noted, some feminists argue that male sexuality is naturally sadistic. Others grant that men's predatory tendencies are a function of sexism, but assume that they are a simple, direct expression of men's (excessive) freedom and power, the implication being that anyone who has the opportunity to dominate and use other people sexually will of course want to take advantage of it.

This assumption is open to serious question. If one pays attention to what men consciously or unwittingly reveal about their sexual attitudes—in their fiction and confessional writing (see *Portnoy's Complaint* and its epigoni), in their political polemics (see George Gilder's *Sexual Suicide*), in sociological and psychological studies (see *The Hite Report on Male Sexuality* or Lillian Rubin's *Worlds of Pain*), in everyday interaction with women—the picture that emerges is far more complicated and ambiguous. Most men, in fact, profess to want and need mutual sexual love, and often behave accordingly, though they have plenty of opportunity to do otherwise. Many men experience both tender and predatory sexual feelings, toward the same or different women, and find the contradiction bewildering and disturbing; others express enormous pain over their inability to combine sex with love. Often men's impulses to coerce and degrade women seem to express not a confident assumption of dominance but a desire to retaliate for feelings of rejection, humiliation, and impotence: as many men see it, they need women sexually more than women need them, an intolerable imbalance of power.[8] Furthermore, much male sexual behavior clearly reflects men's irrational fears that loss of dominance means loss of maleness itself, that their choice is to "act like a man" or be castrated,[8] embrace the role of oppressor or be degraded to the status of victim.

None of this is to deny men's objective social power over women, their reluctance to give up that power, or their tendency to blame women for their unhappiness rather than recognize that their own oppressive behavior is largely responsible for women's sexual diffidence. My point is only that the behavior that causes women so much grief evidently brings men very little joy; on the contrary, men appear to be consumed with sexual frustration, rage, and anxiety. With their compulsive assertions of power they continually sabotage their efforts to love and be loved. Such self-defeating behavior cannot, in any meaningful sense, be described as free. Rather it suggests that for all the unquestionable advantages men derive from "acting like a man" in a male-supremacist society, the price is repression and deformation of spontaneous sexual feeling.

The idea that untrammeled male sexuality must inevitably be oppressive is rooted in one of our most universal cultural assumptions: that the sexual drive itself (that is, "pure" passion unanchored to the "higher" purposes of marriage and procreation) is inherently

anti-social, separate from love, and connected with aggressive, destructive impulses. (In providing a modern, secular rationale for this
idea, Freud reinforced—even as he demystified—traditional Judeo-
Christian morality.) Sexual liberals have promoted the competing
assumption that sex is simply a healthy, enjoyable biological function with no intrinsic moral connotations. But this bland view not
only violates most people's sense that their sexuality is not an isolated "function," that it is bound up with their emotions, their values,
their very being; it also evades the question of sexual destructiveness.
In practice, sexual liberals often refuse to acknowledge the hostile,
alienated, and exploitative impulses that attend contemporary sexual
"freedom." As a result, people who experience their own sexuality
as corrupted by those impulses, or who feel victimized by the sexual
behavior of others, tend to fall back on some version of the old conservative idea.

There is, however, another possibility, advanced by a minority of
utopians, romantics, and cultural radicals: that sexual desire, tender-
ness, and empathy are aspects of a unified erotic impulse; that the
splitting of this impulse and the attendant perversion of sexual desire
into exploitative, solipsistic lust are an artificial social product. This
thesis has been most systematically and convincingly elaborated in
Wilhelm Reich's radical critique of Freud.[9] In essence, Reich argued
that parental condemnation of infantile genital desires and sensations
forces the child to split (bad) sex from (good) love. The child reacts
to this thwarting of its sexual expression with frustration, rage, and a
desire for revenge. These feelings modify the sexual impulse itself; the
child's sexuality becomes sadistic. If the sadistic feelings are also forbidden they turn inward, producing guilt and masochism. People's
guilt at their own overt or repressed sadism, along with their observation of other people's anti-social behavior, prompts the conviction
that sex is inherently destructive. Yet that conviction rests on a piece
of circular reasoning: repression creates the destructiveness that is
then cited as proof of the eternal need for repression. In this way,
sexual repression becomes the self-perpetuating basis of a sadomasochistic psychology[10] that is in turn crucial to the maintenance of an
authoritarian, hierarchical social order.

Reich contended that people with an anti-sexual upbringing tend to uphold established authority—even when the practical conditions for rebellion exist—because that authority fulfills several functions: it reinforces people's inner controls over their sadistic impulses and protects them from the uncontrolled sadism of others; it invites people to express sadistic feelings vicariously by identifying with authority; and it permits people to vent those feelings directly on whoever is below them in the social hierarchy. In this way the anger that should inspire social rebellion is transformed into a conservative force, impelling people to submit masochistically to their oppressors while bullying their "inferiors." Yet even for ruling classes, Reich maintained, power is at best a substitute for genuine fulfillment.

Reich's concept of a basic erotic unity shattered by genital repression has radical implications for feminist sexual politics. I have tried to show how efforts to control male sexuality undermine women's struggle for freedom and equality, and vice versa. To take the argument a step further, if the sexual impulse is intrinsically selfish and aggressive, there are two possible explanations for why men's sexuality, far more than women's, has displayed these characteristics. One is that sexual desire, per se, is inherently male; the pitfalls of this idea have been discussed at length. The other is that women have simply not been allowed to be as selfish and exploitative as men; to adopt this notion puts feminists in the position of agreeing with conservatives that liberating women from the feminine role would destroy the social cement that keeps civilization going. If, on the other hand, sexual destructiveness can be seen as a perversion that both reflects and perpetuates a repressive system, it is possible to envision a coherent feminist politics in which a commitment to sexual freedom plays an integral part.

Similarly, if parents, by rejecting their children's genitality, atomize the erotic impulse and direct infantile sexuality into a sadistic mode, the source of the difference between "masculine" and "feminine" sexual patterns seems clear. While boys are permitted, indeed encouraged, to incorporate their sadistic impulses into their sexual identities and to express them in socially approved ways, girls' aggression is no more tolerated than their genitality. Like men, women experience a split between lust and love, but the lustful component of their sexuality is subjected to severe inhibition. Women who do not suppress their lustful feelings altogether—or sublimate them into disembodied romanticism or mother love—usually feel free to express them only in the relatively safe and socially validated context of marriage or a quasi-marital commitment: what looks like women's superior ability to integrate sex and love is only a more hidden form of alienation.

I I I

I want to argue, then, that male and female children develop masculine and feminine sexual psychologies thorough a systematic (though largely unconscious) process of parental intimidation, in which sexual repression and sexism function symbiotically. But before I go on, I ought to note that its controversial premises aside, my thesis has another difficulty. Like psychoanalysis itself, my argument invokes a model of family that is in rapid decline in this country and arguably has never applied to large sections of the American (let alone the world's) population: the "ideal" nuclear family, in which the parents provide a traditional model of sexual roles and attitudes toward sex, and dispense strict but loving parental discipline. Freud and Reich developed their theories in the context of Victorian middle-class family life. I grew up in the '40s and '50s, when the male breadwinner/dependent wife pattern was still hegemonic (if far from universal), and my ideas about sexual character formation have been strongly influenced by insights from my own psychotherapy. How, then, can I presume to generalize beyond these culturally specific milieus?

My presumption starts with the idea that whatever their differences, all patriarchal cultures uphold—indeed are defined by—certain basic institutional norms. One is male supremacy and its psychic concomitants, masculine and feminine identity. Another is the underlying denigration (often masked by surface acceptance) of genital sexuality. The third is familialism, a system in which children belong legally and socially to their parents (with varying ties to other biological kin), while the society as a whole has only the most minimal responsibility for their welfare—which means that they depend for survival on parental love and, particularly when very young, are subject to virtually unlimited parental control. In my view, the cultural ingredients of the repressive symbiosis I'm about to describe are precisely these ubiquitous norms. Furthermore, while the patriarchal family has taken many forms and served a variety of social and economic functions in different times and places and among different social groups, its constant essential task has been to care for and socialize children, thereby perpetuating its norms from one generation to the next. Granted that this process too has been subject to countless variations, produced by historical, class, racial, religious and other cultural differences, surely it must also have crucial common elements. And my speculation is that the nuclear household reveals, or at least suggests, such commonalities, for precisely the same reason it inspired psychoanalysis in the first place: the family in its mom-dad-kids configuration, stripped of extended family relationships and preindustrial socioeconomic baggage, confined within a privatized domestic environment and devoted almost exclusively to its bedrock purpose, can make its psychic dynamics uniquely visible.

In the contemporary American context, this analysis implies that the sexual psychology of the iconic white middle class suburban family of the '50s still has something to do with our own reality despite three decades of massive social change that includes black rejection of the presumed superiority of white middle class culture, feminism, gay liberation, the normalization of women (particularly mothers) in the work force, sexual liberalism, easy divorce, the weakening of parental authority, and the rising incidence of single motherhood (which among the urban black poor amounts to the virtual demise of the patriarchal family in any form). Just as the new right charges, all such changes destabilize and threaten to undermine the process of "normal" sexual character formation. Yet this remains a sexist and sex-negative culture, and, as the condition of millions of poor children attests, a dogmatically familialist one.

To understand how sexism and sexual repression converge in the child's mind, it is necessary, in my view, to rethink two Freudian concepts that most feminists have either rejected or interpreted in purely symbolic terms—castration anxiety and penis envy. My contention is that children subjected to the three social conditions I've enumerated develop a quite literal belief in the reality or threat of an

attack on their genitals as pleasure-giving organs, as well as an artificial valuation of the penis as an indicator of social power and worth.[11]
From infancy children absorb two sets of messages about their sexual
organs. As soon as they discover genital desire and pleasure, they
learn that such feelings are forbidden. Masturbation and interest in
their own, their parents' or other children's genitals provoke parental
anxiety and discomfort if not outright displeasure. Their frustrated
desire excites aggressive, vengeful feelings and fantasies that are even
more taboo, so that their infantile experience of genitality is thoroughly permeated with a sense of danger. Meanwhile, they have been
learning—by observing the behavior of their parents, their siblings,
and the world at large—about the social differences between the
sexes. At some point, they come to understand that there are two
classes of people, one superior and dominant, one inferior and subordinate, distinguished by the presence or absence of the penis. It
seems entirely reasonable that children's efforts to piece together all
this disturbing information about sex and gender should lead them
to the terrible conclusion that girls have been physically mutilated
and socially devalued for bad sexual desires, and that boys risk being
punished for their badness in similar fashion.

   This perceived catastrophe drastically alters the child's relation to
the world. The child already knows that its parents have the fearful
power to deprive it of love, protection, even life, but that knowledge
is typically leavened by confidence in the parents' love. The apparent
evidence of female castration convinces the child, far more effectively
than normal parental discipline could do, that even the most loving
parents are willing to use their power in a truly terrifying way. This in
turn suggests to the child that its badness must be utter depravity; the
other logical possibility—that the parents are not really loving at all,
but capriciously, monstrously cruel—is too frightening to contemplate. The child may at first deny the evidence, or its full import, or
its irrevocability, but eventually the bad news sinks in and becomes a
traumatic blow to the child's lingering hopes of beating the system.
In accepting the awful truth, the child undergoes a kind of conversion to the parents' sexual values. After that, though he or she may
still rebel, it will be with a sense of moral illegitimacy.

   Since the child's sexual desires do not go away, but continue to
evoke anxiety and guilt, its only choice is to repress the whole com-

plex of feelings, especially the traumatic discovery with which they are connected; this ensures that the infantile interpretation of sexual difference will remain impervious to rational correction. But the impact of the trauma, and the degree of sexual repression it generates, are not the same for both sexes. For one thing, their earlier experience has been different: from the beginning, girls' sexual and aggressive impulses are restricted more severely. In addition, there is an enormous emotional difference between fear of mutilation and the conviction that one has already been mutilated. The boy's fear of castration is softened by the knowledge that so far he has been bad and gotten away with it; the girl imagines that her defiance has provoked terrible retribution. The boy fears a punishment that, bad as it is, is specific and limited; the girl's speculation on what might happen to her if she persists in incurring parental wrath is limited only by her imagination and capacity for terror. The boy feels impotent, humiliated by his parents' ability to frighten him into submission; the girl suffers, in addition, the far more devastating humiliation of consignment to an inferior class. Furthermore, her terror and humiliation are compounded by other intensely powerful emotions: violation, grief, despair.

The children's subsequent experience will reinforce these sexual differences. The boy will see that within prescribed limits he can safely express his "bad" impulses toward women outside the family, with greater or lesser freedom depending on the women's social status. Given this outlet, his fear will actually stimulate his sexual aggression: by "acting like a man" he can continually assure himself that he is not a woman, while maintaining vigilant control over these castrated beings who must surely hate him and covet his precious organ. The girl, in contrast, will observe that male power often expresses itself in sexual hostility and aggression; she will see that men punish rebellious women with contempt, rejection, and violence. When she grasps the concept of rape she will understand it as a reenactment of her original violation. All this will add to her terror and give it concrete form. In the interest of survival she must at all costs suppress her bitterness, hatred, envy, vengefulness, and predatory lust and accept her subordination. She must desperately direct her energies toward being *good*.

The castration trauma can be seen as the pivotal event of an ongoing process of acculturation in which parents prepare their children to "freely" embrace a masculine or feminine identity—that is, to see conventional sexual behavior and attitudes as the only tenable alternative and to repress feelings that do not fit the mold. In large part, parents accomplish this simply by acting out their own masculine and feminine patterns in relation to the child. That parents unconsciously assume toward their children their entire complex of cultural attitudes toward men, women, and sexuality would explain the common observation that in relating to a child of the other sex, heterosexual parents undercut their sexual prohibitions with covert seductiveness, while in relating to a child of the same sex, they augment the prohibitions with covert hostility based on competitiveness and, no doubt, defenses against forbidden homosexual feelings. Since the parents have internalized the cultural atomization of the erotic, their seductiveness—split off from acceptably sexless parental love—will have a predatory aspect, accentuated by the power differential between adult and child.

This configuration suggests a particular view of another Freudian construction, the Oedipus complex. Though children undoubtedly feel a spontaneous erotic attraction to their parents (especially, given the present system of childrearing, their mothers), there is no reason to believe that intense, exclusive heterosexual desire for one parent and jealous hatred of the other necessarily follow, even for boys, while Freud himself acknowledged that the Oedipus complex in girls required further explanation. On the contrary, it seems likely that parents instigate the Oedipal triangle, encouraging the other-sex child's fantasies with their seductiveness (while at the same time their disapproval inhibits the child's sexual explorations in general), and provoking or exacerbating same-sex rivalry with their own hostile, competitive behavior.

If the castration trauma terrorizes children into foreclosing certain psychic possibilities (accepting sexual desire as good and natural, seeing male-female difference as a morally neutral fact), the function of the Oedipal situation, as I will try to show, is to channel their response to the trauma in socially approved directions, beginning, most obviously, with heterosexuality. Under "normal" circumstances the child, in coping with the desire, fear, rage, guilt, and disappoint-

ment the triangle generates, will eventually come to identify with the
prescribed sexual roles because they represent the path of least resistance, offering the least risk of punishment, the most relief from
guilt, and the most compensatory satisfactions. If something goes
wrong (if, for instance, a child remains unconvinced that conformity
offers any rewards worth having; if disappointment with the parent
of the other sex is too overwhelming, or conversely the attraction is
too strong; if fear of the same-sex parent is excessive or insufficient;
if the parents are truly cruel or neglectful; if actual incest occurs)
he or she may balk at the final giving over to conventional mascu-
line/feminine identity. In adult life the recalcitrant child may prefer
homosexuality or some other form of "deviance"; develop a sexual
personality defined by overt emotional conflict and "maladjustment";
or withdraw from the sexual arena altogether. In practice, of course,
these choices overlap and form a continuum, from a decisive commitment to masculinity or femininity, with more or less successful
repression of conflicting desires, to total refusal, generally disastrous
to the individual concerned, to be conscripted into the sexual culture.

What follows is an attempt to outline the paradigmatic "successful" working out of the Oedipus complex for both sexes. The discussion assumes two heterosexual parents in the home, with the mother
as primary caretaker—even now the situation of most young children. As I've suggested, families that diverge significantly from this
model should logically produce a wider, less predictable range of
sexual psychologies, a prospect of major concern to social conservatives. But there is a complication to keep in mind. Sexual acculturation has never been more than relatively successful, even in societies
enforcing rigid adherence to traditional patriarchal standards. However thorough the imposition of psychic repression and guilt, "illicit"
sexual desire and rage continually threaten to break through, which is
why internal controls must be reinforced by external social sanctions.
The system's failures, its "bad" and "deviant" products, do not really
contradict the norm, only invite its enforcement. Similarly, individual
families or even familial cultures that deviate from the norm do not
exist in a vacuum. They are situated in a dominant culture that affects both parental behavior and attitudes and children's perceptions
of how families are supposed to work, as well as a cultural history

that has shaped the parents' emotional makeup. For a child brought up by a single parent with a conventional sexual identity in a conventional environment, a fantasy of the missing parent may in crucial respects substitute for the actual person; even if the child has never met the absent parent, and if the caretaking parent does not have lovers on whom the child's imagination can focus, he or she may construct a workable fantasy out of parental and social messages about what mothers or fathers are like. (Conversely, in a standard nuclear family whose emotional undercurrents are greatly at odds with the facade of normality, the child's experience and consequent path may be far less typical.) As for urban black cultures stigmatized as deviant because of (among other things) their "matriarchal structures" and "absent fathers," the resulting differences in sexual patterns fit comfortably within the dominant culture's images of badness and otherness. What I'm proposing is that the psychology perpetuated by the "ideal" Oedipus conflict defines a sexual norm that, however attacked and eroded, still exerts a powerful influence on most people's behavior and unconscious predispositions. In fact, I would question whether people whose childhood experience departed so radically from the paradigm that it has no emotional resonance for them can function in this culture even as deviants.

In the "normal" case, the mother's role in the family insures that from the beginning boys and girls get different signals about sex. To the boy, the mother conveys a complex and contradictory message of affection, seduction, and rejection. In the context of her maternal love and his infantile dependence, her seductiveness, with its admixture of aggression, makes her an embodiment of erotic power that is both irresistible and scary; at the same time her disapproving rejection of his sexual response frustrates and confuses him. His father, on the other hand, is more clearly censorious, more emotionally distant (since he is less involved in the child's day-to-day care), and much more powerful: the mother, so potent a figure in relation to the boy, is obviously subject to the father's control. It is also clear that father has claimed mother for himself, and that the sexual prohibitions he enforces on the rest of the family do not apply to him.

The boy's discovery of his mother's "castration" puts all this in a new light: mother belongs to the deprived class, therefore she must envy and hate his maleness. This explains both the predatory element in her desire—which he interprets now as a potential attack on his penis, stemming from a wish to appropriate the prized object—and, in part, her sexual rejection. He is outraged at his mother's betrayal in condemning the "badness" she has encouraged—and of which she is equally guilty, as her penisless condition attests. But he also understands her behavior as a means of protecting both of them from his father. For father is obviously responsible for mother's punishment, and by far the greater threat to his own manhood.

In response to this threat, the boy represses his guilty desire and his rage at his father. He accepts his father's moral authority and adopts him as a model, a strategy that is at once a form of appeasement and of acceptable competition. But he can allow himself to feel considerable anger at his less dangerous mother. By deprecating her (she is after all "only a woman") he takes revenge, reduces the danger still further, comforts himself for his loss, and compensates for the humiliation of having to submit to his father. Yet he also idealizes her: out of guilt and the need to renounce their sexual bond (and also as a way of negating his father's victory), he denies her seductive attitude and transforms her into the pure woman who rejects men's bad impulses for their own good.

The mother is more unambiguously hostile to her daughter's sexuality. Besides seeing the girl as a rival and a doubly taboo sexual object, she feels freer to exercise power over a (mere) girl. We can also assume that she identifies more with a daughter, and that the girl's naive desire threatens to undermine her own hard-won inhibitions. Finally, it is mother's job to enforce the sexual double standard. The likely result is that the girl will blame her mother for her mutilation, while her father's seductiveness gives rise to the hope that he, as the real authority in the family, will rescind the punishment. Disillusioned with mother (her first love), she diverts her passion to father and imagines that he will side with her because she is willing to be "bad" with him in defiance of spiteful mother (who, as the girl sees it, wants her child to share her own deprived state). Also, since she has not yet accepted her inferior status as irrevocable or deserved, she believes that she is worthy of her father, while her mother is clearly not his equal. Her moment of awful truth comes when she understands that her father will neither restore her penis nor choose her over her mother. Though he has encouraged her badness, he nonetheless condemns it and stands with his wife, the good woman, against her. She realizes now that the powerful man she counted on to protect her may abandon or turn on her instead.

With this realization, her perception of the aggressiveness in her father's desire translates into a threat of rape, or even death. With horror and panic she imagines that having alienated her mother and failed to win her father she is an outcast, alone, powerless, contemptible. Her only recourse is to devote herself to appeasing her parents in the hope of regaining some sense of a secure place in the world, and, despite her humiliating demotion, some kind of self-respect. She adopts her mother's sexual righteousness, not only out of fear and guilt but because she has begun to believe that her mother punished her out of love, to warn her and keep her from inciting her father to rape and murder. On one level the girl's loyalties revert to a pre-Oedipal pattern, in which father was if anything an unwelcome rival for mother's attention: she sees herself and her mother as fellow victims of male power. Yet she does not completely suppress her desire for her father, who continues to be seductive as well as rejecting. Rather, she represses the self-willed aggression at the core of her "badness" and, again taking her mother as a model, expresses her sexual response in an indirect, muted—i.e., feminine—way. Thus she propitiates her father while simultaneously placating and competing with her mother.

In the girl's case, the most dangerous emotion is not her Oedipal desire, in itself, but her subversive wish to reject her female destiny. She can admit (much more readily than the boy can admit of his mother) that she is sexually attracted to her father and craves his sexual approval; what she cannot afford to recognize is her fury at not getting satisfaction, at being forced into passivity with the threat of violence. Like the boy, she is often able to express a modicum of anger at mother, who is less powerful and, she surmises, has already done her worst; such anger usually takes the form of competitiveness, disparagement of mother's inferior feminine traits, and complaints about being dominated, unloved, or misunderstood. But it is a superficial, ambivalent anger, for the daughter's deepest feelings of rage and betrayal must remain buried if she is to do what she has to do: be a woman.

For both sexes, the incentive to identify with the same-sex parent and embrace a conventional sexual role is not only fear of punishment but the prospect of psychic and social rewards. For the boy the rewards are greater, more direct, and more obvious. He will be able to express his aggressive impulses, his needs for both autonomy and power, in a wide range of non-sexual activities in the larger world (which activities and how wide a range will depend on his position in the class and racial hierarchy, but his opportunity will always exceed that of women in comparable social categories). He will have authority over women, the power to punish them if they forget their place, and a gratifying feeling of superiority. He will have considerable leeway in demanding and taking sexual pleasure, which, however morally dubious, even in his own eyes, is nonetheless a prerogative and an imperative of manhood.

For the girl, the male-dominated world outside the home promises little in the way of power, material reward, or self-esteem. Direct, aggressive pursuit of sexual gratification or personal power over men is taboo. Given these strictures, the role of good woman has significant advantages.[12] It allows her to exercise a certain amount of power by withholding sex and manipulating men's desire. It enables her to marry: with luck her husband will provide indirect access to the resources of the male world, a vicarious outlet for her impulses to worldly participation and power, disguised sexual fulfillment in the form of romantic ecstasy and (if she is really lucky) actual sexual satisfaction within permissible bounds. Marriage carries with it the privilege of motherhood, which will become her greatest and most socially legitimate source of power, as well as a source of erotic pleasure. Finally, goodness offers her a means to retrieve her shattered pride. If she is good, men will respect her; in fact, she can claim moral superiority to men with their animal urges. In the name of morality she can, if she chooses, crusade against vice, bully "bad" women, and even make men feel guilty—another socially acceptable way to vent aggression and exercise power.

Since the sexual formations of women and men are complementary, each sex to a large extent meets the expectations (positive and negative, overt and repressed) of the other; the child's experience with the other-sex parent "works" when applied to other heterosexual objects (which is why, just by "acting naturally," each new generation of parents recreates that experience with its children). In adult life, the masculine man displaces most of his feelings about his mother to his relations with other women, carrying with him the emotional contradictions of his childhood. His experience ensures that women can do nothing right, that he will always feel cheated: sexual rejection or reserve evokes the primal disappointment, while ready acceptance (let alone active seduction) revives the castration fear. To complicate matters, he assumes that marriage and procreation legitimize his lust (father is allowed to fuck mother), yet to marry a woman and have children with her defines her as good, hence sexually taboo. His unconscious confusions reinforced by social mores, he treats "good" women with "respect"; the rage their reserve provokes he directs—in the form of sexual predation and contempt—toward the "bad" women who respond to him, thereby transgressing their prescribed role and challenging his authority. He tends, in other words, to arrange his sex life on the principle that he wouldn't want to join any club that would have him as a member. When he marries he demands his wife's sexual compliance, yet cannot tolerate any display of "excessive" sexual enthusiasm, initiative, or self-assertion. Then, finding domestic sex boring and his wife's "goodness" inhibiting, he sleeps with (or has fantasies of) more exciting women to whom he need recognize no loyalty or commitment. He feels guilty about his own "bad" desires, yet also proud of them since they confirm his manhood. He considers the "good" woman morally superior to himself, yet has a deep conviction that all women are secretly bad, that their goodness is a hypocritical facade. If he transgresses the bounds of respectful behavior with the good woman, he rationalizes that he could only get away with it because she was really bad all along. At its extreme this is the psychology of the rapist and the wife-beater.

The same double binds ensure that the woman's claim to goodness, hence her safety and legitimacy, is never secure. In the first place, she knows on some level that her goodness *is* phony—that deep down she is indeed lustful, angry, rebellious—and she feels guilty about it. As a result she will often accept the judgment of the rapist or wife-beater that she somehow asked for or deserved punishment. Furthermore, the requirements of goodness are contradictory. The good woman must defer to men, do their will; she must also curb her sexual desire; yet part of what men will is that women not only sleep with them but desire them. Her father wanted her to desire him, but when she went too far (and how far was that? where did she cross the line?) love turned into rejection and threat. As she grows up she will encounter the same dilemma: the boys demand that she be attractive and sexy, but if she goes too far they label her easy; if, on the other hand, she goes too far in the other direction—too aloof, too indifferent—they condemn her as a cold bitch or a sexual failure. In marriage the good woman must not refuse her husband but must not demand too much. Always she must walk the elusive line between being too good, therefore bad, and not good enough. The line shifts with history and circumstance, the particular man or his particular mood; the more freedom women achieve the more tenuous the line becomes. The anxiety this uncertainty provokes functions actively as a means of social control; women can never stop trying to be *better*, to escape an inescapable taint. Given this impossible situation, it is no wonder that so many feminists are more preoccupied with their fears of male violence than with their hopes for sexual freedom. Indeed, women's quest for security—futile by the very nature of the system—not only discourages women from demanding freedom but often moves them to defend rigid standards of sexual morality and resist any blurring of the line between good and bad women. In doing so, they shore up the very system that punishes them. Finally, the only way women will ever break out of this trap is to end the association between sex and badness.

Sexual liberals have tried to dismiss that association as an unenlightened remnant of our puritanical past. But since the cultural unconscious cannot be erased by fiat, they have succeeded mainly in damaging their credibility. In a sense, sexual liberalism creates its own backlash. Men scoff at the idea of the good woman—and find that they are terrified by the specter of the bad woman, self-willed, demanding, perhaps insatiable. Women try to be free—and end up being punished. Both sexes equate sexual freedom with a license to be bad—and feel guilty. The power imbalance between the sexes remains. As a result, the symbiosis of sexism and sexual repression continues to recreate a complex of patriarchal emotions that increasingly conflict with our rational ideas and aspirations and with the actual conditions of our lives. It is in fact the social instability and psychological tensions this conflict produces that have made people so receptive to "pro-family" ideology. The right proposes to resolve the conflict by changing social reality to conform to our most conservative emotions. Feminist politics, in contrast, often seem to embody the conflict instead of offering an alternative solution. Nor is this any wonder, if such a solution must include a fundamental transformation in people's sexual psychology. Yet however overwhelming and frightening, it is precisely this issue that we must somehow begin to address.

The first step, I believe, is simply to affirm the validity, in principle, of sexual liberation as a feminist goal. This in itself will clarify many confusions and contradictions in current feminist thinking, and indicate practical political directions. For instance, my analysis suggests that crusading against pornography as a symbol of male violence will impede feminism rather than advance it; that focusing *primarily* on issues of women's safety (like rape) may be more problematic and less effective than focusing on issues of women's sexual freedom (like abortion rights); that it is important for feminists to defend people's (including men's) freedom to engage in consensual sexual activity, including acts we may find distasteful. In short, it is a losing proposition for feminists to compete with the right in trying to soothe women's fears of sexual anarchy. We must of course acknowledge those fears and the legitimate reasons for them, but our interest as feminists is to demonstrate that a law-and-order approach to sex can only result in a drastic curtailment of our freedom. In the long run, we can win only if women (and men) want freedom (and love) more than they fear its consequences.

N O T E S

1. Some radical feminists argued that there was nothing wrong with marriage, per se, only with sex roles within marriage. (In a sense this position was an early version of Betty Friedan's "pro-family" feminism, minus the sentimental glossing over of

male power.) Others maintained that while sexual freedom in the context of women's liberation was an ultimate goal, for now it was in our interest to resist the sexual revolution. See, for example, Shulamith Firestone, *The Dialectic of Sex* (Morrow, 1970), pp. 160–163. Another version of this argument was advanced by Kathie Sarachild, an influential theorist in the early movement, in "Hot and Cold Flashes," *The Newsletter*, vol. I, no. 3, May 1, 1969. "We women can use marriage as the 'dictatorship of the proletariat' in the family revolution. When male supremacy is completely eliminated, marriage, like the state, will wither away."

2. Of the early radical feminist groups taking a female separatist position, the most influential were The Feminists in New York City and Cell 16 in Boston.

3. For a lucid exposition of this distinction I am indebted to Alice Echols' "The New Feminism of Yin and Yang," in *Powers of Desire*, ed. Ann Snitow, Christine Stansell, and Sharon Thompson (Monthly Review Press, 1983).

4. The best known exponents of these views were Ti-Grace Atkinson, of The Feminists, and Dana Densmore, of Cell 16.

5. The following is a good example of this kind of thinking: ". . . if we are going to destroy the effects of pornography in our lives . . . We must each be able to visualize on a grand scale what it is that we want for ourselves and for our society . . . Would you try now to think of what it would be like to live in a society in which we are not, every minute, bombarded with sexual violence? Would you try to visualize what it would be like to go to the movies and not see it, to be able to walk home and not be afraid of it . . . If we set that as our goal and demand nothing less, we will not stop fighting until we've achieved it."—Kathleen Barry, "Beyond Pornography: From Defensive Politics to Creating a Vision," in *Take Back The Night: Women on Pornography*, ed. Laura Lederer (Morrow, 1980), p. 312.

6. The June, 1981, issue of the feminist newspaper *off our backs* published two letters to the editor on this theme. One of the writers, while affirming her unequivocal stand in favor of legal abortion, protests, "Why are we fighting so hard to make it 'safe' to fuck with men? . . . Why don't we focus on eliminating the need for abortion and birth control?" The other letter states, "Compulsory pregnancy results from compulsory penetration . . . So I'm getting impatient to know when we will really take control over our bodies and not let ourselves be penetrated?" and goes on to assert "the inescapable fact that since I did not allow men to have control over my body, I could not then turn around and claim control over my baby's body."

7. In the ongoing debate over "the epidemic of teenage pregnancy" and whether it is best dealt with by providing teenagers with contraceptives or giving them lectures on chastity, birth control advocates have argued that access to contraception does not increase teenage sexual activity. So far as I know, no "responsible" organization has dared to suggest that adolescents have sexual needs and should have the right to satisfy them.

8. Shere Hite's *Hite Report on Male Sexuality* (Knopf, 1981) includes many revealing comments from men on this particular theme: see her chapters on "Men's View of Women and Sex" and "Rape, Paying Women for Sex, and Pornography."

9. Reich's basic argument is laid out in *The Function of the Orgasm*, *The Sexual Revolution*, and *The Mass Psychology of Fascism*.

10. Sadomasochism as a consensual sexual practice has recently been a subject of controversy in the women's movement, and among anti-pornography activists "sado-

masochism" has become something of a code word for any form of sexuality condemned by neo-Victorian standards. To avoid confusion, I want to make clear what I mean by "sadomasochistic psychology": an emotional attitude consisting of the impulse to dominate, hurt, or revenge oneself on others, along with a reactive guilt manifested in the impulse to submit to others and seek their protection, while embracing pain and suffering as evidence of one's moral purity. In my view—and Reich's—this attitude is the inner emotional analogue of social hierarchy. In a sense, psychic sadism and masochism are perversions of the impulses to assertive, autonomous activity and emotional giving, respectively—impulses that are inevitably corrupted by social inequality and coercion.

From this perspective, sadomasochism is a universal cultural attitude, expressed in a myriad of sexual and nonsexual, overt and unconscious, acted and fantasized, public and private, harmful and harmless ways. The neo-Victorian attitude, compounded of sentimentalized feminine eroticism and punitive moralism, is itself rooted in sadomasochism.

11. Feminist theorists who agree on the importance of female "castration" as a determinant of feminine psychology have tended to adopt a Lacanian perspective, attributing significance to the phallus as cultural metaphor, rather than the penis as anatomical fact. See especially Juliet Mitchell, *Psychoanalysis and Feminism* (Random House, 1974), and Gayle Rubin, "The Traffic in Women," in *Toward an Anthropology of Women*, ed. Rayna R. Reiter (Monthly Review Press, 1975).

12. Accordingly, this role is not equally available to all women: men of dominant classes and races have typically regarded women of subordinate classes and races as "bad" by cultural definition, and therefore fair game for sexual and economic exploitation. For an excellent analysis of how black women have been systematically denied "good woman" status, see Bell Hooks, *Ain't I a Woman: Black Women and Feminism* (South End Press, 1981).

The Last Unmarried

Person in America

The great marriage boom of '84 began shortly after Congress passed the historic National Family Security Act. Though most of its provisions merely took care of old, long overdue business— abolishing divorce, enabling local communities to prosecute single people as vagrants, requiring applicants for civil service jobs to sign a monogamy oath, making the interstate sale of quiche a federal offense, and so on—two revolutionary clauses cleared the way toward making a reality of what had until then been an impossible dream: universal marriage.

The child purity provision, popularly known as the Down-There Amendment, prevents premarital sex by allowing parents to marry a child to a suitable mate as soon as he or she shows signs of prurient interests—"After all, it's better to marry than to burn," as President Ray Gun so eloquently observed. (An amendment that would have included the unborn in this provision was defeated on the grounds that it cast aspersions on fetal innocence.) Another landmark is the act's legalization of homosexual marriage. This was the most controversial aspect of the bill, splitting the pro-family movement into two camps—the purists, who insisted that homosexuality was a sin, period, and the pragmatists, who pointed out that denying homosexuals the sacrament of marriage discouraged their impulses toward decent respectability, kept dens of iniquity like Greenwich Village in business, and played into the hands of feminists who claimed that women didn't really want to get married anyway. In the end a compromise was reached: homosexuals who swore not to have sex would be permitted to marry, and those who declined to take advantage of this privilege would be deported to Saudi Arabia.

The week after President Gun signed the bill into law, we interviewed a number of the happy couples who had been standing on line at City Hall for up to three days waiting to apply for marriage licenses. The heterosexuals all insisted the Family Security Act had nothing to do with their decision to tie the knot. "It was a totally spontaneous thing," said one radiant young woman. "We were ready to make a commitment."

"My landlord was going to double my rent," her radiant young fiance explained. "He feels, and I can't say I really blame him, that single men attract quiche-eaters to the area. It got me thinking, and I realized that I really wanted to settle down."

"It was so cute the way he proposed," the young woman broke in. "He came over one afternoon while I was sewing scarlet S's on my clothes—it was the day before the deadline, and I'd been procrastinating, as usual. He kissed me and said, 'Why spend your time doing that, when you could be sewing on my buttons instead?'"

We talked next to a pair of radiant young lesbians who proclaimed this the happiest day of their lives. To our delicate inquiry as to whether it would bother them not to have sex, one of the women replied coldly, "That is a bigoted, heterosexist question. Why do straight people always assume we're dying for sex? We think sex is dirty just like you do."

"We're getting married for love," her fiancee declared, "and for children."

"Do you plan to adopt," we asked, "or to be artificially inseminated?"

"Don't be ridiculous! We're going to have our own. The idea that women need men to have babies is patriarchal propaganda. Do you still believe that fairytale about God being Jesus' father?"

On June 30, after a month in which clergymen and government officials worked around the clock to meet the demand for weddings, riots erupted in two cities where laboratory equipment needed for blood tests broke down from overuse, and the last shipment of degenerate sex fiends was dispatched to the Middle East, the president announced proudly that the goal for which all Americans were praying had been achieved: everyone in the 50 states and the District of Columbia was married. The next day our newspaper received an indignant phone call.

"Tuesday here," said a voice that sounded like a cross between a purr and a bark. "I'm calling you guys because you have a reputation for being openminded. Didn't your editor come out for allowing divorce to save the lives of the children?"

"Not divorce," we said. "Just separation."

"Okay. But you agree that what's going on is just a little excessive?"

"Look, Mr.—Mrs.?—ah, Tuesday," we said nervously, "why exactly are you calling?"

"*Mrs.*, my ass!" our caller exclaimed. "*That's* why I'm calling. The president is a liar! As he knows perfectly well, since his Secret Service thugs argued with me for five hours yesterday, I'm as single as the day I was born. And I have no plans to get married, either."

This *was* news. Minutes later we were on our way to an exclusive interview with Ruby Tuesday, the last unmarried person in America. We caught up with Ruby, who makes her home in an empty car of the Lexington Avenue IRT, at the Union Square station. She was a striking-looking woman. It wasn't the green hair so much as the fact that instead of the one scarlet S required by law—a requirement we had naively imagined was obsolete—she wore a see-through satin jumpsuit made entirely of scarlet S's sewn together.

"Come on in," she said. "Have a quiche. It's okay—I make my own."

She was still shaking her head at the chutzpah of the president and the Secret Service. "To think that I *voted* for the guy. He promised to get the government off my back—what did I know? This thing has, whadayucall it, *radicalized* me. Do you know what these fuckers wanted to do? Get some poor slob who couldn't stand the plumbing in Saudi Arabia to come back and marry me, and have Jerry Falwell do it on TV, right before the president's announcement. The Soviets would shit, they said. Ha!"

"We take it you don't agree with that analysis?"

"Listen, don't get me wrong. I'm no Communist! No way! But what could be more communistic than trying to get everybody to *live* with each other? Besides, I'm Jewish."

We asked Ruby why she had such strong objections to marriage.

"It's taken me 15 years to get this car just the way I like it," she said. "Why should I share it with some asshole?"

"Don't you feel a need for intimacy? Community? Commitment?"

"Nah."

"Would you call yourself a narcissist?"

Ruby raised her eyebrows. "I know you're just doing your job," she said, "but let's not get insulting. I'm as kinky as the next one, but some things I won't do even for money."

We apologized. "Would you mind telling us your sexual preference?"

"Hm. Well, sometimes I can really get into plain old-fashioned fucking. Then again there's nothing quite like having your ass licked and your cunt sucked at the same time."

"Actually, what we meant was, do you prefer men or women?"

"Yes," said Ruby enthusiastically.

We decided to take another tack, and asked her how the public was reacting to her refusal to perform what most of us considered a patriotic duty, necessary to end our humiliating dependence on Japanese moral fiber. Ruby rolled her eyes.

"I've done without moral fiber all my life, and I've never felt better," she said. "But try to convince people of that nowadays! I have to admit I'm not too popular. Everybody's paranoid about me. The wives think I'm after their husbands and the husbands think I'm after their wives. I don't believe in homewrecking, but what am I supposed to do? There's nothing but husbands and wives *left*."

"Are you now or have you ever been a feminist?"

"I'm for equal pay for equal work," said Ruby with conviction, "and anybody who doesn't like it can get fucked. About all the other stuff, I don't know. I went to a meeting of Women Against Pornography once, but that was mostly to meet girls."

"Aren't you worried about getting picked up on a vagrancy rap?"

"Nah. They can't touch me. I looked it up: the Supreme Court decided I can't be busted unless I do something, like ask a child for directions. And only two justices have been assassinated since then."

"But the Family Security Act overrules that decision. It says, 'Congress finds that the rotten Supreme Court decision allowing dangerous marriage-dodgers to stalk our streets is full of shit!'"

Ruby shook her head stubbornly. "It won't stick, until they kill at least one more justice."

"When that happens, will you go under—er, into hiding?"

"The fuck I will! This used to be a free country! They'll have to drag me away."

The rhinestones on Ruby's eyelashes gleamed defiantly. We noticed that she was looking us up and down. "Are you married?" she demanded.

"Of course we're married," we said. What was she driving at?

"So they managed to intimidate you," said Ruby, giving us a pitying look.

"Not at all!" we said hotly. "We got married because we wanted to! We needed intimacy and community and commitment!"

"Bullshit," said Ruby, continuing to look at us in a way we were beginning to find unnerving. "Are you really going to tell me that getting a deportation order had nothing to do with it?"

We turned bright red. "How did you know?" we said finally. "We haven't told a soul."

"Oh, I can always tell when I'm turning somebody on," said Ruby, smiling indulgently. "You know, I find you quite attractive, too."

Feeling a little weak, we made an attempt to pull ourselves together and act professional. "Thank you for your time," we said loftily. "We'll be going now."

"Stay here tonight," Ruby said. "You won't regret it."

"Well—we'd like to, but—no. No, we just can't do it."

"Why not?"

"It's too risky. Suppose the National News Council found out?"

"I'm very discreet. The only thing you have to worry about is the picket line outside. But a bag over your head should take care of that."

"No—no, really—" By this time Ruby was stroking our back and kissing our ear. Our heart thumped. "Have another quiche," she whispered.

July 1981

Peace in Our Time?

The Greening of Betty Friedan

The classic blind spot of liberals is their faith that all social conflicts can be settled by peaceful compromise. However bitter the differences, whatever the imbalance of power between opposing parties, one need only apply ingenuity and good will, reject "extremists on both sides," and the lion will sit down with the lamb. No matter how many lambs get eaten, liberals never learn. Faced with an enemy who won't play by their rules, who responds to all their placating gestures with more bids for power, they get irrational. Either they keep ceding more and more ground, or they proclaim that the battle is irrelevant and the real issues lie elsewhere, or both. The response of liberal feminists to the relentless right-wing assault on women's rights is a depressing example. A couple of years ago, NOW president Eleanor Smeal set up a meeting between feminists and leaders of the right-to-life movement to discuss how the two groups might defuse the "polarization" over abortion and work together to advance their common interests. Work together, indeed: the right-to-lifers used the meeting to get some dramatic publicity by bringing in two dead fetuses and denouncing "baby-killers." Now Betty Friedan, in her new state-of-the-movement manifesto, *The Second Stage*, lauds this humiliating event as a model of how feminists and traditionalists can transcend their differences and march hand in hand into the new age.

The Second Stage is a case study in the crisis of liberal feminism. Its outstanding characteristic is incoherence. At first the unwary reader may imagine that the icon of us all, who has made a career of defending "responsible" feminism against those bra-burning, man-hating, dyke-loving radicals, has undergone a sudden conversion to the cause of social revolution. Friedan begins by observing, accurately enough, that women's increased opportunity to pursue careers and maintain independent identities has not brought genuine liberation. Rather, in the absence of changes in the structure of work, family life, and child rearing, women are faced with a series of no-win "choices" between two sets of needs—work and autonomy on the one hand, love and children on the other. Neither the successful professional woman who finds herself unwillingly alone and childless, nor the traditional wife and mother who finds herself divorced and without marketable skills, nor the superwoman who drives herself crazy trying to "have it all," can rightly be described as free. Furthermore, women who gain political power within the present system cannot be trusted to support women's interests, and career women intent on beating the competition are disinclined to let sisterhood stand in their way. Friedan believes this situation has led to a widespread disillusionment with feminism, and is responsible for the movement's current malaise. The solution, she argues, is to launch a "second stage" movement whose aim is to "restructure institutions," "create new forms of family," come to "new terms with love and with work."

Friedan, who has never lacked for chutzpah, presents these ideas as her own, the product of painful soul-searching. In fact, they are a reductive and vulgarized rehash of arguments radical feminists have been making since the '60s, when the women's liberation movement first suggested—to the dismay of Friedan and her fellow responsibles —that careerism and room-at-the-top liberal integrationist politics were a dead end. The radical critique of male supremacy paid particular attention to the family and the need to transform domestic life. As we saw it, women's traditional familial role as wife, mother, and all-purpose selfless nurturer not only deprived them of an independent life outside the home, but stifled their sexual and emotional needs. Equality in sex and love, we argued, was every bit as important as equality on the job. And neither could be achieved without the equal sharing of housework and child care.

Is Friedan then ready to admit, if only tacitly, that the radicals were right? That we saw something she didn't? On the contrary, radical feminism (which is equated with the most extreme versions of separatism; Friedan has the impression that all radical feminists live in basements on a diet of male babies) is, as usual, the main target of her polemic. It was the radicals' anti-male, anti-marriage-

and-motherhood propaganda, she contends, that led to the movement's one-sided emphasis on worldly success. This creative attempt
to merge the image of the monastic revolutinary with that of the
lonely corporate striver produces some unwitting comedy, as when
she writes of a young woman, concerned that commitment to her
work may preclude having a family: "She complains that the older
woman vice-president, one of the early radical feminists who vowed
never to marry or have children, didn't understand her quandary.
'All she wants,' the executive assistant says, 'is more power in the
company.'"

While Friedan absurdly blames radicals for the narrow focus of
establishment feminism, she simultaneously accuses us of diverting
the feminist movement from the "main thrust" of the drive for
equality to irrelevant sexual issues. (How we managed to spare the
time from fighting our way up the corporate ladder goes unex-
plained.) Here she reverts to familiar arguments: calling men oppressors is extremist nonsense; demands for sexual freedom and pleasure
are "not political at all, merely personal"; insisting on the right to be
openly lesbian is exhibitionistic. Besides, such unseemly dwelling on
sex has enabled antifeminists to insinuate that feminism is somehow
at odds with conventional morality. The Equal Rights Amendment,
Friedan declares, "has nothing to do with either abortion or homosexuality—in fact it has nothing to do with sexual behavior at all."
Nonetheless, "sexual politics . . . made it easy for the so-called Moral
Majority to lump ERA with homosexual rights and abortion into one
explosive package of licentious, family-threatening sex." And "Such
slogans as 'free abortion on demand' had connotations of sexual licen-
tiousness . . . implying a certain lack of respect for the values of life
and the mysteries of conception and birth." To advocate ERA, legal
abortion, or child care "solely in individualistic terms"—i.e., in terms
of freedom and equality—"aborts our own moral majority"; instead
we should argue that such reforms are vital to "the very survival of
the family." In other words, the way to beat the right is to me-too
it to death—never mind that the suppression of women's sexual and
personal freedom in the name of "family survival" and "the values of
life" is the first principle of sexism.

Friedan devotes a good deal of space to protesting that feminism,

far from being in any way opposed to the family, is its salvation: because the right is committed to preserving a rigid traditional family
structure that is fast becoming obsolete, it refuses to deal with the
problems (like child care for working couples) of actual families,
while the agenda of the women's movement would meet the needs
of a "diversity of families." And since this diversity can include "new
family forms" free of the old sex roles, there is no reason for feminists
to be against it.

The trouble with this argument is that Friedan, like other liberals
who hope to "take the family away from the right," uses rhetoric
about diversity to forestall debate on the real issue—the laws, social
practices, and prejudices that favor the conventional family and dis-
courage or punish alternatives. Friedan herself reinforces this bias by
repeatedly equating marriage and the nuclear family with intimacy
and nurturance per se. She also dogmatically assumes that any woman
who lives alone is "yearning for some form of family or family substitute." Having made her gesture to "new forms," she feels free to
denounce, in the most bullying terms, feminists who persist in criticizing the family, not as a catch-all synonym for intimate community,
but as a specific social institution: we are "locked in violent reaction"
against the wife and mother role, "resisting the tests of evolving life,"
and so on. (One of her targets is an article of mine, in which I argue
that the family as we know it offers its emotional and social support
at the expense of autonomy and sexual passion, and that women who
try to live by the latter values pay a high price. According to Friedan,
the piece typifies radical feminists' denial of women's need for love.)
The depth of her commitment to fostering diversity can be deduced
from her answer to a lesbian activist who suggested that her pro-
family talk was exclusionary: "'Why?' I asked. 'Don't you have family
needs? The family is who you come home to.' 'Then why don't you
talk more about gay families?' she asked. 'Because it twists the focus
to sexual politics,' I said." Oh.

In her determination to achieve total sexual equality without challenging men, criticizing traditional family values, or talking about
s-e-x, Friedan flounders like a skier whose legs have taken off in two
directions. She admits that "the price of motherhood is still too high
for most women," yet accuses women who don't want children of

"blind reaction" to "past dangers" and "false fears." She notes that "control and manipulation of sexuality and the family" have always been "key elements in authoritarian power," yet insists that sex isn't political. She affirms that sexual privacy is precious—and argues that lesbians should safeguard it by staying in the closet. She agrees that women should control their own bodies—but abortion has nothing to do with equal rights.

Defending abortion without defending sex or freedom isn't easy, but Friedan gives it a shot. She lists control of the reproductive process as one of the "mainstream" goals that radical feminists neglected for sexual politics (never mind that it was radicals, with their "licentious" slogans, who galvanized the abortion law repeal movement) and finally settles on this rationale: "I am not *for abortion*—I am for the *choice to have children*." We need the option of abortion, she explains, because the pill and the IUD can threaten women's health and interfere with their future childbearing.

This sort of sophistry does nothing to combat the right-to-lifers' charges that abortion is murder, or that it promotes sexual "self-indulgence" and undermines women's God-given role in the family. But then Friedan doesn't take the opposition or its ideas too seriously. In her view the antifeminist backlash does not reflect a real social schism over the role of women, the family, and sexual morality; rather it is a conspiracy of right-wing extremists who are fomenting conflict over these issues in order to distract people from the economic crisis. In support of this position Friedan cites a study on women's ideas about feminism and the family, based on interviews with a group of Michigan mothers. The researchers found that their subjects' attitudes and behavior invariably reflected efforts to reconcile two opposing propositions: that a woman should place the needs of her husband and children above all else, and that the needs of the individual woman are equally important. From this Friedan concludes not that these women are ambivalent, or trying their best to work out a livable compromise, but that the contradiction between "familial" and "individualistic" ideologies exists only in the abstract, not in women's real lives.

It follows that for feminists to encourage "polarization"—i.e., to forthrightly defend feminist principles against the right's attack—is to fight on the enemy's terms. Instead, the movement should seek to "transcend" these "diversionary" battles: "Why don't we join forces with all who have true reverence for life, including Catholics who oppose abortion, and fight for the choice to have children?" Presumably the antiabortionists in the coalition will happily agree that the choice to have children is the same as the choice not to have them, and the Schlaflyites will be left muttering, "Foiled again!" "Do they really want to outlaw abortion?" Friedan asks rhetorically, and suggests that if the Human Life Amendment passed, the right would "lose the abortion issue as a scapegoat." By this logic we ought to support the amendment, call the right's bluff, and force it to hunt for new scapegoats—contraception, say, or divorce.

Friedan's brand of revolution without tears also dismisses struggles with men as an irrelevance to be "transcended." Far from resisting women's encroachments on their power and privilege, men are eager to exchange it all for the right to cry; in fact, "Men may be at the cutting edge of the second stage." (Apparently gremlins are responsible for what Friedan refers to as "the remaining barriers of insidious sex discrimination.") And though she chastises feminists for worrying about trivialities like sex when the economy is in such bad shape, Friedan brushes aside the notion that capitalism might be an obstacle to the new order. In fact, the only obstacle she does discern is women themselves—those stubborn radicals and conservatives who believe their disagreements matter. "Stripped of polarizing rhetoric, the practical problems of restructuring home and work may not be as difficult as they now seem," she assures us, and predicts that by the year 2000, "The arguments about equal rights for women will be nostalgic history."

It turns out that what Friedan means by "restructuring" is reforms like child-care programs and flexible working hours. While women would certainly benefit from many of the measures she suggests, they leave the basic institutional structures pretty much intact. Friedan does not understand sexism in structural terms; she sees it as a series of "practical problems" to be solved piecemeal, without reference to "ideology." This is, of course, precisely the approach advocated by liberal social scientists at the end of the '50s. The difference is that in a prosperous and relatively quiescent era, the claim that ideology is passé was superficially plausible; at a time when the economy is wobbling and right-wing ideologues are making frightening gains, that claim has all the marks of a desperate flight from reality.

Friedan's politics have always been confused. The experience that shaped her feminism—and inspired the eloquent indignation of *The Feminine Mystique*—was the suburban wife's confinement to marginality and isolation. From that perspective the promise of feminism was escape from the sidelines. The rhetoric Friedan uses to describe the aims of "first stage" feminism is all about getting *in*— "in the mainstream, inside the party, the political process, the business world." Radical women's liberationists rudely insisted that, on the contrary, to oppose sexual inequality was to challenge men and the whole fabric of male-female relations, which by definition meant taking a stand outside the mainstream. Since the radicals had militant energy and an analysis of women's condition, both of which the liberals lacked, they immediately took center stage, capturing the public's and the media's imagination, pushing NOW and other liberal groups to take bolder positions. All this put Friedan in a terrible double bind. To associate herself with radicalism was to exchange the marginality of a housewife for the marginality of a rebel. But to ignore it was to risk being left behind, relegated to marginality within the movement itself.

From the beginning, Friedan's response to this dilemma was to attack and misrepresent radical feminists while shamelessly co-opting their ideas. Ironically, the decline of radical feminism and the rise of the new right have, if anything, exaggerated these tropisms. Since Friedan sees that liberal feminist assumptions do not address the issues of family and morality—and that the right will swamp the movement unless it addresses those issues—she is viscerally drawn to more radical formulations. But to follow the logic of her perceptions would mean facing down her fears—of alienating men, offending Peoria, standing alone—in an atmosphere infinitely more hostile to dissidents than the 1960s. And so her second stage becomes a hodgepodge of pseudo-radical global optimism, modest reformism, and craven appeasement. Reading her book reminded me of an old joke about a pulp magazine serial. An installment ends with the hero bound hand and foot and thrown into a pit with poisonous snakes.

Circling the rim of the pit are enemy warriors with spears drawn. The following month readers rush to their newstands to see how the hero gets out of this hopeless situation. The new installment begins, "Once out of the pit. . . ."

November 1981

Marriage on the Rocks

Occasionally when I give a talk on "the crisis in the family," someone in the audience asks me what I think is the main cause of divorce. "Marriage," I say. I get a laugh, but a nervous one. For the first time in history, marriage has become, for masses of people, a voluntary association rather than a social and economic necessity; as both a cause and a consequence of this development, divorce has become an increasingly ordinary fact of life. It is still the common sense of our culture that divorce is tragic, that we should be happily married for a lifetime, and that most of us *could* be, if only—well, if only we were different (less "narcissistic," more realistic in our expectations, more self-disciplined and willing to work at a relationship, more able to take pop psychologists' advice on intimacy); or if only our society were more "pro-family" (in the muddied waters of contemporary political debate, this label has been promiscuously attached to social causes that range from stopping ERA to expanding the welfare state). Yet, as Lenore J. Weitzman observes in her illuminating book, *The Divorce Revolution*, the ease and prevalence of divorce can't help but transform marriage itself.

In 1970, California passed the country's first no-fault divorce law, allowing either party—without the other's consent—to get a divorce on the grounds of "irreconcilable differences." Under the no-fault system, marital property was supposed to be divided on the basis of need and ability to pay, rather than used to reward "innocence" and punish "guilt." Furthermore, decisions about alimony, property, and child custody would treat men and women as equals rather than assume traditional sexual roles. Since then, nearly every state has adopted some version of these reforms, with immense social consequences. Weitzman's book studies the impact of the historic California law, focusing on the fate of women and children caught in the middle of a social revolution. She concludes that for all its humane goals, divorce reform in practice has eroded women's power to bargain for a decent financial settlement, and so has contributed to the feminization of poverty; while men's standard of living usually rises after a divorce, women's and children's drastically falls.

Besides being punitive and degrading for both sexes, traditional divorce laws, with their patriarchal definitions of marital guilt and innocence, had special pitfalls for women. Men who had no grounds for divorcing reluctant wives could and often did abandon them, but economically dependent wives were trapped, since they could not get court-ordered support without proving their husbands guilty of infidelity or abuse (an expensive proposition even if the charges were true). And a woman who was divorced for infidelity—or for not doing the housework or for refusing to live where her husband wanted—could be cut off without a penny, perhaps even lose her children. Yet the laws' paternalistic assumptions also gave economically powerless women some leverage: if the husband wanted the divorce, an "innocent" wife could demand a price for her cooperation in the necessary legal charades, and even a "guilty" one could threaten an expensive court fight. In addition, the "innocent" wife, whose dependence was taken for granted, could expect to be awarded the family home and the bulk of marital property; some women (usually the wives of rich or upper-middle-class men) received lifetime alimony.

No-fault, sex-neutral, "equitable distribution" divorce laws—and, even more important, the mostly male judges who apply them— take little account of the realities of institutional sexism. Increasingly, divorce settlements assume that the woman can and should be entirely self-supporting, an assumption that's particularly unrealistic for older housewives and mothers of young children. In general, they ignore the fact that women's unpaid labor as housewives and mothers typically enhances their husbands' value in the marketplace while reducing or destroying their own. Nor do they recognize that the great majority of ex-wives who have custody of their children are doing a job that deserves compensation. Child support awards are ridiculously low, in part because they're based on subsistence-level criteria of need, rather than children's right to as high a standard of living as *both* parents can provide. As for sex-neutral custody standards, their main practical effect has been to intimidate many women into giving up their rightful share of property for fear of losing the children who have been the center of their lives.

On one level, this is the familiar story of how attempts to legislate equal rights and enlightened moral attitudes can backfire when they disregard inequalities build into the social structure. Weitzman argues that further reform is needed, and makes some good suggestions: in divorces involving children and/or long-term marriages the goal of the settlement should be equal standards of living for both post-divorce households; wives should be compensated for their investment in their husbands' educations and careers; the children's primary caretaker should have preference for custody; the laws should be specific enough to prevent judges from imposing their own male-biased notions of what's equitable.

My guess is that such proposals will be politically popular, for people are starting to be alarmed by the impoverishment of erstwhile middle-class women and the social instability it invites. In 1985 the New York State Court of Appeals upheld a three-year-old divorce decree awarding Loretta O'Brien, who had deferred her own education to support her husband through medical school, a share in Dr. O'Brien's medical license equal to 40 percent of its worth. (The dollar amount hasn't yet been determined, though the lower court that made the original ruling suggested $188,000.) All the publicity I saw was favorable.

Hmm. When a decision that redistributes considerable wealth from a man to a woman—a decision that must surely chill the hearts of thousands of married male professionals-in-training—is so complaisantly greeted (at least in public), I can't help sniffing a bit of noblesse oblige. It's easier, after all, to approve of compensating women for inequality than to contemplate ending it. Weitzman notes that one mistake the original divorce reformers made was imagining that sexual equality was just around the corner. Now that it's clearly miles away, perhaps sheer relief is making men feel generous.

The ironies of divorce reform also provide a tempting opportunity to needle feminists by implying that they're more cause than cure of women's problems. Thus Peter Schrag, reviewing *The Divorce Revo-*

lution in *The Nation*: "It would not be stretching things to say . . . that the treatment of women and children in divorce is one of the great embarrassments of the modern feminist movement." Actually, it would be stretching things a lot. At the time the no-fault laws were in the works, the feminist movement—especially its radical wing— was quite alert to the complexities of divorce for women in a sexist society; if we had been in charge of drafting the laws they would have been very different. The perversion of divorce reform is one of the great embarrassments of modern liberalism, with its faith in legisla- tion and its naiveté about power. Besides, much of the push for no- fault came from men convinced that the divorce laws discriminated against *them*, that women were sucking their lifeblood in the form of huge and undeserved property and alimony awards. (Weitzman's statistics show that this idea was strictly a self-serving myth.)

But divorce is not only a feminist issue. Feminists may agree that women need more power in divorce negotiations, but they're as divided and ambivalent as everyone else on the larger question posed by the "divorce revolution": how are we to resolve the ten- sion between familial commitments and personal freedom and inde- pendence? Weitzman argues that the new divorce laws, along with social acceptance of divorce, are effectively changing marriage from a committed partnership with lifetime obligations to a provisional arrangement subordinate to individual desires and less central to people's lives.

No-fault laws don't enforce the traditional marriage contract with financial rewards and punishments. They encourage divorce by mak- ing the process cheaper and easier and shifting the balance of power from the spouse who wants to preserve the marriage to the one who wants out. The pattern of divorce settlements under no-fault discour- ages women from investing energy in marriage and children at the expense of their careers and gives men a financial incentive to get di- vorced rather than stay married and share their incomes with their families. Finally, that pattern devalues child-rearing: while exempt- ing most divorced fathers from a serious financial commitment to the children or any day-to-day responsibility for their care, no-fault settlements require most mothers to work outside the home to make ends meet.

Weitzman is disturbed by the decline of marriage as a partnership; she thinks it hurts women, at least in the short run, erodes our commitment to children, and (though she never says this outright) leads to a culture of joyless individual striving. Yet she holds no brief for the old divorce laws or the myth of the harmonious traditional family, "that 'classical family of western nostalgia,' to use Professor William J. Goode's term." Like most people, she would like to see some livable compromise between familial cohesion and individual freedom. She clearly hopes that her proposed reforms, by keeping the principle of no-fault but eliminating gross inequities in its application, will serve that end, though she's sensible enough to know that no legislation can attain it.

Reforms of the kind Weitzman suggests and the O'Brien decision represents are needed to ease the trauma of women's historic transition from patriarchal wifehood to full equality, but they won't encourage marital partnership. If anything, making it harder to avoid permanent entanglement will encourage men—and the increasing number of career-oriented women—not to marry at all. Extending marital obligations after divorce may make sense economically and politically, but it's incongruous psychologically; there's something necrophilic about it. I can believe that Loretta O'Brien's investment in her husband—measured not only by what she spent but by what she could have been doing instead—is worth almost $200,000. But for Michael O'Brien, as for the lifelong housewife admonished to go out and earn a living, the court's decision changes the rules in the middle of the game. If he had it to do over again, he would probably decide it was cheaper to take out a loan. The O'Brien ruling makes it less risky to give to your partner, but more risky to take anything you can't easily pay back.

What no one except the cultural right wants to admit is that marriage as a social institution (an economic partnership, a secure context for child-rearing) only works when it's more or less compulsory, as it has been until the last 15 or 20 years. Marriages held together solely by desire are by definition unpredictable; as thrice-married Margaret Mead once blurted out to psychologist and divorce counselor Judith S. Wallerstein, "Judy, there is no society in the world where people have stayed married without enormous community pressure to do so."

Conservatives, as usual, have a coherent, if quixotic (I hope), position on this issue: restore the social centrality of marriage by reversing the trends toward personal freedom and sexual equality that have undermined it. Liberals, as usual, do a lot of agonizing and hand-wringing—especially sociologists and psychologists. Their research or clinical experience compels them to see that marriage as an institution is self-destructing; they believe in marriage and the family and deplore the destruction; but they're also for feminism and the right to pursue happiness.

This dilemma pervades Wallerstein's new study, which through periodic interviews traces each member of 60 mostly white, mostly middle-class divorced families over 15 years, beginning in 1971. The awkward check-and-balance wordiness with which the author titles (and subtitles and sub-subtitles) her book—*Second Chances: Men, Women & Children a Decade After Divorce: Who Wins, Who Loses— and Why*, coauthored by Sandra Blakeslee—seems designed to defuse the passions aroused by her subject and ward off the predictable appropriation of her results. Fat chance! *The New York Times Magazine* got straight to the point when it ran an excerpt from the book as a cover story headlined "Children of Divorce." *Second Chances* is also about adults, the "winners" who thrive after their divorces and the "losers" who don't. But what's drawn the media attention is Wallerstein's most controversial finding: contrary to the conventional wisdom of the educated, socially liberal middle class, which had shaped her own expectations, divorce for the children in her study was not only an immediate, devastating trauma (only one in 10, "mostly older children in families where there had been open violence," felt relieved that their parents' marriages had ended) but had a long-term negative impact on their lives.

In the neotraditionalist climate of the day, this message is what a lot of people want to hear. It will no doubt wend its way into the popular folklore of "family issues," boiled down to "Divorce is bad for kids"—yet another installment in the ongoing I-hate-to-say-this-but-I-have-to-be-honest series that includes "Day care is bad for kids," "Single parenthood is bad for kids," and "Adultery is bad for kids even when they don't know about it." Wallerstein will feel misused. After all, she is not arguing against divorce ("Given the egalitarian nature of American life and the rights of individuals, divorce is here to stay") or disparaging the needs and feelings of the divorcing parents, only pointing out that there's no free lunch. But as often happens with such emotionally and politically charged subjects, the author is up to her neck in the contradictions she thinks she's examining.

The most obvious flaw in Wallerstein's study is that it has no control group of families that stayed together. "Because so little was known about divorce," she says, "it was premature to plan a control group. . . . From the findings of [this] study we hoped to generate hypotheses that could then be tested in a more focused way. . . ." Her findings, however, are presented not as tentative hypotheses that warrant further study but as alarming conclusions that urgently require attention.

Nor does Wallerstein limit her comments about the children to those aspects of their experience directly linked with the divorce— their intense, long-lived, and often denied or displaced feelings, their economic deprivation and changed relationships with parents, their tendency to blame their problems on the divorce and invoke it as a metaphor for the uncertainties and disappointments of life. She goes much further, making global judgments about their impaired ability to love and work. Many, Wallerstein claims, "entered adulthood as worried, underachieving, self-deprecating" people and have had trouble forming intimate bonds. But without controls, how can she presume to attribute such effects to divorce, rather than to living with unhappily married parents and/or growing up in a generation shaped by the vicissitudes of the past 20 years—social upheaval and conservative crackdown, open conflict between the sexes that's nowhere near resolution, the fragmentation of communities (familial and otherwise), and, of course, a downward economic mobility by no means limited to the divorced?

Which raises a more basic issue: though Wallerstein is quite aware of the larger social context of divorce, she doesn't recognize how seriously it complicates her project. On the contrary, she often writes as if the changes in the social world were simply the breakup of individual families writ large. "It is a world," she declares in her introduction, "in which our trust in the reliability of relationships has been shaken, especially those that are most fundamental and intimate. 'I'm afraid to use the word *love*,' says a young adult who remembers her parents' divorce as if it happened yesterday. 'You can hope for love, but you can't expect it.'" How much do this woman's feelings have to do with her parents' divorce (or marriage), how much with a realistic appraisal of the conditions of her life? And has she lowered her expectations simply out of conviction that love doesn't last—or also because the influence of feminism has raised her standards about what kind of relationship deserves to be called love?

I'm not talking about self-conscious feminist politics; I assume that by "love," the young woman means romantic love in a more or less conventional sense. I assume this because Wallerstein makes a point of observing that the children of divorce are more morally conservative than their parents: "As a group, they want what their parents did not achieve—a good marriage, commitment, romantic love that lasts, and faithfulness. . . . They are disdainful of concepts like serial monogamy and open marriage. . . ."

As Wallerstein sees it, one of the great ironies of these children's lives is that "their own gut-wrenching unhappiness over the experience of divorce" leads them toward traditional values while crippling their ability to put those values into practice: "They seem propelled by despair and anxiety as they search for what they fear they will never find. They abhor cheating yet find themselves in multiple relationships that lead to cheating. They want marriage but are terrified of it. They detest divorce but end up divorced." It never occurs to her that what she is really describing is a pervasive cultural schizophrenia: the moralistic reaction against the countercultural values of the '60s spreads and builds in intensity even as the landscape of sexual and domestic life is inexorably transformed.

Indeed, schizophrenic is not a bad description of Wallerstein's own attitudes. She shakes her head at people's refusal "to acknowledge the widening gap between our belief systems and our everyday lives." She says of the idealized family à la Bill Cosby, "It is what we yearn for in our fantasies, even though . . . we know it doesn't exist, if in fact it ever did." She insists she wouldn't want to go back to the old ways even if we could: "It is not useful to provide children with a model of adult behavior that avoids problem solving and stresses martyrdom, violence, or apathy." But her criteria for judging the "success" or "failure" of the children of divorce are essentially those of the '50s: how well they are doing at being "open to love, commitment . . . and fidelity," which is to say permanent monogamous marriage (at one point she lumps "multiple relationships" together with short-lived impulsive marriages as forms of maladjustment), and at getting a "good" education and an upper-middle-class job. If there are any homosexuals in her sample of kids, we don't (or she didn't) hear about them. And her language is loaded with the moralism ("With divorce comes an erosion of commitments to our partners . . . of our unspoken moral commitments to our children . . .") and nostalgia ("Our fragile family structures have gotten out of sync with our emotional needs") that she purports to reject.

In short, *Second Chances* is a conceptually incoherent, cryptotraditionalist book. And yet, speaking of contradictions, it is also enlightening—even unwittingly subversive. What saves it are the interviews themselves. Wallerstein draws on material from all the families in her study, while focusing on three whose experience she considers exemplary. She lets her people talk, interviewing each parent and child separately, recording their clashing perceptions of the same events, and constructing a rich, nuanced picture of contemporary social dislocation.

Though the disaster of male-female relations is much in evidence, the most powerful theme that emerges from these interviews is the wreckage produced by the colliding needs of adults and kids. In the aftermath of divorce, children need all the support they can get in coping with their terror and bewilderment at the fact that that small community called the family—the only one they belong to by right, the only one society holds responsible for their well-being— has fallen apart. Yet typically, they have no one to turn to but the very people who have precipitated their trauma and whose own resources are strained to the limit.

Struggling to heal their wounds and put their lives together —often making a desperate bid for happiness after years of self-abnegation—divorced parents tend to have less time and energy for their children. Many mothers get jobs for the first time, or work longer hours. Most fathers, the interviews show, drift away from their kids even when they were close to them before, see them less and less, and feel correspondingly less responsible for them economically (two-thirds of fathers in the study who could afford to contribute to their children's college expenses did not do so). It seems that outside the context of a home held together emotionally and socially by a woman, most men can't figure out how to be parents; they end up retreating from their awkwardness and confusion by staying away. The children not only feel abandoned and rejected by one or both parents, but resent the breach of what they understood to be the social contract: that, as Wallerstein puts it, "parents are supposed to make sacrifices for their children, not the other way around."

All this painful stuff is not just a commentary on divorce; on a deeper level it exposes the zero-sum games and oppressive power relations that define family life. Parents stifle their own needs and desires for the sake of the children (in which case the kids, if they're lucky, will merely suffer from the "normal" chronic intergenerational hostilities and guilts)—or they demand their due in life and the children pay. Women put up with/hang on to their husbands, or they bring up their children alone. Deprived of its patriarchal trappings, fatherhood withers away. Women have less power than men to determine the shape of their lives, and children have hardly any power at all.

For me the implications are clear: the family is a dying beast. Somehow, we must find another way, a better way, to do it—to love, to rear children, to find community in a postfamilial world. But for Wallerstein the family is a given, which puts her in a bind: there is the "intact family," which is disintegrating, or the "broken family," which has abdicated its functions. After making a number of squirt-gun suggestions about learning why bad marriages fail and good ones work (presumably the idea is to help people stay together, *pace* Margaret Mead), and increasing social supports for divorced families, she arrives at a conclusion. We need, she tells us, to "support and

strengthen the family—all families." In the gap between the misery .
all our well-intentioned Wallersteins reveal and the triviality of their
responses to it, the right-wing demagogues flourish.

This essay combines two columns from
The Village Voice *January 1986 and April 1989*

Putting Women Back in

the Abortion Debate

Some years ago I attended a New York Institute for the Humanities seminar on the new right. We were a fairly heterogeneous group of liberals and lefties, feminists and gay activists, but on one point nearly all of us agreed: the right-to-life movement was a dangerous antifeminist crusade. At one session I argued that the attack on abortion had significance far beyond itself, that it was the linchpin of the right's social agenda. I got a lot of supporting comments and approving nods. It was too much for Peter Steinfels, a liberal Catholic, author of *The Neoconservatives*, and executive editor of *Commonweal*. Right-to-lifers were not all right-wing fanatics, he protested. "You have to understand," he said plaintively, "that many of us see abortion as a *human life issue*." What I remember best was his air of frustrated isolation. I don't think he came back to the seminar after that.

Things are different now. I often feel isolated when I insist that abortion is, above all, a *feminist issue*. Once people took for granted that abortion was an issue of sexual politics and morality. Now, abortion is most often discussed as a question of "life" in the abstract. Public concern over abortion centers almost exclusively on fetuses; women and their bodies are merely the stage on which the drama of fetal life and death takes place. Debate about abortion—if not its reality—has become sexlessly scholastic. And the people most responsible for this turn of events are, like Peter Steinfels, on the left.

The left wing of the right-to-life movement is a small, seemingly eccentric minority in both "progressive" and antiabortion camps. Yet it has played a critical role in the movement: by arguing that opposition to abortion can be separated from the right's antifeminist program, it has given antiabortion sentiment legitimacy in left-symp and (putatively) profeminist circles. While left antiabortionists are hardly alone in emphasizing fetal life, their innovation has been to claim that a consistent "prolife" stand involves opposing capital punishment, supporting disarmament, demanding government programs to end poverty, and so on. This is of course a leap the right is neither able nor willing to make. It's been liberals—from Garry Wills to the Catholic bishops—who have supplied the mass media with the idea that prohibiting abortion is part of a "seamless garment" of respect for human life.

Having invented this counter-context for the abortion controversy, left antiabortionists are trying to impose it as the only legitimate context for debate. Those of us who won't accept their terms and persist in seeing opposition to abortion, antifeminism, sexual repression, and religious sectarianism as the real seamless garment have been accused of obscuring the issue with demagoguery. Last year *Commonweal*—perhaps the most important current forum for left antiabortion opinion—ran an editorial demanding that we shape up: "Those who hold that abortion is immoral believe that the biological dividing lines of birth or viability should no more determine whether a developing member of the species is denied or accorded essential rights than should the biological dividing lines of sex or race or disability or old age. This argument is open to challenge. Perhaps the dividing lines are sufficiently different. Pro-choice advocates should state their reasons for believing so. They should meet the argument on its own grounds. . . ."

In other words, the only question we're allowed to debate—or the only one *Commonweal* is willing to entertain—is "Are fetuses the moral equivalent of born human beings?" And I can't meet the argument on its own grounds because I don't agree that this is the key question, whose answer determines whether one supports abortion or opposes it. I don't doubt that fetuses are alive, or that they're biologically human—what else would they be? I do consider the life of a fertilized egg less precious than the well-being of a woman with feelings, self-consciousness, a history, social ties; and I think fetuses get closer to being human in a moral sense as they come closer to birth. But to me these propositions are intuitively self-evident. I wouldn't know how to justify them to a "nonbeliever," nor do I see the point of trying.

I believe the debate has to start in a different place—with the recognition that fertilized eggs develop into infants inside the bodies of women. Pregnancy and birth are active processes in which a woman's body shelters, nourishes, and expels a new life; for nine months she is immersed in the most intimate possible relationship with another being. The growing fetus makes considerable demands on her physical and emotional resources, culminating in the cataclysmic experience of birth. And childbearing has unpredictable consequences; it always entails some risk of injury or death.

For me all this has a new concreteness: I had a baby last year. My much-desired and relatively easy pregnancy was full of what anti-abortionists like to call "inconveniences." I was always tired, short of breath; my digestion was never right; for three months I endured a state of hormonal siege; later I had pains in my fingers, swelling feet, numb spots on my legs, the dread hemorrhoids. I had to think about everything I ate. I developed borderline glucose intolerance. I gained 50 pounds and am still overweight; my shape has changed in other ways that may well be permanent. Psychologically, my pregnancy consumed me—though I'd happily bought the seat on the roller coaster, I was still terrified to be so out of control of my normally tractable body. It was all bearable, even interesting—even, at times, transcendent—because I wanted a baby. Birth was painful, exhausting, and wonderful. If I hadn't wanted a baby it would only have been painful and exhausting—or worse. I can hardly imagine what it's like to have your body and mind taken over in this way when you not only don't look forward to the result, but positively dread it. The thought appalls me. So as I see it, the key question is "Can it be moral, under any circumstances, to make a woman bear a child against her will?"

From this vantage point, *Commonweal*'s argument is irrelevant, for in a society that respects the individual, no "member of the species" in *any* stage of development has an "essential right" to make use of someone else's body, let alone in such all-encompassing fashion, without that person's consent. You can't make a case against abortion by applying a general principle about everybody's human rights; you have to show exactly the opposite—that the relationship between fetus and pregnant woman is an exception, one that justifies depriving women of their right to bodily integrity. And in fact all antiabortion ideology rests on the premise—acknowledged or simply assumed—that women's unique capacity to bring life into the world carries with it a unique obligation; that women cannot be allowed to "play God" and launch only the lives they welcome.

Yet the alternative to allowing women this power is to make them impotent. Criminalizing abortion doesn't just harm individual women with unwanted pregnancies, it affects all women's sense of themselves. Without control of our fertility we can never envision ourselves as free, for our biology makes us constantly vulnerable. Simply because we are female our physical integrity can be violated, our lives disrupted and transformed, at any time. Our ability to act in the world is hopelessly compromised by our sexual being.

Ah, sex—it does have a way of coming up in these discussions, despite all. When pressed, right-to-lifers of whatever political persuasion invariably point out that pregnancy doesn't happen by itself. The leftists often give patronizing lectures on contraception (though some find only "natural birth control" acceptable), but remain unmoved when reminded that contraceptives fail. Openly or implicitly they argue that people shouldn't have sex unless they're prepared to procreate. (They are quick to profess a single standard—men as well as women should be sexually "responsible." Yes, and the rich as well as the poor should be allowed to sleep under bridges.) Which amounts to saying that if women want to lead heterosexual lives they must give up any claim to self-determination, and that they have no right to sexual pleasure without fear.

Opposing abortion, then, means accepting that women must suffer sexual disempowerment and a radical loss of autonomy relative to men: if fetal life is sacred, the self-denial basic to women's oppression is also basic to the moral order. Opposing abortion means embracing a conservative sexual morality, one that subordinates pleasure to reproduction: if fetal life is sacred, there is no room for the view that sexual passion—or even sexual love—for its own sake is a human need and a human right. Opposing abortion means tolerating the inevitable double standard, by which men may accept or reject sexual restrictions in accordance with their beliefs, while women must bow to them out of fear—or defy them at great risk. However much *Commonweal*'s editors and those of like mind want to believe their opposition to abortion is simply about saving lives, the truth is that in the real world they are shoring up a particular sexual culture, whose rules are stacked against women. I have yet to hear any left right-to-lifers take full responsibility for that fact or deal seriously with its political implications.

Unfortunately, their fuzziness has not lessened their appeal—if anything it's done the opposite. In increasing numbers liberals and leftists, while opposing antiabortion laws, have come to view abortion as an "agonizing moral issue" with some justice on both sides, rather than an issue—however emotionally complex—of freedom versus repression, or equality versus hierarchy, that affects their political self-definition. This above-the-battle stance is attractive to leftists who want to be feminist good guys but are uneasy or ambivalent about sexual issues, not to mention those who want to ally with "progressive" factions of the Catholic church on Central America, nuclear disarmament, or populist economics without that sticky abortion question getting in the way.

Such neutrality is a way of avoiding the painful conflict over cultural issues that continually smolders on the left. It can also be a way of coping with the contradictions of personal life at a time when liberation is a dream deferred. To me the fight for abortion has always been the cutting edge of feminism, precisely because it denies that anatomy is destiny, that female biology dictates women's subordinate status. Yet recently I've found it hard to focus on the issue, let alone summon up the militance needed to stop the antiabortion tanks. In part that has to do with second-round weariness—do we really have to go through all these things twice?—in part with my life now.

Since my daughter's birth my feelings about abortion—not as a political demand but as a personal choice—have changed. In this society, the difference between the situation of a childless woman and of a mother is immense; the fear that having a child will dislodge one's tenuous hold on a nontraditional life is excruciating. This terror of being forced into the sea-change of motherhood gave a special edge to my convictions about abortion. Since I've made that plunge voluntarily, with consequences still unfolding, the terror is gone; I might not want another child, for all sorts of reasons, but I will never again feel that my identity is at stake. Different battles with the culture absorb my energy now. Besides, since I've experienced the pri-

mal, sensual passion of caring for an infant, there will always be part
of me that does want another. If I had an abortion today, it would
be with conflict and sadness unknown to me when I had an abortion
a decade ago. And the antiabortionists' imagery of dead babies hits
me with new force. Do many women—left, feminist women—have
such feelings? Is this the sort of "ambivalence about abortion" that
in the present atmosphere slides so easily into self-flagellating guilt?

Some left antiabortionists, mainly pacifists—Juli Loesch, Mary
Meehan, and other "feminists for life"; Jim Wallis and various writers
for Wallis's radical evangelical journal *Sojourners*—have tried to square
their position with concern for women. They blame the prevalence of
abortion on oppressive conditions—economic injustice, lack of child
care and other social supports for mothers, the devaluation of child-
rearing, men's exploitative sexual behavior and refusal to take equal
responsibility for children. They disagree on whether to criminalize
abortion now (since murder is intolerable no matter what the cause)
or to build a long-term moral consensus (since stopping abortion requires a general social transformation), but they all regard abortion
as a desperate solution to desperate problems, and the women who
resort to it as more sinned against than sinning.

This analysis grasps an essential feminist truth: that in a male-
supremacist society no choice a woman makes is genuinely free or
entirely in her interest. Certainly many women have had abortions
they didn't want or wouldn't have wanted if they had any plausible
means of caring for a child; and countless others wouldn't have gotten
pregnant in the first place were it not for inadequate contraception,
sexual confusion and guilt, male pressure, and other stigmata of
female powerlessness. Yet forcing a woman to bear a child she doesn't
want can only add injury to insult, while refusing to go through with
such a pregnancy can be a woman's first step toward taking hold of
her life. And many women who have abortions are "victims" only
of ordinary human miscalculation, technological failure, or the va-
garies of passion, all bound to exist in any society, however utopian.
There will always be women who, at any given moment, want sex
but don't want a child; some of these women will get pregnant; some
of them will have abortions. Behind the victim theory of abortion
is the implicit belief that women are always ready to be mothers, if
only conditions are right, and that sex for pleasure rather than pro-

creation is not only "irresponsible" (i.e., bad) but something men impose on women, never something women actively seek. Ironically, left right-to-lifers see abortion as always coerced (it's "exploitation" and "violence against women"), yet regard motherhood—which for most women throughout history has been inescapable, and is still our most socially approved role—as a positive choice. The analogy to the feminist antipornography movement goes beyond borrowed rhetoric: the antiporners, too, see active female lust as surrender to male domination and traditionally feminine sexual attitudes as expressions of women's true nature.

This Orwellian version of feminism, which glorifies "female values" and dismisses women's struggles for freedom—particularly sexual freedom—as a male plot, has become all too familiar in recent years. But its use in the abortion debate has been especially muddleheaded. Somehow we're supposed to leap from an oppressive patriarchal society to the egalitarian one that will supposedly make abortion obsolete without ever allowing women to see themselves as people entitled to control their reproductive function rather than be controlled by it. How women who have no power in this most personal of areas can effectively fight for power in the larger society is left to our imagination. A "New Zealand feminist" quoted by Mary Meehan in a 1980 article in *The Progressive* says, "Accepting short-term solutions like abortion only delays the implementation of real reforms like decent maternity and paternity leaves, job protection, high-quality child care, community responsibility for dependent people of all ages, and recognition of the economic contribution of childminders"—as if these causes were progressing nicely before legal abortion came along. On the contrary, the fight for reproductive freedom is the foundation of all the others, which is why antifeminists resist it so fiercely.

As "prolife" pacifists have been particularly concerned with refuting charges of misogyny, the liberal Catholics at *Commonweal* are most exercised by the claim that antiabortion laws violate religious freedom. The editorial quoted above hurled another challenge at the proabortion forces:

It is time, finally, for the pro-choice advocates and editorial writers to abandon, once and for all, the argument that abortion [sic] is a religious "doctrine" of a single or several churches being imposed on those of other persuasions in violation of the First Amendment. . . . Catholics and their bishops are accused of imposing their "doctrine" on abortion, but not their "doctrine" on the needs of the poor, or their "doctrine" on the arms race, or their "doctrine" on human rights in Central America. . . .

The briefest investigation into Catholic teaching would show that the church's case against abortion is utterly unlike, say, its belief in the Real Presence, known with the eyes of faith alone, or its insistence on a Sunday obligation, applicable only to the faithful. The church's moral teaching on abortion . . . is for the most part like its teaching on racism, warfare, and capital punishment, based on ordinary reasoning common to believers and nonbelievers. . . .

This is one more example of right-to-lifers' tendency to ignore the sexual ideology underlying their stand. Interesting isn't it, how the editorial neglects to mention that the church's moral teaching on abortion jibes neatly with its teaching on birth control, sex, divorce, and the role of women. The traditional, patriarchal sexual morality common to these teachings is explicitly religious, and its chief defenders in modern times have been the more conservative churches. The Catholic and evangelical Christian churches are the backbone of the organized right-to-life movement and—a few Nathansons and Hentoffs notwithstanding—have provided most of the movement's activists and spokespeople.

Furthermore, the Catholic hierarchy has made opposition to abortion a litmus test of loyalty to the church in a way it has done with no other political issue—witness Archbishop O'Connor's harassment of Geraldine Ferraro during her vice-presidential campaign. It's unthinkable that a Catholic bishop would publicly excoriate a Catholic officeholder or candidate for taking a hawkish position on the arms race or Central America or capital punishment. Nor do I notice anyone trying to read William F. Buckley out of the church for his views on welfare. The fact is there is no accepted Catholic "doctrine" on these matters comparable to the church's absolutist condemnation of abortion. And while differing attitudes toward war, racism, and poverty cut across religious and secular lines, the sexual values that mandate opposition to abortion are the bedrock of the traditional religious world view, the source of the most bitter conflict with secular and religious modernists. When churches devote their considerable political power, organizational resources, and money to translating those values into law, I call that imposing their religious beliefs on me—whether or not such laws technically violate the First Amendment.

Statistical studies have repeatedly shown that people's views on abortion are best predicted by their opinions on sex and "family" issues, not on "life" issues like nuclear weapons or the death penalty. That's not because we're inconsistent but because we comprehend what's really at stake in the abortion fight. It's the antiabortion left that refuses to face the contradiction in its own position: you can't be wholeheartedly for "life"—or for such progressive aspirations as free-dom, democracy, equality—and condone the subjugation of women. The seamless garment is full of holes.

July 1985

Looking for Mr. Good Dad

Though the two are easily confused, female cynicism about men is not an expression of feminism. The cynic assumes that men will always have power over women and the will to exploit it, that if things change it can only be for the worse. But since few people can live entirely without hope, she tends to displace hers onto the past. For the feminist's utopian vision, she substitutes a romantic nostalgia for patriarchal paternalism; she imagines that by pursuing freedom we've gained nothing, only sacrificed the "respect" and "protection" and "commitment" that were once our due. This is the familiar stuff of female antifeminism. But it can get complicated, because sometimes the feminist and the cynic are the same person. Such schizophrenia is rampant in these backward-looking times, and while I haven't taken any polls, I think it's especially rampant among younger women. Younger from my 43-year-old standpoint means too young to have experienced the feminist explosion at its peak or to remember what women's lives were like before the libertarian ferment of the '60s.

Juli Loesch, at 33, is that young. Loesch is a writer, peace activist, and "prolife feminist" whose polemics against abortion have appeared in various lefty publications. Recently she wrote me a letter, which she's agreed to let me take issue with in print. "In the past," it reads, "people assumed that by having heterosexual relations . . . they acquired parental obligations if pregnancy resulted." But with legal abortion, "obligations now result not from the decision to have sex, but from the decision to have a baby." This means that for a woman the legal obligations of parenthood arise from her choice to bear the child; but for a man they arise from the woman's choice. Does this

not, Loesch inquires with heavy irony, violate his sexual autonomy?
    The letter goes on:

There will always be men who, at any given moment, want sex but don't want a child; some of these men will get women pregnant. But sex and pregnancy imply—exactly nothing, no responsibility. It's only the woman's subsequent and separate choice that determines everything. That being the case, why should any man feel he's acquired an obligation? Because he deposited sperm in some woman's vagina? Don't be medieval.

    Am I predicting that men are losing whatever tenuous hold they had on parental obligation? That the men are going to take off, and not only that, but feel *justified* about it? Hell, no . . . I'm *reporting* it. I do women's shelter work. I see it all the time. A couple has a child. Three years down the line he decides he isn't cut out to be a father. "But you can't just walk out. This is your child, too!" "Yeah? But it was *your choice.*"

    . . . You know, most male commitment to the long-term responsibilities of child rearing is not obtained through court order. Most of it is obtained voluntarily, through a man's sense, bolstered by society, that this is right and fair, that it's his child as well as the woman's, because they both brought the child into being by their knowing act.

    Concluding, Loesch refers to the paternity suit against Frank Ser-pico, which caused a small flap a few years ago. He contested his girl-friend's claim to support for their child on the grounds that having the baby was her choice, not his. "What would you say to him?" Loesch asks. "Perhaps he's right?"

    Before I can sensibly answer that question, I have to sort out reality from Loesch's blinky-eyed rhetoric. To begin with, in the past people assumed that by having heterosexual relations *the woman* ac-quired obligations if pregnancy resulted. For the most part, the man was held responsible only if he was married to the woman, willing to marry her, or forced by family and community pressure to marry her. (Such pressure was of course exerted on behalf of "respectable" women only: if she was the "wrong" class or race or had a "bad reputation" she was on her own.) Nor have idealistic scruples about the connection between sex and procreation ever deterred men from sleeping with women they had no intention of marrying. Loesch can romanticize the past because she never had to live through it as a sexually active adult—she was 21 when *Roe* v. *Wade* came down.

18 when New York passed its liberal abortion law. I grew up in the days of forced marriages, illegal abortions, virginity fetishism, sexual guilt and panic and disgrace. I became a feminist during the period when women were supposed to have sexual freedom, but if we got pregnant, too bad. My only feelings about those years are relief that they're gone and fear that they might come back.

Not that the present is so terrific. I have no quarrel with Loesch's anger at male irresponsibility, just with her lack of historical and political perspective. Her view of men reminds me of George "It's a Jungle Out There" Gilder's: Basically men are moral cretins who have a "tenuous hold" on parental responsibility and feel justified in walking out on a three-year-old child because it could have been an abortion. To imagine that they might hang around because they care about their children or partners, or that they're capable of empathy with a woman's need to control her fertility, is to mistake the nature of the beast. In certain circumstances, however—namely, when women renounce any claim to autonomy and rely on their protection—men become honorable creatures ready to do the right thing, the fair thing.

Unlike Loesch, though, Gilder at least recognizes that men have had more concrete incentives than moral uplift for "voluntarily" committing themselves (forgetting for a moment about those shotgun weddings) to marriage and fatherhood. Historically, marriage has been a very good deal for men, offering them considerable status, power, and privilege. In return for their acceptance of parental obligations, their wives have done the nitty-gritty tasks of child rearing, maintained their homes, seen to their physical comfort and emotional well-being—I wouldn't turn it down, myself. However, it's only recently, and only in some cultures and classes, that marriage and parenthood have been truly voluntary for large numbers of men. Having a family used to be the ticket to adulthood and full membership in the community. Bachelorhood was suspect. Divorce was hard to get, stigmatized, and expensive; society couldn't afford to have too many dependent women and children lose their patrons.

While Loesch's idea of the contract between men and women is impossibly sentimental, like a lot of other people she sees that it's breaking down. In the jargon of the day, we are suffering a "crisis in the family," whose central figure is the impoverished single mother. This crisis can hardly be blamed on legal abortion—it was brewing long before *Roe* v. *Wade* was a gleam in some feminist lawyer's eye— but in a way abortion isn't a bad metaphor. For what's happening, over the long term, is that women's continuing struggle for independence and power over their lives is destabilizing the system. Women are demanding a new deal and men are resisting by any means available, including picking up their marbles and leaving home. What Juli Loesch has tuned in to is the sound of male backlash: "You want *choice*? I'll show you *choice*! No more Mr. Nice Guy."

Women have been worrying about male backlash for a long time. In the 19th century, when some feminists supported efforts to ease divorce laws so that women could get out of intolerable marriages, others argued that divorce was a license for men to shuck their familial responsibilities. More recently, many feminists have dismissed the liberalization of sexual mores, which established women's right to have sex outside marriage without social ostracism, as nothing but a means of encouraging and legitimizing men's sexual exploitation of women. Their view echoes that of antifeminist women who believe traditional moral standards protect nice girls from lustful men— just as Loesch's view of abortion echoes the right-wing charge that contraception weakens the family and encourages male irresponsibility. Similarly, female opponents of ERA warned that if women pursued economic equality, men would stop supporting their wives, leaving women with children stranded.

The threat that men will abandon all responsibility for children is potent indeed. But the problem is not that women's demands for freedom are rocking the boat; it's that men have the power to set the terms of their participation in child rearing and women don't. So long as mothers must depend on the "voluntary commitment" of men who can withdraw it without negotiation at any time, we're in trouble no matter what we do. After all, there have always been men who abandoned their families. Maybe they used to feel guiltier— noblesse oblige is the first thing to go when the serfs start getting ungrateful—but as I see it, male guilt and a token will put me on the subway.

So the question a feminist ought to be asking is this: Why do men and women have such an unequal relation to parenthood? Is it biology—we bear children, they don't? Actually, this difference becomes inequality only in the context of a specific social system for rearing children—the family, or, to be more precise, familialism (since I'm talking about a system that affects us all, whether we're in actual families or not). A familialist society assigns legal responsibility for children to the biological parents; the society as a whole has only minimal obligations to its children, and people rarely make deep commitments to children outside their families. This system puts women at an inherent disadvantage: Since it's obvious who a child's mother is, her parental responsibility is automatic; the father's is not. And so the burden has always been on women to get men to do right by them.

Loesch takes familialism for granted. Nearly everyone does. After all, the family is so ancient, so apparently universal, that it seems as natural and fixed as sexual difference itself. Yet a mere 15 years ago it didn't seem that way at all. Feminists and other cultural radicals were pointing out that the family is a social arrangement, invented by human beings, subject to criticism and change. All sorts of radical ideas got a serious hearing: that children should be considered members of the community, rather than wards of their parents; that they are properly a collective responsibility; that every child ought to have a socially guaranteed right to be supported and genuinely cared for. Some of us envisioned a society organized around communal households, in which adults as a matter of course were committed to sharing in child rearing, whether or not they had biological children. With the conservative onslaught, debate on these ideas has been choked off so thoroughly that you would never know, unless you were there, that for a time they had real currency in the culture. That they were far from being realized isn't the point. They provided a touchstone, a perspective from which to analyze the pains of the present and plan the direction of our movement. If men's nature is to hit and run, if aversion to attachment is in their genes, then the best women can do is bribe them, placate them, and guilt-trip them like crazy. But if the fault lies with the social structure that gives men too much power—and we know that power corrupts—we can start talking politics.

Which brings me to the feckless Frank Serpico. His case is only the *reductio ad absurdum* of a fundamentally inequitable system. It's sexist in the first place that a mother must assume the entire burden of parenthood unless she knows and can prove who the father is. It's outrageous to suggest that because she didn't have to have the child she should be denied even that avenue of relief. And at the same time, yes, it's unfair to the Serpicos that all the men whose sexual activity hasn't happened to result in unwanted fatherhood can say, "Tough luck, buddy, but it's not my problem." Loesch has a point when she argues that it's inconsistent to endorse sexual freedom and systematically break the links between sex and procreation, then turn around and say this child is *your* responsibility because it's the product of *your* sexual act. But it doesn't occur to her that responsibility could be extended rather than abdicated. Juli Loesch is of her time, an era when the utopian imagination has failed. And that's a great loss for all of us.

September 1985

From Forced Pregnancy to

Forced Surgery

For once I did not feel isolated in my outrage: the courts ruled, and virtually everyone agreed, that in the Nancy Klein case the right-to-life movement had gone too far. A stranger purporting to represent the fetus of a comatose woman and challenging her husband's right to authorize an abortion on her behalf so violated accepted canons of privacy that even Cardinal O'Connor felt constrained to say he understood the husband's action, though of course he could not condone it.

The case was a particular embarrassment to those who argue that opposition to abortion expresses concern for all life. Doctors who testified in court were divided on whether an abortion would aid Klein's recovery, as her husband contended; in any case, it doesn't take medical expertise to surmise that when a woman has suffered a massive brain injury, the extra strain pregnancy puts on the body can hardly help her struggle to heal. But to the would-be guardian of her fetus, Klein's health and for all practical purposes her life were expendable. From his perspective the question was not why take any risk, however small, that continuing the pregnancy could impede Klein's recovery, but why put the interests of this woman, whose prognosis is poor anyway, above her usefulness as a vessel. It reminded me of the debates on criteria for publicly funded abortions that went on in Congress and the state legislatures a decade or so ago—in particular, I recall one legislator suggesting that the government should pay for an abortion only if the chance of the "mother's" dying from the pregnancy was at least 50 percent.

Ironically, the grossness of the Klein case tended to obscure a more basic issue: What was it doing in court in the first place? Since Nancy Klein would have had a clear legal right to demand an abortion, the normal procedure—as for any other treatment—would have been to allow her husband to act as her surrogate in making the decision. Nor was he under any legal obligation to prove the operation would help her recover. (Suppose he "merely" believed that she would not want to have a baby while facing severe disability—or that she would want her husband to be free to concentrate on caring for *her*?) Yet the hospital administration refused to permit an abortion without a court order. This action and the subsequent harassment of Klein's husband (which is what the court fight amounted to) reflect not only the antiabortionists' success at creating a political atmosphere that subverts the intent of *Roe* v. *Wade*, but the impact of a much more ambitious—and dangerous—movement for "fetal rights."

The right-to-life movement has always claimed to be demanding equal legal rights for an unrecognized class of people. But even assuming the full human status of fetuses—an assumption I'm willing to entertain for the sake of the argument—there is a fundamental flaw in the movement's logic. Every fetus grows inside a woman, making active demands on her body and mind, and there is no such thing in our legal system as a human right to appropriate someone else's body for one's own use. No one, for instance, can be forced to donate a kidney, or for that matter undergo such an innocuous procedure as giving blood, even to save a life. We may admire people who make physical sacrifices or take physical risks on behalf of their fellow human beings—and we may, depending on the circumstances, deeply disapprove of those who don't—but most of us recognize that to compel such generosity would be to deprive people of an essential freedom.

What right-to-lifers are really demanding is that we make an exception for fetuses—or rather, continue making the exception that's always been implied in women's traditional obligation to nurture life regardless of their own needs. It's feminists who are insisting that the treatment of a class of people—women—be brought into line with accepted standards of human rights.

The idea that the fetus is a separate individual with rights that must be weighed against the interests of the woman who carries it has implications far beyond abortion prohibition. After all, if the fetus has a right to life, why not a right to health? Certainly, even those of us who believe in the unconditional right to abortion would agree that a woman who decides to have a baby has a moral responsibility to do what she can to protect that future baby's well-being. During my own pregnancy, I monitored everything that went into my mouth. I don't drink or smoke anyway, but not eating rare meat, limiting my coffee intake, and fulfilling my calcium quota was a drag. I also took vitamin supplements, didn't take cold pills, went to the doctor religiously, took all the tests she recommended, wouldn't work on a computer terminal because of the radiation, and used no anesthetics during the birth. Happily, the question of whether I needed a cesarean never came up.

I did all this voluntarily, of course, and without separating my own stake in having a healthy child from some abstract consideration of its "rights." But what of the pregnant woman who doesn't? Should the state take steps to prevent her from drinking, smoking, eating the wrong foods, gaining too much or too little weight, working or exercising too strenuously, refusing medical advice, or engaging in any other behavior that could—in some authority's opinion—endanger her fetus? Should she be forced to undergo any prenatal tests or medical treatments, including surgery, that her doctor believes are necessary for a healthy birth? Should she be required to stay in bed or abstain from sex to avoid a threatened miscarriage? If she needs medical treatment (for cancer, say) that could have adverse effects on the fetus, should she have to get a judge's permission? If her baby is born dead or with defects or health problems, should she be investigated for possible prenatal child abuse? Should she, in short, be subjected to totalitarian control of her reproductive life?

All this may sound like the far reaches of someone's dystopian nightmare—in fact it used to be my *reductio ad absurdum* argument against forced childbearing. But no such luck: during the past few years, controlling women's behavior during pregnancy has become a serious item on the "prolife" agenda. A smattering of court decisions and a growing body of writing in legal and medical journals claim that the state may—or even must—hold women civilly and criminally liable for harming or failing to protect their fetuses. Specifically, articles by fetal-rights advocates have argued that pregnant women can be forced to have cesarean sections, forbidden to give birth at home, subjected to mandatory prenatal testing, force-fed if they are anorexic, excluded from the provisions of "living wills" that allow patients to forgo artificial life supports or other life-prolonging measures, and sued by their children—or prosecuted under child welfare laws—for drinking and other prenatal derelictions. And a number of these arguments have found their way into the courts.

Since 1981, according to a survey in the *New England Journal of Medicine*, courts in various states have received 15 requests to order a cesarean against the pregnant woman's will. Typically, the doctor felt that attempting a vaginal birth would endanger the fetus, and the woman refused a cesarean because of religious beliefs, fear of surgery, or disagreement with the doctor's judgment. Judges granted 13 of the requests, accepting some version of the argument that the duty of the state to protect a viable fetus outweighed the intrusion of forced major surgery. (In several cases the orders came from juvenile court, which had been asked to accept jurisdiction over the fetus.) As one judge put it, "All that stood between the . . . fetus and its independent existence, separate from its mother, was, put simply, a doctor's scalpel. In these circumstances, the life of the infant inside its mother's womb was entitled to be protected"—and the mother's slashed belly be damned. In at least two other cases, doctors have dispensed with the formality of getting a court order and simply performed cesareans over their patients' protests.

The misogyny that pervades these medical rapes is shocking in its crudity. In a 1982 case in Michigan, a judge not only ordered a pregnant woman to submit to a cesarean, but told her that if she did not come to the hospital at the appointed time, the police would pick her up and take her there. In 1984, a Chicago woman who had been hospitalized in anticipation of the imminent birth of triplets refused to consent to a cesarean. Without telling her (which would have given her a chance to go elsewhere), the hospital convinced a court to grant it temporary custody of the fetuses and permit the operation. When the woman and her husband realized what was happening, they became belligerent, whereupon she was tied down by the wrists and ankles and he was thrown out of the hospital. The cesarean was performed.

A particularly egregious example of forced surgery—comparable to the Klein case in its blatant devaluation of a woman's life—took place in Washington, D.C., in 1987. As a teenager, Angela Carder had been diagnosed as having terminal bone cancer; after years of surgery and other treatment she had survived. She was 27 years old and 25 weeks pregnant when her doctors at George Washington University Hospital's obstetrics clinic found a metastasized tumor in her lung, and again the prognosis was death. Carder's longtime cancer specialist, who did not have privileges at the hospital, recommended an emergency regimen of chemotherapy to prolong her life. But although Carder and her GWU doctors apparently agreed, the treatment was not carried out. The doctors did not consider a cesarean, however, because the fetus was too immature and the surgery too risky for someone in Carder's weakened condition.

Five days after Carder's admission to the hospital, when her death seemed imminent, the hospital asked a judge to rule on whether it should intervene to save the fetus. The judge appointed a lawyer for the fetus, who argued for the need to "balance the interest of a probably viable fetus . . . with whatever life is left for the fetus's mother," and concluded that since Carder was going to die anyway, the court should choose the fetus. Despite Carder's refusal to consent to a cesarean and the unanimous opposition of the obstetrics staff, the judge ordered the operation. It was performed after a three-judge panel from the D.C. court of appeals denied Carder's court-appointed lawyer a request to stay the order so that he could appeal. The whole process was over so quickly that there was no time to call witnesses, including the cancer specialist, who later testified that in his opinion, Carder's condition had not been terminal.

Carder's fetus was not viable and died two-and-a-half hours after the birth; Carder herself died two days later, her death certificate listing surgery as a contributing cause of death. In a written opinion justifying the decision to deny a stay, Court of Appeals judge Frank Nebeker wrote, "We well know that we may have shortened A.C.'s life span by a few hours. . . . With a viable fetus, a balancing of interest must replace the single interest of the mother, and as in this case, time can be a critical factor." The opinion caused a public furor. Shortly afterward, the Court of Appeals granted the ACLU's petition for a rehearing by the full nine-member court, which was held last fall. A decision has not yet come down.*

Less dramatic forms of pregnancy policing have also been gaining legal validation. Over the past decade, courts in various states have granted a man an order compelling his wife to have surgery to prevent a miscarriage (the decision was overturned on appeal), allowed a father to sue the mother of his son for "prenatal negligence" on the grounds that her use of the antibiotic tetracycline had discolored the son's teeth, ordered a pregnant woman hospitalized after a social agency charged that she could not take care of herself, ordered women to undergo intrauterine transfusions for Rh sensitization, and allowed hospitals to forcibly detain diabetic women whose neglect of their condition allegedly endangered their fetuses.

The need to protect fetuses from drug abuse is an emerging theme in fetal-rights advocacy. Last year, a Washington, D.C., judge jailed a pregnant woman who had tested positive for cocaine while waiting to be sentenced for forging checks; *The Washington Post* reported that he "seemed genuinely perplexed by the public clamor and said he and his colleagues had done this before . . . and would probably do it again." A Florida woman who gave birth to a cocaine-exposed baby was recently charged with child abuse and felony drug delivery, which carries a 30-year sentence.

The best-known prosecution of a woman for crimes against her fetus also began as a drug case. In 1985, Pamela Rae Stewart of San Diego gave birth to a son; because of a hemorrhage caused by the placenta's detaching from the uterus, the baby was born brain-dead and succumbed to pneumonia five weeks later. According to Angela Bonavoglia, who wrote a detailed profile of Stewart for *Ms.* magazine, Paul Zlotnik, the medical director of the neonatal care unit where the baby was born, suspected drug use and ordered tests that revealed traces of amphetamines in the infant. He reported his findings to Child Protective Services, adding indignantly that informa-

---

* In 1990, the court ruled seven to one against the original decision. Its finding that a woman cannot be forced to have a Caesarean is binding only in D.C.

tion Stewart's husband had given him proved her to be "extremely negligent": she had, Zlotnik said, violated her doctor's orders by neglecting to take medication he had prescribed, having sex, and not going to the hospital immediately when she started bleeding.

Stewart was arrested and charged with the baby's death under a child-support statute that had been amended to include the unborn (the purpose of the change was to allow women to begin receiving support payments while they were pregnant). Unable to post bail immediately, she stayed in jail for six days. Two years later a judge dismissed the charges on the grounds that the statute did not apply— and suggested that new legislation was the proper remedy.

Well, but . . . some of you are saying; I'm for women's rights, but what about those dead or damaged or drug-poisoned babies? Is there nothing we can do to save them—do we just shrug and say "tough luck"? And if tying a woman down and cutting her open sounds horrifying, what about the horror of the doctor forced to stand by and let a baby die? I'm not minimizing these concerns. I believe we have a collective, social responsibility to support the birth of healthy babies. But despite appearances, the fetal-rights movement is not really about protecting babies—it's about shifting power away from women to doctors, hospitals, and courts, which is by no means the same thing. If the movement has its way, a small number of babies will benefit, but the overall prospects for babies will be no better, and in some ways they will be worse.

Babies are not served by the movement's most basic assumption: that women are irresponsible and can't be trusted to manage their pregnancies; therefore, doctors' orders should have the force of law. This is, among other things, a backlash against the successful struggles of pregnant women, and patients generally, to establish their right to question doctors' judgment and control their medical treatment. Certainly women can make mistakes, but at this late date—after the DES scandal, the shift from worrying about gaining too much weight during pregnancy to gaining too little, the discrediting of the slogan "once a cesarean, always a cesarean," the explosion of concern over the high cesarean rate—it should hardly be necessary to point out that today's medical orthodoxy is tomorrow's malpractice suit. Furthermore, there is almost always some element of uncertainty in medical decision-making (in several of the cases where hospitals requested or were granted court orders for cesareans, the women ended up having normal vaginal deliveries).

But judgment is not the only issue here; there is also the underlying implication that conscientious doctors must protect fetuses from women's feckless indifference to their fate. In the real world, of course, women who are carrying a wanted baby typically have more of an emotional investment in the outcome of their pregnancy than anyone else, and are willing to do just about anything they believe will insure a healthy birth. Indeed, as women's health advocates have shown, they are usually more ready than they should be to accept aggressive medical intervention. If anything, it is doctors who are more likely to have extraneous motives for their decisions—motives like money, convenience, and avoiding possible lawsuits.

The idea that women are their unborn children's worst enemies is especially ludicrous in the present social context. Millions of women, especially the urban minority poor, have inadequate access (or none at all) to prenatal care and education (or medical care in general), and cannot afford the kind of diet necessary to sustain a healthy pregnancy. Growing numbers of pregnant women are homeless. The correlation of poverty with low birth weight and with infant death, illness, and birth defects is well established. Various forms of environmental pollution also play a part in pregnancy problems; so do violence, stress, and abusive or unsympathetic male partners. (According to the *Ms.* account, Pamela Rae Stewart had a public history of being beaten by her husband; the possible implications for the baby's death were never raised. Nor was Stewart's husband charged for having sex with her, though they both heard the doctor's prohibition.)

People who are genuinely committed to saving babies ought to be addressing themselves to these systemic problems. Punishing and restricting individual pregnant women diverts attention from larger social failures and in effect scapegoats women for those failures— particularly since it is mostly poor, black, and Hispanic pregnant women (Stewart is poor and white) who, because they depend on public hospitals and other government agencies, most often come to the attention of the state. (Of the court-ordered cesareans and other procedures listed in the *New England Journal of Medicine* survey, 81 percent involved black, Hispanic, or Asian women.) In addition, the fetal-rightists' invasive, punitive tactics will only make it more difficult for women to get the help they need. Faced with the risk of forced treatment, intrusions in their personal lives, or criminal prosecution, many women will simply stay away from public hospitals and clinics. They and their babies will both be the worse for it.

Enlisting the fetal-rights approach in the "war on drugs" has especially frightening potential, merging as it does a police-state mentality toward women with the mindless, authoritarian zeal of the antidrug crusade. Already, fetuses are being used to get around prosecutors' frustration at what they consider the law's leniency toward individual drug users: the Florida "felony drug delivery" case mentioned above is one example; another is Pamela Rae Stewart, whose alleged use of amphetamines, according to a doctor interviewed for the *Ms.* article, in all probability had no bearing on her baby's condition. On a deeper level, punishing pregnant drug users will only reinforce the pervasive lack of understanding that the sad spectacle of drugged babies stems, ultimately, from the despair of women who need more, not less, control over their fates.

None of which is to deny that there will always be hard cases—times when a baby will die or suffer because a pregnant woman is negligent, unreasonable, or just plain wrong; when sensitive, dedicated doctors will wish they sold rugs for a living; when the most democratic-minded judge will have the impulse to sanction force. But even in those hard cases, the impulse must be resisted: the price in human freedom and dignity is simply too high. Not only do state controls over pregnancy violate particular women's right to self-determination, bodily integrity, and informed consent to medical treatment, in effect defining them not as people but as fetus-carriers; the degree of surveillance required to enforce such controls would violate the rights of all women of childbearing age.

In justifying their position, fetal-rightists often cite the new medical technology that has increased our ability to observe, test, and treat fetuses inside the womb. But as Judith Levine argued in *The Village Voice* a few years ago, this is less a genuine rationale than an attempt to appeal to the nonreligious through the secular god of science. The real impetus to the fetal-rights campaign has been the appalling success of the antiabortion movement in pushing women, their bodies, and their lives to the periphery of the abortion debate and defining the central issue—really, the only issue—as fetal life. While in one way the assertion of fetal rights is simply an extension of "prolife" ideology, it also seems to be a response to the antiabortionists' frustration at being unable (so far) to recriminalize abortion, an effort to achieve their underlying goal—subordinating women to their childbearing role—by other means. There is a none-too-subtle note of revenge in the argument made by Margery Shaw, a doctor who supports fetal rights, that because women do have the right to abortion, they have more responsibility for the fetuses they choose to carry to term. Shaw has even suggested holding women liable for *not* aborting a defective fetus; this sounds like a contradiction, but what I hear under the surface is, "You want abortion? Okay, bitch, you've got it."

Fetal-rights advocates have also used (or misused) *Roe* v. *Wade* in court, seizing on its finding that the state has a legitimate interest in preserving fetal life after viability. The text of the decision clearly states that this interest only applies to regulating abortion in the third trimester; it also affirms that the woman's interest in her life and health remains paramount. But this has not stopped judges from invoking it to allow forced cesareans.

In the words of Janet Gallagher, who has done extensive research on the fetal rights movement, the legal doctrine it promotes is a "backdoor Human Life Amendment." Though the concept of fetal personhood—which was specifically rejected in the *Roe* v. *Wade* decision—has no basis in present law, the fact that more and more judges are nevertheless invoking that concept in making decisions has the inevitable effect of legitimizing and "normalizing" it, as well as putting pressure on the Supreme Court to reverse itself. Among its many clauses, the Missouri abortion law the court will review this month declares that human life begins at conception. Even among those most fearful—or for that matter hopeful—that the court will limit or overrule *Roe* v. *Wade*, few expect it to take the radical step of declaring the fetus a person. But a few more years of fetal-rights cases and the picture could be very different.

I've been pregnant three times. The first time I had an early abortion; the third time I had a healthy child. In between, I had a miscarriage at five months, for no apparent reason. I have two vivid memories: that my grief was not for the fetus, the dead body I'd expelled, but for the baby that would not be born and perhaps (I was afraid) never would be; and that my sudden sense of freedom to do and eat what I wanted, without worrying about the baby, was one of the worst feelings I'd ever had. But now, reading about fetal-rights cases, I think about something else: when I was pregnant again, routine tests showed that for some months I'd had abnormally high levels of toxoplasmosis antibodies. If this was the answer to the mystery of why I'd lost the other baby (and I'm still not sure), it only raised another question; I'd always heard that the way you got toxoplasmosis was by handling cat litter or eating rare meat, neither of which I'd done. But how could anyone else know that? Suppose obstetricians had to report toxo cases to the health department. Suppose someone had shown up at my door: "Just a routine investigation. . . ." It can't happen here, right?

I am grateful to Lynn Paltrow (who argued the Angela Carder case for the ACLU) and to Janet Gallagher for providing me with a wealth of information on fetal-rights case law and the surrounding debate. Especially helpful in preparing this article were Gallagher's "Fetus as Patient," in the anthology *Reproductive Rights for the 1990s*; "Prenatal Invasions and Interventions: What's Wrong With Fetal Rights," also by Gallagher, in *Harvard Women's Law Journal*; and Paltrow's speech to the National Association of Women and the Law Conference on "Maternal and Fetal Rights."

April 1989

Sisters Under the Skin?

Confronting Race and Sex

Recently, at a feminist meeting, a black woman argued that in American society race is a more absolute division than sex, a more basic determinant of social identity. This started an intense discussion: if someone shook us out of a deep sleep and demanded that we define ourselves, what would we blurt out first? The black woman said "black woman." Most of the white women said "woman"; some said "lesbian." No one said "white person" or "white woman."

I'm not sure it makes sense to say that one social division is more absolute than another. I wonder if it isn't more a matter of different kinds of division. Most blacks and whites live in separate communities, in different social, cultural, and economic worlds, while most women and men share each other's daily, intimate lives and cooperate, even if unequally, in such elemental activities as fucking, procreating, and keeping a household going. On the other hand, a man and a woman can spend their lives together and have such disparate versions of their "common" experience that they might as well live on different planets. Do I feel more distant from black women than from white men? Everything else (class) being equal? (Except that it usually isn't.) In some ways yes, in some ways no. But whatever the objective truth, my sex feels more basic to my identity than my race. This is not surprising: in a sexist society it's impossible to take one's femaleness for granted; in a racist society whiteness is simply generic humanness, entirely unremarkable. Suppose, though, that a black revolution were to seriously challenge my racial privileges? Suppose I had to confront every day, every hour, the question of which side I'm on?

Such questions excite and disturb me. Like talk about sexuality, discussions of the racial-sexual nexus radiate danger and taboo—a sign that the participants are on to something. Lately such discussions, mostly initiated by black women, are happening more often. They raise the heartening possibility of connecting, and in the process revitalizing, the unhappily divergent discourses of feminism and black liberation. This could be the first step toward creating a new feminist radicalism, whose interracial, interclass bonds go deeper than lowest-common-denominator coalition politics.

One of the women at the meeting suggested that I read *Sally Hemings*, Barbara Chase-Riboud's controversial historical novel about Thomas Jefferson's black mistress. I found it a devastating study of the psychology of masters and slaves, the politics of romantic love, the relations between black and white women, and the institution of the family. Much of its power lies in the way the author merges the race and sex of each character into a seamless whole, bringing home the point that to abstract these categories is already to falsify experience. So long as whiteness and maleness remain the norm, white women can think of themselves as "women," black men as "blacks"; but black women, doubly the Other, must be constantly aware of their dual identity at the same time that they suffer from both racial and sexual invisibility. In forcing the rest of us to see them, they also present us with new and far less tidy pictures of ourselves.

This suggests that confronting the oppression of black women means more than taking in new information or taking up new issues. It also means questioning the intellectual frameworks that the (male-dominated) black and (white-dominated) feminist movements have set up. If race and sex are experientially inseparable, can we (should we) still analyze them separately? If all women are subject to male supremacy—yet black and white women play out their relations with men (both inside and outside their own communities) in different ways—do they still have a common core of female experience, a common political oppression *as women*? Theoretically, the different situations of black women and black men should raise the same sort of question. But in practice black women have tended to single out their relation to white women and feminism as the more painful, problematic issue. This subject is now bursting through a decade's sediment of sloganeering, ritualistic condemnations, and liberal apologies to inform some provocative new writing.

But first, I feel I have to say something about Angela Davis. Her *Women, Race and Class* may have been inspired by all this ferment, but the kindest judgment I can make is that it misses the point. From Davis's orthodox Marxist perspective (still CP after all these years!), in which economic relations determine all, while sexual relations have no material status and sexism is merely a set of bad attitudes, the question of how racial and sexual politics interact loses its meaning: Davis strips racism of its psychocultural dimension and treats it strictly as a form of economic exploitation; she tends to ignore sexism altogether, except when invoking it as an excuse for white bourgeois feminists to undermine the struggles of black and working people. (For instance, she rightly condemns the racism of white suffragists outraged at the prospect that black men would get the vote before white women—but rationalizes the sexism that prompted black men to sell out women of both races by agreeing that the black male vote should have priority. Black men's "sexist attitudes," Davis argues, were "hardly a sound reason for arresting the progress of the overall struggle for Black liberation"—and never mind the effect on that struggle of denying the vote to half the black population.) Still, it would be a mistake to simply dismiss Davis's book as an anachronism. In more subtle and ambiguous forms, its brand of left antifeminism continues to influence women's thinking. Besides, Angela Davis is a public figure, and *Women, Race and Class* will undoubtedly outsell both the books I'm about to discuss.

Gloria I. Joseph is black; Jill Lewis is white. In *Common Differences: Conflicts in Black and White Feminist Perspectives*, they attempt to explore their separate histories, confront misunderstandings, and move toward "collaborative struggle." The book has the flavor of an open-ended political conversation; for the most part the authors write separate chapters, each commenting from her own perspective on various aspects of sexual politics. The result is uneven, full of intellectual loose ends and contradictions, and both writers have an unfortunate penchant for clotted, obfuscatory prose. But *Common Differences* does help to clarify touchy areas of black-white conflict. Joseph's chapters—which taught me a lot, especially about black mothers and daughters—are a valuable counterweight (and an implicit rebuke) to the tendency of white feminist theorists to base their generalizations about the female condition on white women's experience. In discussing black women's lives, Joseph uses a time-honored feminist method: she records group discussions and individual comments, picks out common themes and contradictions, and tries to draw conclusions. The immediacy of this material exposes white feminist parochialism more effectively than any abstract argument.

Without denying the movement's shortcomings, Lewis sets out to debunk the stereotype of the spoiled, elitist "women's libber." The feminist movement, she maintains, deserves recognition as the only social movement to challenge the status of women as women. She argues that white feminists have been struggling toward a deeper understanding of race and class, and that even those sectors of the movement most narrowly oriented to white middle-class concerns "have engaged in and won concrete struggles that potentially open up new terrain for *all* women."

In their introduction, Joseph and Lewis agree that "as a political movement, women's liberation did and does touch on questions which in different ways affect *all* women's lives." But *Common Differences* is much more about difference than about commonality. In *Ain't I a Woman: Black Women and Feminism* Bell Hooks strides boldly beyond pluralism to the rockier ground of synthesis. While Hooks also stresses the uniqueness of black women's experience and the ways it has been discounted, her aim is to enlarge the theoretical framework of feminism. To this end she analyzes black women's condition in a historical context, tracing the basic patterns of black female oppression to slavery and developing three intertwined themes: black men's sexism, white women's racism, and the effect of white men's racial-sexual politics on the relations between black and white women. Hooks is a contentious writer, and I don't always agree with her contentions, but *Ain't I a Woman* has an intellectual vitality and daring that should set new standards for the discussion of race and sex.

The central political question these books raise is why the contemporary feminist movement has been so white. Most critics of the movement have offered a simple answer: white feminists' racism has driven black women away. This indictment is true as far as it goes, but it already takes for granted facts that need explaining. Why, in the first place, was it primarily white women, rather than black women or both groups simultaneously, who felt impelled to mobilize against sexism? And why did so many politically conscious black women reject the movement (in some cases the very idea of feminism) out of hand, rather than insisting that it purge its theory and practice of racism, or organizing groups committed to a nonracist feminist politics? Antifeminist leftists have typically argued that sexual politics are inherently a white middle-class crotchet, irrelevant to women who are "really"—i.e., economically and racially—oppressed. Or else (this is Angela Davis's main strategy) they redefine feminism to mean women fighting together against racism and capitalism, and conclude that black and white working-class women have been the leaders of the *real* feminist struggle. Either way they imply that sexism is not a problem for black women, if indeed it is a problem at all.

Hooks, Joseph, and Lewis reject this idea. They assume that black women have a stake in women's liberation, and see white feminists' racism as part of a complex social history that has shaped black women's politics. Bell Hooks argues that estrangement between black and white women goes all the way back to slavery. The terms of the conflict, as she sees it, were defined by white men who applied racism to a Victorian sexual (and class) ideology that divided women into two categories: good (chaste, delicate, to be protected and idealized) and bad (licentious, unrefined, to be exploited and punished). While the white upper-class southern woman represented the feminine ideal, black female slaves were stigmatized, in schizoid fashion, both as bad women—therefore deserving to be raped and beaten— and as nonwomen: in doing the same work as men, black women threatened the ideology of female inferiority, a contradiction resolved by defining them as neuter beasts of burden.

At the same time, the white woman's power to collaborate in oppressing blacks softened and obscured the reality of her own inferior position. She exercised this power most directly over female slaves, whom she often treated with the special viciousness of the insecure boss. No doubt the degraded status of black women also reminded her, subconsciously at least, of what can happen to any female who provokes men into dropping the mask of patriarchal benevolence. As Hooks observes, the manifest cruelty of white women's own husbands, fathers, and brothers "served as a warning of what might be their fate should they not maintain a passive stance. Surely, it must have occurred to white women that were enslaved black women not available to bear the brunt of such intense antiwoman aggression, they themselves might have been the victims." As a result, the very identification that might have led white women to black women's defense probably had the opposite effect. White men's sexual pursuit of black women also exposed white women's humiliating position: they could neither prevent their husbands' behavior nor claim a comparable freedom for themselves. Instead they expressed their anger, salvaged their pride, and defended their own good-woman status by vilifying black women as seducers and sluts.

Hooks shows that what she calls the "devaluation of black womanhood" did not end with slavery but remains a potent source of black women's rage. Her account of how black women are systematically disparaged as whores, castrating matriarchs, and sexless mammies explains a crucial ingredient of black female hostility to the women's movement. Clearly, when white feminists ignored black female experience and in effect equated "woman" with "white woman," the insult had a double meaning for black women: it suggested that we were not only reinforcing white supremacy but trying to have it both ways by preserving our monopoly on femininity and its rewards (respect, status, financial support) while demanding the option of rejecting it. This perception of bad faith fueled the angry denunciations of feminism as "white women's business."

But envying white women's "femininity" is a trap for black women, as Hooks is well aware. Idealization of the white woman's status has tended to divert black women from demanding sexual justice to attacking black men for their inability to support stay-at-home wives. Many black women have endorsed black male demands for female subservience in the hope that at last they would get a crack at the pedestal. At the same time, their envy of white women has been mixed with contempt, an emotion that led some black women to insist they didn't need a movement because they were already liberated. Another illusion in Hooks's relentless catalogue: strength in adversity and the need to make a living are not the same thing as freedom.

Gloria Joseph emphasizes the painful collisions of black and female identity. As she says, "an individual cannot be two separate entities." Yet black women suffer from two modes of oppression and so are implicated, like it or not, in two social movements at once. At best this involves a double burden, at worst a continuing conflict of loyalties and priorities. Joseph shows that deep ambivalences permeate black women's thinking—on black men (distrust and antagonism mixed with solidarity, affection, and protectiveness), on sex ("a 'desirable no-no,' an 'attractive nuisance'"), on feminism itself (most of Joseph's respondents reject the movement but endorse its goals). Her argument suggests that black women have been slow to commit themselves to feminism—especially the more radical aspects of sexual politics—for fear of weakening their ties with the black community and the black struggle. Jill Lewis points out that white middle-class women could focus singlemindedly on feminism because "they did not have the stakes of *racial* unity or solidarity with White men that the Black women had with Black men" and because their privileges left them "free of the survival struggles that are priorities for minority and working-class women." If anything, class and racial privileges (particularly education) spurred their consciousness of sexual injustice by raising expectations that were thwarted purely because they were women.

Ironically, Joseph exemplifies the dilemma she describes: like many other black women who define themselves as feminists, she draws the line at calling black men oppressors. While Joseph and Lewis agree that black and white women are oppressed as women, they uncritically assume that male supremacy is a product of white culture, and that the concept does not really apply to male-female relations among blacks, except insofar as all white institutions and values shape black life. Lewis asserts that institutionalized sexism in America was imported by European immigrants, as if Native American, African, and other nonwhite cultures were free of male dominance. In fact, no anthropologist, feminist or otherwise, has ever come up with convincing evidence of a culture in which some form of male dominance does not exist.

Lewis and Joseph argue that because black men do not have the same worldly power as white men, "Male dominance as a salient problematic factor in male-female sexual relationships cannot be considered as a universal trait applicable to all men." But Joseph's own descriptions of black women's attitudes toward sex, men, and marriage—not to mention their struggles to bring up children alone—belie this view. Rather, her evidence confirms that despite black men's economic and social subordination to whites they share with all men certain male supremacist prerogatives, including physical and sexual aggression, the assumption of male superiority, and refusal to share responsibility for child rearing and housework. Joseph and Lewis also make the puzzling claim that sexist repression is more severe for white women because "Black women can be kept in their places via racism alone." Does racism alone account for black women's oppression as mothers, workers (including domestic workers), welfare recipients, prostitutes, victims of rape and sexual exploitation?

All this adds up to a bad case of conceptual confusion. You can't simultaneously agree that black women need feminism and deny the basic premise of feminism—that men have power over women. Women who engage in this form of doublethink still have a toe or two in the camp of left antifeminism; while rejecting crude economism of the Angela Davis variety, they assume that sexism is perpetuated not by men in general but by a white capitalist ruling class.

Hooks insists on the reality of black male sexism. Discussing the experience of female slaves, she angrily refutes the cliché that "the most cruel and dehumanizing impact of slavery . . . was that black men were stripped of their masculinity." This idea, she argues, merely reflects the sexist assumption that men's experience is more important than women's and that "the worst that can happen to a man is that he be made to assume the social status of woman." In fact, though all slaves suffered brutal oppression, "black men were allowed to maintain some semblance of their societally defined masculine role." Noting that American blacks came from African patriarchal cultures, Hooks rejects the idea that black men learned sexism from whites and the myth (repeated once again by Angela Davis) that within the slave community men and women were equal. On the contrary, the slaves accepted the concept of male superiority, and black families maintained a sexual division of labor, with women doing the cooking, cleaning, and child care. Nor did slaveholders assign black men "women's work." Black women, however, were forced by their white masters to perform both "masculine" and "feminine" functions, working alongside black men at backbreaking labor in the fields, while also serving as houseworkers, breeders, and sexual objects.

Hooks implicitly links what she sees as black women's false consciousness about sexism with their political isolation: while the sexism of black male activists has forced black women to choose between asserting themselves as women and maintaining racial solidarity, the racism of white feminists has reinforced and justified that split. *Ain't I a Woman* describes how this combination of pressures undermined black women's efforts to participate in both 19th and 20th century feminist movements. In dissecting the rhetoric of the contemporary black and women's movements, Hooks shows how sexism has been promoted as a cure for racism, sisterhood as a rationale for ignoring it. Black power advocates, confusing liberation with the assertion of their "manhood," embraced a white man's contention that a black matriarchy was the cause of their problems, and called on black women to advance the black cause by being submissive; some even suggested that sexual equality was a white racist idea, indicative of the white man's effeteness and decadence. Black Muslims tried to reverse the racist Victorian paradigm, defining black women as the feminine ideal and white women as devils (and establishing rigid patriarchal families).

Meanwhile the early radical feminists were claiming that the division between men and women was the most basic social hierarchy, and that since men had ruled every known political system, racism was basically a male problem ("men dominate women, a few men dominate the rest"—Redstockings Manifesto). This analysis, which I and most of my political cohort then subscribed to, has had a good deal of influence on the movement as a whole. It has two erroneous implications: that it's impossible for white women to oppress black men, and that racial conflict between black women and white women has no objective basis, but is (on both sides) an inauthentic antagonism that only serves the interests of men. Radical feminists understood, theoretically, that to build female unity white women had to oppose racism and change their own racist attitudes and behavior. We were sharply critical of liberal feminists who defined women's freedom in terms of professional careers and formal equality within a racist, class-stratified social system. Yet emotionally our belief that sex was a more basic division than race allowed us to evade responsibility for racism. It was tempting to imagine that simply by doing what we wanted most passionately to do—build a radical feminist movement—we would also be fighting racism; tempting, too, to play down how much we benefited from being white. For a while feminism seemed a way out of the classic bind of white middle-class radicals: we no longer had to see ourselves as privileged people wondering where we fit into the revolutionary struggle; we too were part of an oppressed class with a historic destiny.

Hooks's anger at this refusal to be accountable is well-deserved. But when she gets down to specifics, she tends to oversimplify and at times rewrite history. In her indictment of "white upper and middle-class feminists" (Abby Rockefeller aside, who are these upper-class feminists I keep hearing about?), the movement becomes a monolith. The political differences between liberals and radicals, the social conditions that allowed the former to co-opt and isolate the latter, the fierce intramovement debates about race and class are ignored or dismissed. White feminists' main aim, Hooks charges, has been to join the male power structure; the movement has posed no threat to the system.

This is silly. The women's movement has been no more or less opportunistic than the black movement, the labor movement, or any other mass movement successful enough to attract power mongers. Feminists have not succeeded in making a revolution (neither, I believe, has the rest of the left), but—as Jill Lewis ably argues—we did create a new political arena and set a revolutionary process in motion. (Among other things, we established the political context in which a book like *Ain't I a Woman* can be written and read.) The best measure of our threat to the system is the virulence of the reaction against us.

Hooks also indulges in overkill when she tries to explain white feminists' appropriation of female experience in terms of two different, even contradictory forms of racism. My own view is that the right explanation is the obvious one: we were acting on the unconscious racist assumption that our experience was representative, along with the impulse to gloss over racial specificities so as to keep the "complication" of racism from marring our vision of female unity.

Hooks makes these points, but she also argues that white feminists have shared the racist/sexist perception of black women as non-women. In the process she accuses white feminists of claiming that black women are oppressed only by racism, not sexism, and denying that black men can be oppressive. These charges are, to put it mildly, befuddling. If there was any point radical feminists insisted on it was that all women were oppressed because of their sex, and that all men had the power to oppress women. In response, antifeminist black women (along with black and white male leftists) made the arguments Hooks now puts in our mouths, and denounced us as racists for attributing a "white problem" to black people. Inevitably, many white women have echoed these arguments, but it's perverse to blame feminists for them.

In fact, white feminists have generally been quite conscious of black women *as women*; it's their blackness we've had trouble with. Straightforward reactionary racism exaggerates differences and denies commonalities; liberal racism, more typical of white feminists, does the opposite. Since the denial of black women's "femininity" is such a central issue for Hooks, she mistakenly assumes that protecting an exclusive claim to femininity is equally an issue for all white women. On the contrary, white feminists felt free to challenge received definitions of femininity because we took for granted our right to be considered women. And it was precisely because our claim to womanhood was not an issue for us that we were insensitive to black women's pain at being denied it by racial fiat. Many white feminists recognized that the division between white women and black women had something to do with good girls and bad girls. (Shulamith Firestone, in *The Dialectic of Sex*, discusses this idea at length.) What we didn't see was the asymmetry: we could decide to be bad, or play at being bad; black women had no choice.

Hooks's misperception of white feminists' psychology also leads her to argue that their analogies between women and blacks were designed "to evoke in the minds of racist white men an image of white womanhood being degraded" by association with black people, especially black men. Again, the "image of white womanhood" had much less resonance than Hooks imagines, either for white feminists or for the white liberal and leftist men who were our immediate targets.

The main reason that '60s feminists relied so heavily on comparisons between sexism and racism is that white male politicos recognized the race issue as morally legitimate, while dismissing feminism as "a bunch of chicks with personal problems." If anything, we were trying to evoke in these men the same guilt about sexism that they already felt about racism; since we hadn't yet experienced the drawbacks of liberal guilt, we craved its validation. We also hoped, naively enough, to convince black men to renounce their sexism and identify with the feminist cause.

Hooks takes a hard line on analogies between women and blacks. She argues that they always imply a comparison between white women and black men, that they make black women invisible, obscure the issue of white women's racial privilege, and divert attention from racism to white women's problems. Certainly racial-sexual analogies have been misused in all the ways Hooks cites, but I don't see these misuses as either invariable or necessary. Many feminists have made analogies between women and blacks in full awareness that they are talking about two overlapping groups; what they mean to compare is two sets of oppressive relations, male-female and white-black. And though the dynamics and effects of racism and sexism differ in important ways, the parallels—legal, social, ideological—do exist. Which is why antiracist movements have been so instrumental in stimulating feminist consciousness and revolt.

Hooks refuses to recognize this. Scoffing at the idea that abolitionism inspired the first feminist wave, she says, "No 19th century white woman could grow to maturity without an awareness of institutionalized sexism." But of course 19th century white women—and for that matter my generation of white women—did exactly that. It is the essence of institutionalized sexism to pose as the natural order; to experience male dominance is one thing, to understand that it is political, therefore changeable, is quite another. For me and most feminists I know, that politicizing process was very much influenced by the civil rights and black power movements. Conversely, though feminism was not a miraculous antidote to our racist impulses and illusions, it did increase our understanding of racism.

Surely, the answer to exploitative comparisons between women and blacks is not to deny the organic link between antisexist and antiracist politics. Here Hooks, too, gets trapped in contradictory thinking. She argues that the issues of racism and sexism cannot really be separated, yet she repeatedly singles out racism as an issue that is not only separate from sexism but prior to it. According to Hooks, "American society is one in which racial imperialism supersedes sexual imperialism," and all black people, black men included, are absolutely lower on the social scale than any white woman. In other words, it is illegitimate for feminists to regard sexism as a category that can, at least theoretically, be abstracted from (and compared to) racism; but no comparable stricture applies to black liberationists.

Gloria Joseph agrees that, "In the end, it is a question of priorities, and given the nature of racism in this country, it should be obvious that the Black liberation struggle claims first priority." Most black feminists whose views I know about take a similar position. It is easy to see why: because racism is intertwined with, and in part defined by class oppression, black people as a group suffer an excruciating combination of economic hardship and social indignity that white middle-class women and even most white working-class women escape. (Of course this does not necessarily hold true for individuals—it can be argued that a middle-class educated black man is a lot better off than a white welfare mother from an Appalachian rural slum.) Besides, as Hooks points out, women without the insulation of racial or class privilege are also the most vulnerable to sexist oppression: a white professional woman can buy liberation from housework by hiring a black maid; she can also (for the time being) buy the legal abortion Medicaid patients are denied.

Left antifeminists have often used this line of reasoning to suggest that sexual issues should wait until racism and poverty are abolished. Black feminists, by definition, have rejected that idea. But what then does it mean, in practical political terms, to say that despite the irreducibly dual character of black women's oppression, their sex is less immediate an issue than their race? Specifically, what does this imply for the prospect of an antiracist feminist movement, or, more modestly, "collaborative struggle"?

While Hooks never really focuses on strategic questions, Joseph and Lewis often write as if black and white women are on fundamentally separate tracks. They refer, for instance, to "White feminism," a concept as self-contradictory as, say, "male socialism"; while one can speak of a feminism limited and flawed by white racist bias, it is *feminism* only to the extent that it challenges the subjection of women as a group. (The mechanical pluralism underlying the notion of separate-but-equal "White" and "Black" feminisms also impels the authors to capitalize "White." Though capitalizing "Black" may make sense as a polemical device for asserting black pride, racial self-assertion by white people is something else again.) But in discussing abortion, Jill Lewis endorses a specific approach to integrating feminism with race and class struggle. The strategy she describes has developed as a response to the abortion backlash, but the basic idea could be applied to almost any feminist issue. Since I think it's both appealing and fallacious, I want to discuss it in some detail.

Lewis argues that to "isolate" abortion as an issue and defend it in terms of freedom for women betrays a white middle-class bias: since black women suffer not only from being denied safe abortions but from sterilization abuse, inadequate health care, and poverty—all of which impinge on their reproductive choices—a radical approach to "reproductive rights" must address all these concerns. The trouble with this logic is that abortion is not just one of many medical or social services being rolled back by Reaganism; nor does the present opposition to abortion stem from the same sources or political motives as pressure toward sterilization. Abortion is first of all the key issue of the new right's antifeminist campaign, the ground on which a larger battle over the very idea of women's liberation is being fought. In essence, the antiabortionists are arguing that women who assert their free agency and refuse to be defined by their childbearing capacity are immoral. (In contrast, no one defends poverty or forced sterilization on principle.) So long as this moral attack on women is gaining ground, presenting abortion primarily as a health or social welfare measure is ineffective because it evades the underlying issue. Our choice right now is to defend abortion as a pivotal issue of women's freedom, or lose the battle by default. This is not to belittle the urgency of opposing sterilization abuse (which is, among other things, another expression of contempt for black femaleness) or demanding better health care. Nor is it to deny that all these issues are linked in important ways. My point is only that the reproductive rights strategy does not resolve the touchy question of priorities. Rather, while purporting to cover all bases, it submerges sexual politics in an economic and social welfare program.

Is this good for black women? Gloria Joseph points out that on the issue of abortion rights, "Black women have even more at stake, since it is they who suffer more from illegal and abusive abortions." They also suffer more from having unwanted children under horrendous conditions. If a sexual-political strategy offers the only real chance to preserve legal abortion and restore public funding, it is clearly in black women's interest. Since black women are faced with so many urgent problems, they may well have other priorities, but it doesn't follow that white women who concentrate on abortion are indulging a racist bias. On the contrary, they're doing a crucial job that will benefit all women in the end.

All this suggests that the question of whether racism is worse (or more basic, or more pressing) than sexism matters less than the fact that both are intolerable. I don't agree with the white feminists Bell Hooks castigates for dismissing racial differences on the grounds that "oppression cannot be measured." It's clear to me that in demonstrable ways, some oppressed people are worse off than others. But I do question whose interests are really served by the measuring. Once it's established that black women are the most victimized group, and that most black men are more victimized than most white women— then what?

In my experience, this kind of ranking does not lead to a politics of genuine liberation, based on mutual respect and cooperation among oppressed groups, but instead provokes a politics of *ressentiment*, competition, and guilt. Black men tend to react not by recognizing the sexual oppression of black women but by rationalizing their anti-feminism as a legitimate response to white women's privilege. White women who are sensitive to the imputation of racism tend to become hesitant and apologetic about asserting feminist grievances. As for white women who can't see beyond their own immediate interests, attempts to demote them in the ranks of the oppressed do nothing but make them feel unjustly attacked and confirmed in their belief that sexual and racial equality are separate, competing causes. The ultimate results are to reinforce left antifeminism, weaken feminist militance, widen the split between the black and feminist movements, and play into the divide and conquer tactics of white men ("We can do something for blacks or for women, but not both, so you folks fight it out"). Black women, caught in the racial-sexual crossfire, stand to lose the most.

Insistence on a hierarchy of oppression never radicalizes people, because the impulse behind it is moralistic. Its object is to get the "lesser victims" to stop being selfish, to agree that their own pain (however deeply they may feel it) is less serious and less deserving of attention (including their own) than someone else's. Its appeal is that it allows people at the bottom of social hierarchies to turn the tables and rule over a moral hierarchy of suffering and power-lessness. But whatever the emotional comfort of righteousness, it's a poor substitute for real change. And we ought to know by now that effective radical movements are not based on self-abnegation; rather, they emerge from the understanding that unless we heal the divisions among us, none of us can win.

The logic of competing oppressions does not heal divisions but intensifies them, since it invites endless and absurd extension—for every person who has no shoes, there is always someone who has no feet. (One might ask, by this logic, what Bell Hooks has to complain about next to a woman from a dirt-poor Third World country who was sold to her husband and had her clitoris cut off at age four.) White women will not become committed allies of black women because they're told that their own suffering is unimportant. What white women must be convinced of is that it's impossible to have it both ways—that the privileges we cling to are an insuperable obstacle to the freedom and equality we long for. We need to learn this lesson again and again. Good books help.

June 1982

Radical Feminism and

Feminist Radicalism

I was a radical feminist activist in the late '60s. Today I often have the odd feeling that this period, so vivid to me, occurred fifty years ago, not a mere fifteen. Much of the early history of the women's liberation movement, and especially of radical feminism (which was not synonymous with the w.l.m. but a specific political current within it) has been lost, misunderstood or egregiously distorted. The left, the right, and liberal feminists have all for their own reasons contributed to misrepresenting and trivializing radical feminist ideas. To add to the confusion, radical feminism in its original sense barely exists today. The great majority of women who presently call themselves "radical feminists" in fact subscribe to a politics more accurately labeled "cultural feminist." That is, they see the primary goal of feminism as freeing women from the imposition of so-called "male values," and creating an alternative culture based on "female values." While radical feminism was conceived as a political movement to end male supremacy in all areas of social and economic life, and rejected as sexist the whole idea of opposing male and female natures and values, cultural feminism is essentially a moral, countercultural movement aimed at redeeming its participants. Though cultural feminism came out of the radical feminist movement, the premises of the two tendencies are antithetical. Yet on the left and elsewhere the distinction is rarely made.

Along with simply wanting to retrieve this history (my history), I think it's crucial for understanding what happened to the women's movement later, and what's happening now. In the first couple of years of its existence, radical feminism showed every sign of becoming a true mass movement. We had enormous energy and enthusiasm and used a variety of tactics—demonstrations and speakouts;

tireless organizing among friends and coworkers, on street corners, in supermarkets and ladies' rooms; above all, a prodigious output of leaflets, pamphlets, journals, magazine articles, newspaper and radio and TV interviews. The movement exploded into public consciousness, pushed NOW and other liberal feminist organizations way to the left, and grew so fast that existing groups didn't know what to do with the influx of new members. Organized radical feminist activism was most visible and prominent in New York City, Boston and Washington, D.C. and on the West Coast, but myriads of small groups inspired by radical feminist ideas sprang up all over the country.

It was radical feminism that put women's liberation on the map, that got sexual politics recognized as a public issue, that created the vocabulary ("consciousness-raising," "the personal is political," "sisterhood is powerful," etc.) with which the second wave of feminism entered popular culture. Radical feminists sparked the drive to legalize abortion and created the atmosphere of urgency in which liberal feminists were finally able to get the Equal Rights Amendment through Congress and most of the states. Radical feminists were also the first to demand total equality in the so-called private sphere— equal sharing of housework and child care, equal attention to our emotional and sexual needs. It's no exaggeration to say that the immense transformation in women's consciousness over the past fifteen years has been inspired by the issues radical feminists raised. One exasperating example of how easy it is to obliterate history is that Betty Friedan can now get away with the outrageous claim that radical feminist "extremism" turned women off and derailed the movement she built. Radical feminism turned women on, by the thousands.

Yet this movement collapsed as quickly as it had grown. By 1975 radical feminism had given way to cultural feminism. The women's liberation movement had become the women's movement, in which liberals were the dominant, not to say hegemonic force. Socialist and Marxist feminism, which had come out of other tendencies of the w.l.m. and segments of the left influenced by it, were theoretically confused and practically marginal.[1] Feminism had become a reformist politics, a countercultural community, and a network of self-help projects (rape crisis centers, battered women's shelters, women's health clinics, etc.).

How and why did this happen? Like other left social movements, feminism had to contend with the institutional and ideological power of American liberalism, which succeeded in marginalizing radical feminists while channeling the aspirations they aroused into demands for reform on the one hand, a cult of the individual "liberated woman" on the other. In addition, radical feminism had surfaced only a short time before the expansive prosperity and utopian optimism of the '60s succumbed to an era of economic limits and political backlash. The conservative retrenchment of the '70s had a critical negative impact, not only in strengthening political resistance to feminist demands but in constricting women's personal choices, making rebellion of any sort more difficult and risky, and undermining faith in the movement's more radical possibilities. Yet these external pressures, heavy as they were, do not wholly explain why radical feminism fell apart so easily and thoroughly. Contradictions within the movement, problems with its basic assumptions, played a crucial role.

I joined New York Radical Women, the first women's liberation group in New York City, in 1968, about a year after it had started meeting. By that time the group was deeply divided over what came to be called the "politico-feminist split." The primary commitment of the "politicos," as the "feminists" labeled them, was to the new left. They saw capitalism as the source of women's oppression: in their view the ruling class indoctrinated us with oppressive sex roles to promote consumerism and/or keep women a cheap reserve labor force and/or divide the workers; conventional masculine and feminine attitudes were matters of bourgeois conditioning from which we must all liberate ourselves. I sided with the feminists, who at some point began calling themselves "radical feminists." We argued that male supremacy was in itself a systemic form of domination—a set of material, institutionalized relations, not just bad attitudes. Men had power and privilege and like any other ruling class would defend their interests; challenging that power required a revolutionary movement of women. And since the male-dominated left would inevitably resist understanding or opposing male power, the radical feminist movement must be autonomous, create its own theory and set its own priorities. Our model of course was black power—a number of the early radical feminists had been civil rights activists.

Though new leftists immediately accused the radical feminists of being bourgeois and antileft, in fact nearly all of us considered ourselves leftists of one kind or another—socialists, anarchists, pacifists, new leftists of various stripes (my own politics were a somewhat confused blend of cultural radicalism, populism and Marxism). With few exceptions, those of us who first defined radical feminism took for granted that "radical" implied antiracist, anticapitalist, and anti-imperialist. We saw ourselves as radicalizing the left by expanding the definition of radical to include feminism. In accordance with that definition, we agreed that until the left embraced feminism, our movement should not work with leftist men or male-dominated left groups, except perhaps for ad hoc coalitions. Some feminists argued that it was also against women's interests to join left groups as individuals; others continued to work with men on various left issues and projects. Either way, we assumed that building an autonomous radical feminist power base would further the struggle for sexual equality in mixed left organizations, just as in other arenas. We took for granted the need for a radical, feminist left.

What we didn't do—at least not in any systematic way—was tackle the question of how to integrate a feminist perspective with an overall radical politics. At that stage of the movement it would have been premature. Our overriding priority was to argue, against pervasive resistance, that male-female relations were indeed a valid political issue, and to begin describing, analyzing and challenging those relations. We were really on new ground, and trying to explore it while under very heavy pressure from the left and from the "politicos" in the w.l.m. to subordinate feminist questions to traditional leftist concerns. It's hard to convey to people who didn't go through that experience how radical, how unpopular and difficult and scary it was just to get up and say, "Men oppress women. Men have oppressed *me*. Men must take responsibility for their actions instead of blaming them on capitalism. And yes, that means *you*." We were laughed at, patronized, called frigid, emotionally disturbed man-haters and—worst insult of all on the left!—apolitical.

In retrospect I see that we were faced with an insoluble contradiction. To build a women's liberation movement we had to take male supremacy out of the context of social domination in general. Yet from the very beginning we ran into problems of theory and strategy that could only be resolved within a larger context. Radical feminists professed a radical skepticism toward existing political theories, directed as they were toward the study of "man," and emphasized "consciousness-raising"—the process of sharing and analyzing our own experience in a group—as the primary method of understanding women's condition. This process, so often misunderstood and disparaged as a form of therapy, uncovered an enormous amount of information about women's lives and insights into women's oppression, and was the movement's most successful organizing tool. Yet the emphasis on personal experience tended to obscure and mystify the fact that we all interpreted our experience through the filter of prior political and philosophical assumptions. (For that matter, the idea of basing one's theory on shared personal experience came from the Chinese revolution's "Speak pains to recall pains" via the black movement's "Tell it like it is.")

Many debates on feminist issues were really debates about differing overall world views. For example, when a group of radical feminists did consciousness-raising on sex, we discovered that most of the women who testified preferred monogamous relationships, and that pressure for more sexual freedom came mostly from men (at that point, heterosexuality was a more or less unchallenged assumption). There were a lot of arguments about how to interpret that material (did it represent these women's true desires, their objective interest given a sexist culture, or the psychology of the oppressed) and what to make of the minority who disagreed (was the difference in their situation or their emotional makeup, did they have "false consciousness," or what). And to a large extent the differing positions that emerged depended on whether one viewed sexuality from the perspective of psychoanalysis (my own ideas were very much influenced by Wilhelm Reich), behaviorism, Simone de Beauvoirist existential humanism, or an orthodox Marxist rejection of psychological categories as unmaterialist. Despite its oppositional stance toward the existing left, radical feminism was deeply influenced by Marxism. While many w.l.m. "politicos" tried to fit women's liberation into pre-existing Marxist categories, radical feminists appropriated certain Marxist ideas and assumptions (specifically, concepts of class interest, class struggle, and materialism) and applied them to male-female relations. Maoism, especially, was instrumental in shaping radical feminist ideas about the nature of power and oppression.

Though radical feminists did not deny being influenced by the ideas of other radical movements (on the contrary, we often pointed to those continuities as evidence of our own revolutionary commitment), we acted as if it were somehow possible for women to separate their ideas about feminism from their ideas about everything else. There was an unarticulated assumption that we could work out our differences solely within a feminist framework and ignore or agree to disagree on other political issues. Again, I think that assumption was necessary, in order to create a feminist framework to begin with, but it made for a very fragile kind of solidarity—and it also excluded large groups of women. The question of why the radical feminist movement was overwhelmingly white and mostly middle class is complex, but one reason is surely that most black and working-class women could not accept the abstraction of feminist issues from race and class issues, since the latter were so central to their lives.

At the same time, the narrowness of the movement's demographic base limited the value of generalizations about women and men based on feminists' personal experience. So another problem in interpreting data gleaned from consciousness-raising was assessing how much it revealed patterns of male-female relations in general, not just the situation of women in particular social groups. I don't want to be misunderstood—I think consciousness-raising did reveal a lot about male-female relations. In basic ways women's subordination crosses class, racial and cultural lines and it was a strength of radical feminism to insist on that reality. (We also insisted, rightly in my opinion, that male dominance had to be understood as a transhistorical phenomenon, though we didn't use that language. In effect we challenged historicism as an adequate conceptual framework for understanding politics—a challenge that's since arisen in other quarters.) I'll go further and claim that in accumulating detailed information about the interaction of men and women on a day-to-day level, the consciousness-raising process contributed important insights into the nature of power relations in general—not only sexism. Still, our lack of attention to social differences among women did limit and distort both our analysis and our practice, and it's hard to see how that could have been avoided without reference to a politics about other forms of social domination. When the minority of radical feminists who were working class or from working-class backgrounds began to challenge class bias within the movement, the same problem arose: the movement had no agreed-on politics of class that we could refer to, beyond the assumption that class hierarchy was oppressive. And again the dilemma was that to turn our attention to building such a politics would conflict with the imperatives of the specifically feminist project that had just barely begun.

Very early in the game radical feminists tried to make an end run around this problem by advancing the thesis that women's oppression was not only the oldest and most universal form of domination but the primary form. We argued that other kinds of hierarchy grew out of and were modeled on male supremacy—were in effect specialized forms of male supremacy. This idea has a surface logic, given that all the hierarchical systems we know about have been ruled and shaped by men. But it's a false logic, because it assumes that men in creating and maintaining these systems are acting purely *as men*, in accordance with peculiarly male characteristics or specifically male supremacist objectives. It implicitly denies that the impulse to dominate, or to use a more materialist formulation, an authoritarian response to certain conditions of life, could be a universal human characteristic that women share, even if they have mostly lacked the opportunity to exercise it. It's a logic that excludes women from history not only practically but ontologically, and it leads to an unrealistic view of women as a more or less undifferentiated underclass with no real stake in the power struggles of class, race, and so on that go on among groups of men.

This notion of women's oppression as the primary oppression was very appealing for several reasons. It was a way of countering the left's insistence that class oppression was primary and women's liberation at best a subsidiary struggle—we could claim that on the contrary, all previous revolutions were mere reformist preludes to the real thing. It allowed white middle-class women to minimize the ways in which women participated in and benefited from race and class privilege. Most important, I think, it seemed to offer a resolution to the contradiction I've been talking about: it held out the possibility that a feminist theory could also be a general theory of social transformation. For all these reasons I uncritically bought this thesis—helped to sell it, in fact.

By 1969, radical feminists were beginning to meet in their own small groups. The first group to publicly espouse a radical feminist line was Redstockings, a spinoff from New York Radical Women, which Shulamith Firestone and I started early in 1969. Shortly after that, the October 17th Movement, a radical split-off from NOW led by Ti-Grace Atkinson, changed its name to The Feminists and proclaimed itself a radical feminist organization. These groups, which were both very influential in the movement, developed distinctive and opposing political stances.

Redstockings' dominant political tendency was a kind of neo-Maoist materialism. In addition to the belief in personal experience as the bedrock of feminist theory, this perspective was grounded in two basic principles. One was a view of sexual class struggle as the direct exercise of power by men, acting in their economic, social and sexual self-interest, over women. In this view institutions were merely tools of the oppressor and had no political significance in and of themselves. The idea that systems (like the family or capitalism) are in some sense autonomous, that they operate according to a logic that in certain ways constrains the rulers as well as the ruled, was rejected as a mystification and a way of letting men off the hook. To say, for instance, that the family oppressed women was to evade the fact that our husbands and fathers oppressed us; to say that men's sexist behavior was in any way dictated by social or familial norms was to deny that men oppressed women by choice, out of self-interest. The other principle was that women's behavior was always and only a rational, self-interested response to their immediate material conditions, i.e. their oppression by men. When women appeared to consent to their oppression, it was because they saw that individual resistance would not get them what they wanted, but only invite the oppressor's anger and punishment. As we built a movement capable of winning real change, more and more women would feel free to speak up and act collectively in their own behalf. The "pro-woman line," as this position was called, was absolutely antipsychological. It rejected as misogynist psychological explanations for feminine submissiveness or passivity, since they implied that women collaborated in or were responsible for their oppression. Psychological explanations of men's behavior were regarded as yet another way to avoid blaming men for male supremacy.

The most articulate and systematic exponents of these ideas were Kathie Sarachild and Carol Hanisch, both former SNCC activists and founding members of New York Radical Women, Irene Peslikis, who wrote the classic article "Resistances to Consciousness," and Pat Mainardi, author of "The Politics of Housework." While I did not fully share these politics—I believed in the importance of the unconscious and thought the pro-woman line was simplistic—I was profoundly influenced by them. They effectively challenged my tendencies to over-psychologize everything when social explanations were staring me in the face, and to avoid confronting my painful personal relations with men by making abstract arguments about the system. The genius of the Redstockings brand of radical feminist materialism was its concreteness. It demanded that women examine their everyday lives and face the most immediate and direct sources of their pain and anger. For women who responded to that demand, the confrontations inspired a powerful and urgent desire to change things. Activism became a personal emotional necessity—always a more effective spur to organizing than abstract principle or moral sentiment—with specific and immediate as well as long-range goals. As a result the materialist version of radical feminism had by far the most impact on the larger society, in terms of changing women's view of themselves and the world and inspiring both individual rebellion and collective political action.

But the reductionism of the Redstockings line led to basic miscalculations. For one thing, it underestimated the difficulty of change. If, for instance, resistance to feminism or outright antifeminism among women comes solely from rational fears of the consequences of challenging male authority, then the way to combat it is simply to build a movement and convince women that sisterhood really is powerful—that organized and unified we can win. But suppose in addition to the rational fears and hopes, women suffer from deep unconscious convictions of their own powerlessness and worthlessness and the unlimited power of men? Suppose they unconsciously equate being a "good woman" in men's terms not only with survival but with redemption? If that's true, then the successes of a feminist movement may actually intensify women's fears along with their hopes, and provoke unbearable emotional conflict. And that can lead not only to various forms of female antifeminist backlash, but to feminists managing in various ways to sabotage their own movement—even to redefine feminism so that it embraces and glorifies traditional feminine values. Both these things have in fact happened, and are continuing to happen, and it's impossible to understand these developments or confront them politically without a psychological critique. I won't belabor the parallels with the overoptimism of classical Marxism and its inability to explain why large numbers of European workers supported fascism.

Similarly, the dismissal of institutions, particularly the family, as "mere tools" was an obstacle to understanding how change takes place, or fails to. From Redstockings' perspective, the problem with the family was simply male supremacy: women were subordinated within marriage and at the same time forced to marry for economic security and social legitimacy; we were assigned the care of children, but denied control of our fertility. Left criticism of the family per se was dismissed as men's resistance to committing themselves to women and children, emotionally and financially.

This analysis ignored the way the fundamental premise of the family system—the equation of biological and social parenthood—institutionalized the difference in women's and men's biological relation to reproduction as social and political inequality. Since women in a familialist system need marriage to establish the father's social obligation to his children, men have enormous power over the terms of the marriage contract. When women press their demands for equality "too far," the probable result is not an equal marriage, but no marriage at all. And whether it's the woman or the man who leaves, it's the woman who is all too likely to end up an impecunious single parent, or to find her prospects for heterosexual intimacy and children diminishing with age. So long as the family remains an unquestioned given of social relations, women are trapped into choosing between subordination and abandonment. This is the specter haunting contemporary sexual politics: to face it down requires taking institutions seriously.

Of course, a serious critique of the family would have stretched the radical feminist framework, for the family has more than one political dimension. Besides subordinating women, it's also a vehicle for getting children of both sexes to submit to social authority and actively embrace the values of the dominant culture. Among other things that means enlisting both women and men to uphold the family system and its sexual morality, in which sex for its own sake is bad and dangerous and must be subordinated to the "higher" purposes of heterosexual monogamous marriage and procreation. (True, men have always had more license to be "bad" than women. But all this means is that men experience a conflict between their sexual desire and identity and their "higher" nature—not, as radical feminists have tended to assume, that men are free of sexual guilt and repression.) We all to some degree internalize familialist sexual ideology in its feminine or masculine version; to the extent that any of us rejects it, we are rejecting being a woman or a man as the culture defines it and accepting an identity as social, sexual deviants, with all the consequences that entails. We are all oppressed by having this ideology imposed on us, though some groups are particularly oppressed—women, youth, homosexuals and other sexual minorities. So there is a political fault line in the society dividing people who are in one way or another defending this ideology (and the practices that go with it) from people who are in one way or another rebelling against it. This line cuts across gender, and like class or racial difference creates real divisions among women that can't simply be subsumed in an antisexist politics. It also defies analysis strictly in terms of the "self-interest" of one class of people oppressing another. Ultimately the interest of sexual conservatives in suppressing sexual dissidence is their interest in obliterating possibilities they themselves have painfully relinquished. This interest is so powerful that there are few sexual dissidents—and I would call feminists and unapologetic gays dissidents by definition—who are not also conservative in some ways.

While ignoring all these complications, Redstockings' vision of direct confrontation between sexual classes put an enormous premium on unity among women. The idea was that if all women supported each other in demanding equality—if there were no women willing to "scab"—then men would have no choice but to accept the new order. This was the model of struggle put forward in *Fanshen*, William Hinton's account of revolution in a Chinese village, which circulated widely in the movement. It was inspiring reading, but America is not a Chinese village; Hinton's cast of characters, at least as he presented it, was divided by class, sex and age, but not by multiple ethnic and cultural antagonisms.[2] For all the reasons I've been laying out, I don't see universal sisterhood as a practical possibility. Fortunately, men are hardly a monolith—they are deeply divided along various social and political axes, disagree with each other on what "male self-interest" is, and don't necessarily support each other in the face of feminist demands. Feminist struggle will never be a matter of women as a united class confronting men as a united class, but rather of particular groups of women pressing on vulnerable points in the structure of male supremacy and taking advantage of divisions among men. Direct personal pressure on men to change their behavior will be more feasible in some communities than in others. Most early radical feminists operated in a social milieu that was middle-class, educated, culturally liberal and politically leftist. A degree of economic opportunity, access to birth control, and the decline of rigidly familialist mores—along with the fact that most of us were young and as yet uninterested in having children—allowed us a certain amount of independence, therefore power, in dealing with "our" men, and we were also in a position to appeal to their proclaimed belief in democracy and equality.

Even under the best conditions, though, direct confrontation has built-in limits, because it requires a level of day-to-day militance that's impossible to sustain over the long haul. After a while even the most passionate feminists get tired, especially when they see how slow the progress is. As soon as they ease the pressure, men take advantage of it and start a backlash, which then touches off a backlash by *women* who feel they've struggled too hard for not enough result. That's part of the story of the '70s. I'm not saying that personally confronting men is not worth doing, or that our doing it hasn't had lasting effects.

But I think it is basically a minority tactic, and one that flourishes in the exceptional moment, rather than *the* model of revolutionary struggle.

When applied beyond the realm of direct personal combat to feminist demands for changes in public policy, the pure class struggle paradigm becomes much more problematic. These demands operate on two levels. They are aimed at men as a group in that they attack the sexist assumptions embedded in social and economic institutions. But they are also aimed more specifically at men (and the occasional woman) with institutional power—corporate, legal, medical, religious or whatever—who by virtue of their positions represent other interests and ideological commitments besides male privilege. Such interests and commitments may have priority over sexist imperatives or even conflict with them; the alliances and oppositions that form around feminist demands are rarely based strictly on gender or sexual class interest.

For instance, although legal abortion reduces women's subordination to and dependence on men, men as a class have not closed ranks against it. Rather, the active political opposition has come from sexually conservative familialists of both sexes (most but not all of whom are opposed to feminism across the board). Many men have supported legal abortion on civil liberties or sexual libertarian grounds. Others have supported it on racist grounds, as an antiwelfare or population control measure. Male politicians have more often than not based their position on abortion on one simple criterion: what would get them reelected. The medical establishment supports freedom for doctors to perform abortions while opposing feminist demands that paramedics be allowed to perform them. And so on. Most men have at worst been indifferent to or ambivalent about the abortion issue; most women, on the other hand, *have* seen abortion rights as in their female self-interest. Without this asymmetry, it is doubtful that feminists could have won legal abortion or kept it in the face of heavy pressure from the right. As it is, our biggest defeat on this issue, the ban on Medicaid funds for abortion, has clearly involved other factors besides sexism. The new right took advantage of middle-class women's apathy toward the poor, while mobilizing antiwelfare sentiment among people outside the hard-core familialist antiabortion constituency. Often a combination of racist, antipoor and sexist feelings motivated men to opposition in a way sexism alone had not ("Let those irresponsible women have their abortions, but not at my expense"). Battles over measures to combat economic discrimination against women involve similar complexities. Some men, putting economic class loyalty or opposition to corporate power or commitment to economic equality above their specifically male self-interest, support such measures (especially if they hope to get feminist support for their economic agenda); some women oppose them, whether on familialist grounds or because of *their* economic class loyalty and/or ideological belief in a free market economy.

I use examples of struggles for reform because feminists have never yet been in a position to make an active fight for basic structural changes in institutions. Such a fight would be impossible for a feminist movement alone; to envision it presupposes the existence of a left capable of attacking state and corporate power. And in that context, the configuration of alliances and oppositions across gender lines would if anything be much more complicated than it is now.

The Feminists agreed with Redstockings that male domination was the primary oppression and that women and men were political classes. Beyond that the groups diverged. For one thing, The Feminists used the terms "sex role" and "sex class" interchangeably—they identified sexism with particular, complementary patterns of male and female behavior. Redstockings' view of sex roles, like its view of institutions, was that they reflected male power, but were not primary political categories. The Feminists' conflation of role and class provided a basis for rejecting the pro-woman line: if the female role, per se, defined women's oppression, then conforming to the role was upholding the oppression. The Feminists' attitude toward institutions was even more reductive than Redstockings', in the opposite direction. While Redstockings assumed that the sexist dimension of an institution could somehow be abstracted from the institution itself, The Feminists assumed that the primary institutions of women's oppression—which they identified as marriage and the family, prostitution, and heterosexuality—were entirely defined by sexism, that their sole purpose was to perpetuate the "sex-role system." Therefore, radical feminists must destroy them. (The Feminists had a penchant for words like "destroy" and "annihilate.") The group also rejected consciousness-raising in favor of abstract theorizing, but never clearly laid out the philosophical or epistemological basis of its ideas.

For all the limitations of Redstockings' materialism, we at least knew that we had to base a feminist program on women's actual lives and feelings, and that the important thing was to understand women's behavior, not judge it from some utopian moral standpoint. The Feminists were idealist, voluntarist and moralistic in the extreme. They totally disregarded what other women said they wanted or felt, and their idea of organizing was to exhort women to stop submitting to oppression by being subservient or participating in sexist institutions like marriage. Once at an abortion demonstration in front of a legislative committee I had a huge argument with a member of the group who was yelling at the committee's female secretaries and clerks that they were traitors for not walking out on their jobs and joining us. The Feminists were the first radical feminist group to suggest that living or sleeping with men was collaborating with the system. They shocked the rest of the movement by making a rule that no more than a third of their membership could be married or living with a man.

The Feminists, and in particular their best-known theorist, Ti-Grace Atkinson, also developed a set of ideas about sex that will be familiar to anyone who has followed current movement debates. The first radical feminist to talk about heterosexual intercourse as an institution was probably Anne Koedt, a member of New York Radical Women who later joined The Feminists, in her essay "The Myth of the Vaginal Orgasm." Koedt was careful to distinguish between intercourse as an option and as an institutionalized practice defined as synonymous with "normal" sex. She also assumed that the point of sex was pleasure, the point of institutionalized intercourse was male pleasure, and the point of challenging that construct was equal pleasure and orgasm for women. Atkinson wrote an article elaborating on this idea of "the institution of sexual intercourse," but took it in a different direction. As she saw it the purpose of the institution was getting women to reproduce and the concept of sexual need or drive was mere ideology. What erotic pleasure was or whether it existed was unclear, especially in the present social context. In fact, heterosexual intercourse was so thoroughly corrupted by the sex-role system that it was hard to imagine a future for it even as an optional practice.

The Feminists' organizing manifesto condemned the institution of heterosexual sex very much in Atkinson's terms, and added that since sex was part of the marriage contract, marriage meant legalized rape. It also included the statement—tucked in inconspicuously, so it seemed a lot less significant than it does in retrospect—that in the context of freedom, physical relations between individuals of whatever sex would not necessarily emphasize genital contact. The implication was that any special interest in or desire for genital sex, heterosexual or otherwise, was a function of sexism. This was a mental leap that seems to me clearly grounded in unconscious acceptance of a traditional patriarchal assumption, namely that lust is male.

The Feminists' perspective on sex was a minority view within radical feminism, considered provocative but out on some weird edge. The predominant attitudes in Redstockings were more typical: we took for granted women's desire for genital sexual pleasure (the importance of fucking to that pleasure was a matter of debate) and focused our critique on the ways men repressed and frustrated women sexually. Though we theoretically defended women's right to be lesbian or celibate, there was a strong heterosexual presumption underlying Redstockings politics. It was tacitly assumed, and sometimes explicitly argued, that men's need for sexual love from women was our biggest weapon in both individual and collective struggle—and that our own need for *satisfying* sexual love from men was our greatest incentive for maintaining the kind of personal confrontation feminism required. We rejected sexual separatism as a political strategy, on materialist grounds—that simply refusing to be with men was impractical and unappealing for most women, and in itself did nothing to challenge male power. But beyond that we didn't really take it seriously as a personal choice, let alone an expression of militance. On the contrary, we thought of living without men as the bitter price we might have to pay for our militance in demanding equal relationships. Tension over these issues, among others, led an alienated minority to quit Redstockings and join The Feminists.

At that point lesbianism per se had not yet emerged as an issue, but there were pitfalls for lesbians in both groups' ideas. If you accepted Redstockings' assumption that the struggle for equality in hetero-sexual relationships was the nerve center of radical feminism, lesbians were by definition marginal to the movement. The Feminists offered a much more attractive prospect—by their logic lesbians were, simply by virtue of rejecting sexual relationships with men, a liberated van-guard. But there was a catch: the vanguard role was available only to lesbians willing to ignore or play down the element of sexual desire in their lesbian identity. As Alice Echols has pointed out, the conver-gence of homophobic and antisexual pressures from the movement eventually impelled the majority of lesbian feminists to accept this tradeoff and sanitize lesbianism by defining it as a political choice rather than an erotic one.[3] To complicate matters, many of the femi-nists who "converted" to lesbianism in the wake of lesbian separatism did so not to express a compelling sexual inclination but to embrace a political and cultural identity; some of these converts denied that lesbianism was in any sense a sexual definition, and equated their rejection of compulsory heterosexuality with "liberation" from sex itself, at least insofar as it was "genitally oriented." In this atmosphere, lesbians who see freedom to express their unconventional sexuality as an integral part of their feminism have had reason to wonder if the label "male identified" is any improvement over "pervert."

Toward the end of 1969, Shulie Firestone and Anne Koedt started a third group, New York Radical Feminists, which rejected both the pro-woman line and The Feminists' arrogant vanguardism. While most radical feminists assumed men wanted dominance for the sake of material benefits—by which they meant not only the economic, in the broad sense, benefits of the sexual division of labor, but the psychic benefits of having one's emotional needs catered to with-out any obligation to reciprocate, NYRF proposed in essence that men wanted to exercise power for its own sake—that it was intrin-sically satisfying to the ego to dominate others. According to their formulation men did not defend their power in order to get services from women, but demanded services from women in order to affirm their sense of power. The group's other important proposition was its entry in the ongoing debate about why women submit to their oppression. While Redstockings' answer was necessity and The Feminists' implicit answer was cowardice, NYRF insisted that feminine behavior was both enforced and internalized: women were trained from birth both to conform to the feminine role and to accept it as right and natural. This pass at an analysis of male and female behavior was incoherent, implicitly biologistic, and sexist. Besides suggesting that men, by virtue of their maleness, had an inherent predilection for power, NYRF's formulation gave men credit for being active agents while implicitly defining women as passive recipients of social indoctrination. The social-learning model, applied to women, also posed the same problem as all behaviorist psychologies—it could not account for resistance to the system. Inevitably it implied its antinomy, moral voluntarism, since the very existence of a feminist movement meant that some women had in some sense transcended their conditioning.

All the disparate versions of radical feminist analysis shared two basic weaknesses that contributed to the movement's demise. First, commitment to the sex-class paradigm pinned women's hopes for radical change on a millennial unity of women across barriers of class, race, cultural values and sexual orientation. The gap between what radical feminism promised and what it could deliver without a more complex, multivalent theory and strategy was immense. That gap was all too soon filled by attempts at individual liberation through "overcoming female conditioning," fantasies of benevolent matriarchies, the equation of woman-bonding, an alternative women's community and/or a "politically correct lifestyle" with feminism, and moralizing about the iniquity of men and "male values." Underlying these individualist and countercultural revisions of radical feminism was an unadmitted despair of real change. That despair is expressed more overtly in the work of cultural feminist theorists like Andrea Dworkin, who has reified the sex-class paradigm, defining it as a closed system in which the power imbalance between men and women is absolute and all-pervasive. Since the system has no discontinuities or contradictions, there is no possibility of successful struggle against it—at best there can be moral resistance.

The movement's second major weakness was its failure to develop a coherent analysis of either male or female psychology—a failure so total that to me it indicates a willed ignorance rooted in terror. While there was a dissenting minority, radical feminists as a group were dogmatically hostile to Freud and psychoanalysis, and psychoanalytic thought—especially its concept of the unconscious and its emphasis on the role of sexual desire in human motivation—had almost no impact on radical feminist theory. Since I agree with Juliet Mitchell that psychoanalysis is not a defense of patriarchal culture but an analysis of it—though I don't subscribe to her Lacanian interpretation of Freud—I think radical feminists' closed-mindedness on the subject was an intellectual and political disaster.

As I've discussed elsewhere, I basically agree with Freud's model of how children develop a masculine or feminine psychology in response to parental suppression and channeling of infantile sexuality.[4] Of course, as a radical I also believe that the social context in which this takes place is subject to change: male superiority is not a biological fact, and the patriarchal family and sexual repression are not prerequisites of civilization. But Freud's sexism and pessimism are not sufficient to explain why most radical feminists were so blind to his subversive insights, while they had no comparable qualms about selectively criticizing and appropriating other male theorists, Marx, for instance. I believe—and I know this is the kind of circular argument that drives anti-Freudians crazy—that the movement's violent rejection of psychoanalysis was in part a response to its hitting too close to home. At a time when feminism itself was tearing off layers of protective skin and focusing our attention on feelings we'd spent our lives suppressing, it was not surprising that women should resist any further attack on their defenses. To analyze women's behavior psychoanalytically was to risk unmasking all our secret strategies for coping with the traumatic linking of our sexual organs to our class inferiority, and with the resulting unconscious feelings of irrevocable violation, shame, global terror and dangerous rage. And those cherished strategies would not necessarily pass political muster, since—if you accept Freud's basic assumptions—it's precisely through women's attempt to manage their unconscious conflicts that femininity is reproduced. For instance, one typical feminine strategy is to compensate for the humiliation of sexual "inferiority" with self-righteous moralism and asceticism. Whether this is rationalized as religious virtue or feminist militance, the result is to reinforce patriarchal values. As I see it, a psychoanalytic perspective is crucial to understanding and challenging such self-defeating tendencies in feminist politics, and for that reason it is anathema to feminists who confuse the interests of women with their own unconscious agenda.

Redstockings did not succeed in defining psychology as a nonissue. Most radical feminists recognized that there were aspects of male and female feelings and behavior that eluded pragmatic, common-sense explanation. But their attempts to acknowledge the psychological dimension have been fragmented and muddled. In general, the inheritors of the radical feminist movement have followed the path of New York Radical Feminists and endorsed some version of behaviorism, biological determinism, or an ad hoc, contradictory mélange of both. Given the history of biologism as the enemy's weapon, most feminists who draw on it prefer to pretend it's something else, and behaviorist terminology can be useful for this purpose. The present "radical feminist" antipornography movement provides a good example. It claims that pornography conditions men to sexual sadism, which is the foundation and primary expression of their power over women, and conditions women to accept their victimization. But if you examine the argument closely, it doesn't hang together. If men have the power, create the pornography, and define the values it embodies, conditioning might perhaps explain how some men transmit a sadistic mentality to others, but not how or why that mentality arose in the first place. And in fact it is clear from the rest of their rhetoric that antiporn theorists equate male sexuality, per se, with sadism. As for women, the antipornography movement explicitly defines authentic female sexuality as tender, romantic, and nongenitally oriented, despite the suspicious resemblance of this description to the patriarchal stereotype of the good woman. It is only women who disagree with this view of their sexuality who are proclaimed to be victims of male-supremacist conditioning. (How antiporn activists have managed to avoid being conditioned is not explained.) In this case, the language of behaviorism serves not only to deflect charges of biologism, but to inflate the importance of pornography as a target and dismiss political opponents.

The disintegration of radical feminism took several forms. First of all radical feminist ideas caught the attention of large numbers of women, especially educated, upper-middle-class women, who had no radical perspective on other matters and often were uninterested in, if not actively hostile to, left politics as such. These women experienced sexual inequality in their own lives, and radical feminism raised their consciousness. But their awareness of their oppression as women did not make them radicals in the sense of being committed to overall social transformation, as the early radical feminists had naively assumed it would. Instead they seized on the idea of women's oppression as the primary oppression and took it to mean not that feminism was or should be inclusive of other struggles, but that left politics were "male" and could be safely ignored.

This idea became a prominent theme of cultural feminism. It also led to the development of a new kind of liberal feminism. Many women reacted to radical feminism with an intense desire to change their lives, or the social arrangements that immediately affected them, but had no intention of supporting changes that would threaten their (or their husbands') economic and social class status. Many of the same women were reluctant to explicitly attack male power— not only because of the personal consequences of militance, but because the whole subject of power is uncomfortable for people who are basically committed to the existing socioeconomic order. The result was a brand of politics best exemplified by *Ms.* magazine, which began publishing in 1972. The traditional reformism of organizations like NOW was economistic and hostile to the "personal" sexual and emotional issues radical feminists were raising. *Ms.* and the new liberals embraced those issues, but basically ignored the existence of power relations. Though they supported feminist reforms, their main strategy for changing women's lives was individual and collective self-improvement. They were partial to the argument that men and women are fellow victims of sex-role conditioning. But where the "politicos" in the early movement had blamed this conditioning on capitalism, the liberals blamed it vaguely on "society," or the media, or the schools, ignoring the question of who runs these institutions and on whose behalf. In terms of their political ethos and constituency, the difference between the *Ms.*-ites and NOW was roughly analogous to the difference between the McGovern and Humphrey wings of the Democratic Party, and *Ms.* was to radical feminism what the "new politics" Democrats were to the new left.

On one level *Ms.*-ism and cultural feminist anti-leftism were the inevitable and predictable distortions of a radical movement that reaches far beyond its founders. They were testimony to people's desire to have it both ways—to fight their oppression while holding on to their privileges—as well as their tendency to take refuge in simple if illusory solutions. But the specific forms the distortions took were inspired by the idea of sex as the primary division and reflected the inadequacy of the sex-class paradigm as the basis for a radical movement. Although the early radical feminists were appalled by these uses of our ideas, we can't avoid some responsibility for them.

Within the radical feminist movement itself, the original momentum almost immediately began giving way to a bitter, immobilizing factionalism. The first issue to create permanent rifts was equality in the movement. Partly out of rebellion against hierarchical structures (especially in the new left), partly because consciousness-raising required informality, radical feminists, like the w.l.m. as a whole, had chosen the putatively structureless small group as their main form of organization. Yet every group had developed an informal leadership, a core of women—I was part of that core in Redstockings—who had the most to do with setting and articulating the direction of the group. Women who felt excluded from equal participation challenged not only the existing leaders but the concept of leadership as a holdover from male-dominated organizations. Debates about group process, the oppressive behavior of some members toward others, and leaders' alleged exploitation of the movement for personal ends began to dominate meetings, to the exclusion of any engagement with sexism in the outside world.

The problems of elitism, class bias, differences in power within the movement, and opportunism were certainly real—they were much the same kinds of problems that had surfaced elsewhere on the left—but by and large the attempts to confront them were ineffective and in the long run disastrous. Obviously, there are inherent difficulties in trying to build a democratic movement. You can't create a perfect society in microcosm while the larger society remains the same, and you can't change the larger society if you spend all your time and energy trying to create a utopian microcosm. The goal should be to strike a balance—work on finding ways to extend skills, experience and confidence to everyone, but at the same time encourage people who already have these assets to use them for the movement's benefit, provided they are accountable for *how* they use them in the movement's name. What makes this so difficult is not only the leaders' desire for personal power or their resistance to being held accountable and sharing their skills, but the rage of those who find themselves at the bottom of yet another hierarchy. They tend to want instant redress, and since there's no way to instantly create a situation where everyone has equal power—because the differences come from years of differential opportunities—some people resort to the pseudo-solution of demanding that those who have the skills or other forms of social power not use them, either for the movement or for themselves. Which is a dead end in terms of creating an effective movement, as well as an unreasonable demand on individuals trying to live their lives within the present social system.

These issues come up in all egalitarian movements, but the premises of radical feminism made them especially intense. The assumption that women's oppression is primary, and that the differences among women can be worked out entirely within an antisexist context, shaped the movement's predominant view of women and class: that a woman's position in the class hierarchy derived solely from the men she was attached to, that women could oppress other women by virtue of their class status but not men, that class conflict among women was a product of false consciousness, and that any form of class striving or power-mongering was therefore "male-identified" behavior. For some women this category extended to any form of individual achievement, intellectual activity, articulateness or self-assertion, the assumption being that these could only derive from some unholy connection with male power. The implicit corollary was that traditionally feminine behavior was the only truly sisterly behavior. These ideas too became staples of cultural feminism. Of course, many radical feminists disagreed and pointed out that charges of pushiness and overachieving were always used by dominant groups to keep oppressed groups in their place. But since the dissenters were operating out of the same basic framework as their adversaries, they tended to adopt some version of the mirror-image position that since women's common interest transcended class differences, this democracy in the movement business must be a sexist plot to cut down feminist leadership and keep the movement weak.

Though this idea was literally absurd, there was a grain of emotional truth in it. Much of the opposition to elitism took the form of unworkable, mechanistic demands for an absolutely random division of labor, taking no account of differences in skill, experience or even inclination. (As usual, The Feminists carried this tendency the furthest, instituting a strict lot system for the distribution of all tasks. When the group decided that no member could talk to the media unless chosen by lot, Ti-Grace Atkinson quit.) These demands were often coupled with personal attacks on individuals that were little more than outbursts of fury and *ressentiment* against any woman who seemed to have achieved some measure of autonomy, recognition or influence. Some feminist leaders reacted with defiance, some quit the movement, and others—myself included—tried to respond to the criticism by echoing it and withdrawing from our leadership roles, in classic guilty liberal fashion. With all the accusations and breast-beating, there was relatively little honest effort to deal with the concrete problems involved in creating a movement that was both egalitarian and effective. The result was not democracy but paralysis. And part of the reason, I'm convinced, was unconscious fear that feminists' demands for freedom and power would provoke devastating retribution. The movement was stripping away our protective mask of feminine compliance, and its leaders were the most visible symbol of that.

During the same period, working-class women in the movement began talking to each other about their experience with class oppression and confronting middle-class feminists. This new application of the consciousness-raising process educated feminists about the workings of the class system on the level of personal relations, but it did not significantly change class relations in the movement or help to unify women across class lines. As I've noted, there was no way within the bounds of radical feminism to connect the struggle for internal democracy with active opposition to the class system per se. This split between internal and externally oriented politics was exacerbated by a total emphasis on class as a set of oppressive personal relations. It was assumed that the strategy of challenging men's sexist behavior could be applied with equal success to challenging women's class-biased behavior. But this assumption overlooked fundamental differences in the dynamics of class and sexual politics. While the basic institutions of sexist oppression are located in personal life, a realm in which men have a great deal of personal power, the basic institutions of class oppression are located in the public world of the political economy, where middle-class people (women, especially) have little power. That does not mean there is no personal aspect to class oppression, but it does suggest that personal politics are not the cutting edge of class struggle.

For some radical feminists, however, consciousness-raising about class led to a political identity crisis. I was one of those who became convinced that women *were* implicated in the class system and had real class interests, that women could oppress men on the basis of class, and that class differences among women could not be resolved within a feminist context alone. Which meant that a feminist movement purporting to represent all women had to connect in some organic way to a workers' movement, and by extension to a black liberation movement and other movements of oppressed groups—in short, to a left. Some women reacted to this realization by going back to the existing left to promote feminism from within; some moved off in search of a socialist-feminist synthesis. My own experience left me with a lot of new questions and no answers. In the fall of 1969 I had moved to Colorado Springs to work in a G.I. organizing project, intending at the same time to start a radical feminist movement in the area. Obviously, I was already interested in somehow combining feminist and leftist organizing, less out of any abstract commitment to the idea than from the impulse to integrate different sides of my life and politics. A radical feminist from New York who was working-class and had raised the class issue in Redstockings came out to work with me. She began confronting the oppressive class relations between middle-class and working-class members of the project and between civilians and G.I.s. After going through this confrontation in a sexually mixed group, in which the women were also raising feminist issues, I had no doubt that the standard radical feminist line on class was wrong.

Unlike my friend, who later became active in Youth Against War and Fascism, I continued to regard myself as a radical feminist. I still believed that male supremacy was a structure of domination at least as basic as class or race, and so far as I could tell neither the "male" left nor the socialist-feminists—who struck me as updated versions of '60s politicos—agreed. But I rejected the idea of the primacy of women's oppression and began reluctantly to reject the global sister-hood model of feminist revolution. I saw that the fate of feminism at any given time and place was bound up with the fate of the larger left, though I had no idea how to translate this perception into a politi-cal strategy: at this point—1971—our G.I. project had fallen apart along with the rest of the new left, radical feminism was doing the same, and the prospects for any kind of radical politics looked grim.

The final blow to the radical feminist movement as a vital political force was the gay-straight split, which took place in the early '70s. Lesbian separatists added a crucial ingredient to existing female sepa-ratist ideology—a positive vision of community. While early separat-ism offered only the moral reward of revolutionary purity, lesbian feminism offered in addition the more concrete social and sexual benefits of a women's counterculture. It then defined that culture not simply as a strategy for achieving women's liberation or as a form of sustenance for its troops but as the meaning and purpose of feminism.

At a time when the enormous obstacles facing the movement were becoming apparent, this vision had an understandable appeal. And while it had particular advantages for women already committed to lesbianism (and oppressed as lesbians), it could not have been a transforming influence on the movement if it had not exerted a strong pull on the feelings of radical feminists generally. Not only did many women break with heterosexuality to join the lesbian feminist counterculture, and even more experiment with it; many feminists who remained practicing heterosexuals identified with that culture and its ideology and considered themselves failed or incomplete femi-nists. Others argued that sexual orientation was irrelevant; what mat-tered was whether a woman accepted the *values* of female culture. By this route, cultural feminism evolved into a politics that anyone could embrace, that had little to do with sexual separatism or lesbianism as a sexual practice. The "female values" cultural feminists proclaimed— either with openly biologistic arguments, as in Jane Alpert's influential article, "Mother Right," or with behaviorist window dressing—were none other than the traditional feminine virtues. Once again we were alleged to be loving, nurturing, in tune with nature, intuitive and spiritual rather than genital in our eroticism, while men were violent, predatory, alienated from nature, committed to a sterile rationalism and obsessed with genital sex. (There was some disagreement on whether men were hopeless cases or whether women could teach them female values and thereby "humanize" them.) "Radical feminism" had come full circle, from challenging the polarization of the sexes to affirming it and embracing a reverse sexism.

Insofar as cultural feminists translated their ideas into political activism, their chief focus was male violence against women. Radical feminists had defined rape and other forms of male aggression as weapons for enforcing male dominance—for punishing "uppity" female behavior or simply reminding women who was boss. But their lack of attention to psychology had left a gap in their analysis: in discussing sexual violence as a more or less deliberate, instrumental choice, they ignored it as a sexual and emotional experience. The movement was inconsistent in its view of the relation between rape and sexuality. On the one hand it noted the continuity between rape and "normal" male sexual aggressiveness, and the resulting social tendency to rationalize rape as fun and games. Yet in reaction to this confusion, and to the related myth that men rape out of uncontrollable sexual need, the radical feminist mainstream asserted that "rape is violence, not sex"—a tidy slogan that avoided disturbing "unmaterialist" questions about the nature of male desire, the relationship of pleasure to power. And the iconoclastic Feminists, who implicitly equated heterosexuality with rape, declined to recognize sexual pleasure as a motive in either.

Cultural feminists leaped into this psychological breach, rightly (and therefore effectively) insisting on the reality of sexual violence as an erotic experience, an end in itself. Unfortunately, they proceeded to incorporate this insight into their neo-Victorian caricature of men's sexual nature and to generalize it to all patriarchal relations. New York Radical Feminists had broken with earlier radical feminist thought to argue that men wanted power for its intrinsic satisfactions, not its concomitant rewards; cultural feminists spelled out the implication of this position—that all sexist behavior is an extension of the paradigmatic act of rape. From this standpoint sexual violence was the essence and purpose of male dominance, the paradigmatic "male value," and therefore feminism's central concern.

In the late '70s, cultural feminists' emphasis shifted from actual violence against women to representation of sexual violence in the media and then to pornography. Groups like Women Against Pornography and Women Against Violence in Pornography and Media adopted pornography as the quintessential symbol of a male sexuality assumed to be inherently violent and oppressive, then made that symbol the focus of a moral crusade reminiscent of the 19th-century social purity and temperance movements. Predictably, they have aimed their attack not only at male producers and consumers of porn, but at women who refuse to define lust as male or pornography as rape and insist without apology on their own sexual desires. While continuing to call itself radical feminist—indeed, claiming that it represents the only truly feminist position—the antiporn movement has in effect collaborated with the right in pressuring women to conform to conventionally feminine attitudes.

Though there was surprisingly little resistance to the collapse of radical feminism, some movement activists did fight back. In 1973 Kathie Sarachild, Carol Hanisch, and several other women revived Redstockings, which had disbanded three years before, and in 1975 they published a journal, *Feminist Revolution. FR* was an ambitious attempt to analyze the deradicalization of the movement and contained the first major critiques of cultural feminism and *Ms.* liberalism. Its publication was an important political act, especially for those of us who felt alienated from what was passing for the radical feminist movement—or, as it was coming to be called, the "feminist community"—and were trying without the help of any ongoing group to make sense of what had gone wrong. But the journal also revealed the limitations of Redstockings politics when carried to their logical conclusions. *FR*'s critique did not contain any second thoughts about the premises of radical feminist materialism, including its rejection of psychology. On the contrary, the editors blamed the devolution of radical feminism entirely on deviations from these premises. From this unreconstructed viewpoint they could explain the deviations only as deliberate sabotage by "Agents, Opportunists, and Fools" (a section heading). One article, which provoked brief but intense controversy in the "feminist community" and eventually led Gloria Steinem to threaten a libel suit, contained a detailed account of *Ms.*'s corporate connections and Steinem's past work with the Independent Research Service, an outfit that had received CIA funds, with Steinem's knowledge, to send students to European youth festivals. While the information provided useful commentary on *Ms.*'s and Steinem's political perspective, many of the implications drawn from it were tortuous at best, including the overall implication that Steinem's ascendancy as a feminist leader, and *Ms.* itself, were a government and/or corporate plot to supplant radical feminism with liberalism.[5]

The implicit heterosexual chauvinism of the original Redstockings became overt homophobia in *FR*. Like the dominant tendency in lesbian feminism, Redstockings talked about sexual orientation in terms of political choice rather than sexual desire. But where orthodox lesbian feminists defined heterosexuality as entirely political, a patriarchal imposition on women, Redstockings took heterosexuality for granted and argued that homosexuality, both male and female, was a product of male supremacy. For the *FR* editors, lesbianism was at best one of the many compromises women made with a sexist system, a substitute for the equal heterosexual relationships we all really wanted. At worst it was a copout, a futile attempt to escape from men and male supremacy instead of struggling. By the same logic, *FR* condemned male homosexuality as a form of male supremacy: it was misogynist in that it did not simply subordinate women as lovers and sexual partners but rejected them altogether; and it was a resistance to feminism in that it allowed men to evade women's demands for equality by turning to each other. In a sense, *FR* implied, men who did not need women were the greatest threat of all. Like their cultural feminist opponents the *FR* editors filled the gap in their understanding of sexual psychology with political reductionism on the one hand and biological determinism on the other. But their uncritical acceptance of the concept of a natural, normative heterosexuality was especially ironic for self-proclaimed materialists.

Feminist Revolution crystallized my opposition to cultural feminism and stimulated a long-dormant desire to think seriously about the state of the movement and its future. But it also reinforced my suspicion that simply reviving the old-time radical feminist religion was not the answer, that while we needed to affirm and learn from what we had accomplished, we also needed to move on—to what, was still unclear. I had similar reactions to *Meeting Ground*, a radical feminist and socialist journal that Carol Hanisch began publishing in 1977. Though *MG* was intended as a forum for debate and hopefully an impetus to renewed organizing—Hanisch and her coeditors solicited readers' articles and comments—for the most part its content reflected Redstockings' orthodoxy and embattled isolation. And though it was concerned with exploring the connections between feminism and antiracist, anticapitalist politics—a concern I shared—its conception of socialist revolution was based on Marxist-Leninist-Maoist assumptions with which I had little sympathy.

Yet another attempt to reconstitute a radical feminist movement began in 1980, when Brooke, a radical feminist, a lesbian, and one of the earliest critics of cultural feminism (her essay, "The Retreat to Cultural Feminism," appeared in *Feminist Revolution*), published an article in a feminist newspaper calling for a new radical offensive. Response to the piece led its author and several other women to form the Radical Feminist Organizing Committee, which set out to create a network of radical feminists by circulating a newsletter, *Feminism Lives!*, and inviting readers' responses. RFOC's basic stance is materialist; besides opposing cultural feminism and lesbian vanguardism it has taken an explicit stand against heterosexual chauvinism (Brooke broke with Redstockings over its line on homosexuality). Otherwise the group does not have developed positions; it is at the stage where virtually everything but opposition to male supremacy is open for discussion. As a result, *Feminism Lives!* has been largely free of the sectarian, defensive tone that *Feminist Revolution* and *Meeting Ground* tended to fall into.

A more publicly visible challenge to cultural feminism, and to the antisexual strain in radical feminist thought that dates back to Ti-Grace Atkinson, has come from feminist opposition to the antipornography movement. The antiporn groups, which emerged as an organized political force in 1979, quickly captured the attention of the media and dominated public discussion of feminism and sexuality. Because their ideas resonated with the conservative social climate and appealed to women's fears at a time when real freedom and equality seemed increasingly remote, they exerted a strong influence on the liberal mainstream of the women's movement and on the public perception of feminism. I found these developments alarming, as did many other women who felt that feminists should be fighting the right's assault on women's sexual freedom, not reinforcing it.

The sex debate has recapitulated the old division between those radical feminists who emphasized women's right to equal sexual pleasure and those who viewed sex primarily in negative terms, as an instrument of sexist exploitation and abuse. But contemporary "pro-sex" feminists (as the dissidents have been labeled) are also doing something new—placing a specifically feminist commitment to women's sexual autonomy in the context of a more general sexual radicalism. Bound by its theoretical framework, the radical feminist movement analyzed sexuality as a function of sex class; it did not concern itself with sexual repression versus liberation as a problematic distinct from that of male power over women. Accordingly, most radical feminists in all factions equated women's sexual oppression with male domination and rejected the idea of sexual liberation for men as at best redundant, at worst a euphemism for license to exploit women with impunity. Within this framework there was no way to discuss the common elements in women's and men's (particularly gay men's) subjection to sexual repression; or to explore the extent to which men's sexual guilt, fear and frustration contribute to their sexism (and specifically to sexual violence); or to understand the complexities of lesbian sexuality; or to examine other variables besides sexism that influence sexual formation—such as the parent-child relationship, race, class and anxieties shared by both sexes about the body, pleasure, emotional vulnerability and loss of control.

The pro-sex feminists are raising all these questions and others, provoking an explosion of intellectual activity and reintroducing the spirit of critical inquiry to a movement all but ossified by cultural feminist dogma. The emphasis has been on questions rather than answers. There is a good deal of ideological diversity within the pro-sex camp, a loose, informal network that consists mostly of lesbian dissenters from the lesbian feminist consensus, women with political roots in early radical feminism, and feminist academics influenced by Marxism, structuralism, and psychoanalysis. We also maintain friendly relations and an ongoing exchange of ideas with parallel tendencies in the gay movement and the neo-Marxist left.

At the same time, black women and other women of color have begun to create the context for a feminist radicalism based on efforts to analyze the web of race, class and sex/gender relations. Like pro-sex theorizing, these explorations break with prevailing assumptions —in this case the competing orthodoxies of radical and cultural feminism, black nationalism and Marxist socialism. Each of these movements has insisted on hierarchies of oppression and primary causes, forcing women who suffer from racial and class oppression to subordinate some aspects of their identity to others or be political schizophrenics. While socialist feminists have purported to address this dilemma, in practice their economistic bias has tended not only to vitiate their feminist analysis but to reduce racism to its economic component. Many women of color have shared this perspective and its limitations. What is novel and exciting about the current discussions is their concern with the totality of a culture and their recognition that sexism, heterosexism, racism, capitalism and imperialism intersect in complex, often contradictory ways. When this multidimensional analysis is applied to bedrock issues of sexual politics—marriage and motherhood, sexual repression and violence, reproductive freedom, homophobia—it does not simply correct for white middle-class feminists' neglect of other women's experience; it shows that whatever a woman's particular social vantage point, her experience of femaleness is charged with class and racial meanings.

Though the emergence of this tendency and the burgeoning of the predominantly white pro-sex coalition happened independently (a small number of black and Hispanic women have been involved in both) they end up raising many of the same questions from different angles. They also reflect a common impulse toward a decentered radicalism sensitive to difference, ambiguity and contradiction, and critical of all forms of hierarchical thinking. The same impulse informs contemporary cultural radical revisions of Marxist and Marxist-feminist theory. It seems to me that these convergences represent a first fragile step toward the creation of a multiracial left that will include feminism as a basic assumption. At the moment, helping this process along is my own political priority; I think a "new new left" is the prerequisite for a third feminist wave.

Still, the paradox posed by early radical feminism remains unresolved and may be unresolvable in any definitive way. An antisexist politics abstracted from a critique of familialism, a commitment to sexual liberation, and race and class struggle cannot sustain itself as a radical force; a movement that attempts such an abstraction is bound to fragment into bitterly opposed factions and/or turn conservative. Yet so long as sexist power relations exist there will be a need for an autonomous, specifically feminist women's movement. It is the legacy of radical feminism that makes it possible to talk even tentatively of a feminist left. And it would be naive to imagine that a left intellectually committed to feminism would automatically be free of sexism either in theory or in practice. In the foreseeable future, any feminist movement that aims to be radical will somehow have to negotiate this tension between the need to preserve its political boundaries and the need to extend them. It will help to remember that radical feminism named the boundaries in the first place.

1984

NOTES

1. In this essay, as in common usage on the left, the term "socialist feminism" refers primarily to an activist tendency and "Marxist feminism" to a body of theory. There is of course some overlap between the two, but by no means a one-to-one correspondence. As a movement, socialist feminism has generally been more socialist than feminist, assuming that economic relations are fundamental, while sexual political questions are "cultural" or "ideological," i.e., epiphenomenal. Often socialist-feminists have adopted a cultural feminist view of these "ideological" questions and thereby reduced feminism to a matter of lifestyle.

Marxist feminism has displayed a similar weakness for economic reductionism, but it has also used Marxist methodology to expand feminist theory; in recent years, especially, Marxist feminists have both influenced and been influenced by the cultural radical critiques that have generated the "crisis in Marxism" debate. On the other hand, since Marxist-feminist theorizing has been carried on mostly in the academy, it has suffered badly from lack of contact with any organized feminist movement.

2. In any case, postrevolutionary China is hardly a model for those of us whose definition of liberation includes individual freedom. This does not invalidate the process of self-assertion by peasants against landlords, women against men and autocratic matriarchs that Hinton describes. But it does raise the question of whether the Maoist model of struggle can have more than limited success only in a revolution in which individual autonomy and cultural diversity are not important values.

3. Alice Echols, "The New Feminism of Yin and Yang," in *Powers of Desire: The Politics of Sexuality*, ed. Christine Stansell, Ann Snitow and Sharon Thompson (Monthly Review Press, 1983).

4. Ellen Willis, "Toward a Feminist Sexual Revolution," *Social Text*, 6, Fall 1982.

5. Before publishing *Feminist Revolution*, Redstockings held a press conference on the Steinem-CIA connection and distributed copies of the *FR* article. At the time I was working part-time at *Ms.*, editing book reviews, and had just concluded that I ought to quit, having come to the limits of my tolerance for the constant (and usually losing) battles involved in being the token radical on a magazine with mushy corporate liberal politics. The Redstockings flap pushed me over the edge. I had mixed feelings about the article and was upset about the press conference, which by villainizing Steinem and implying a conspiracy could only undercut the credibility of Redstockings' valid critique of *Ms.*'s politics and impact on the movement. But I was incensed by Steinem's response, a disdainful who-are-these-people dismissal of Sarachild, Hanisch et al. as crazies and not real Redstockings. I resigned from *Ms.* and wrote an open letter to the movement press detailing my own criticisms of the magazine and its editor. Redstockings included it in *FR*.

In 1979, Random House published an "abridged edition with additional writings" of *Feminist Revolution*. The chief abridgement was "Gloria Steinem and the CIA," which Random House deleted in response to Steinem's threat to sue, although the facts of her involvement with IRS had long been public information and the article had already survived a libel reading. Though Redstockings organized a protest, this act of censorship provoked little interest outside of radical and cultural feminist circles, and cultural feminists mostly supported Steinem. In the end, the entire episode was a depressing defeat for radical feminism, albeit largely self-inflicted. Not only did Redstockings fail to provoke significant debate about *Ms.*-ism; most people who heard about the controversy at all were left with the impression that Steinem had been attacked by a lunatic fringe.

Feminism Without Freedom

During the earliest skirmishes between the women's liberation movement and its new left progenitors, one of the charges that flew our way, along with "man-hater" and "lesbian," was "bourgeois individualist." Ever since, left criticism of the movement has focused on one or another version of the argument that feminism (at least in its present forms) is merely an extension of liberal individualism and that, largely for this reason, it is a movement of, by, and for white upper-middle-class career women. At first this attack was crude and frankly preventive, aimed at heading off the whole idea of feminism as serious radical politics before it got started. Later, as the power of that idea became ineluctable, as leftist women—even those who were hostile or ambivalent to begin with—began to take it for granted as a reference point, the argument was tempered and recast as dissent over the meaning of feminism and its proper direction. But the basic issue remains: whether the demands for independence, personal and sexual freedom, the right to pursue happiness that have set the tone of feminism's second wave are the cutting edge of cultural revolution, or on the contrary, socially irresponsible and irrelevant to most women's economic and familial concerns. That there are self-proclaimed feminists and leftists on both sides of this debate is symptomatic of a larger division—the split between cultural radicals and left cultural conservatives that has been widening for years and is now taking on the proportions of a major political realignment.

Elizabeth Fox-Genovese's presumptuously titled *Feminism Without Illusions: A Critique of Individualism*—haven't we had enough of intellectuals who imagine they have no illusions?—dives into these roiling waters. The author, who describes herself as "temperamentally and culturally conservative" and committed to feminism "despite firm opposition to some of its tendencies that I regard as irrational, ir-responsible, and dangerous," rejects the liberal democratic proposi-tion that individuals have inalienable natural rights and therefore the idea that women have an inherent right to self-determination. Insist-ing that the claims of society are prior to individual rights, and that all such rights are socially derived, she calls on the feminist move-ment to break with its individualist roots and find a rationale for women's rights in collectively determined values and interests. Nor, in Fox-Genovese's view, may the collectivity in question be women as a group: for her the concept of sisterhood, whether defined as politi-cal solidarity in fighting male supremacy or as commonality based on some version of "female values" (she makes no distinction between the two) is itself an extension of individualism that obscures differ-ences of race and class while denying women's stake in a common human culture and the legitimate claims of society as a whole.

Feminism Without Illusions is not a systematic argument but a series of loosely related essays with considerable overlap, held together (often just barely) by a sensibility—characteristic of con-temporary left conservatism—that merges two disparate strains of anti-individualist thought. One is a socialist materialism that defines human rights primarily in terms of distributive justice, the other a communitarian, cryptoreligious moralism that laments the decline of traditional forms of social authority, especially the family. Neither philosophy has much use for individual freedom, which is seen mainly as a threat to the social fabric. Both endow human beings with an amoral, insatiable will to power that must be subject to external con-trols. Both object to the capitalist marketplace on the grounds that it unleashes the individual and undermines social and moral order. Both evince a puritanical suspicion of pleasure, particularly sexuality, that powerful manifestation of the anarchic, imperial will. For the socialist in Fox-Genovese, individualism leads to Hobbes's nightmare war of all against all; for the communitarian, to a disastrous denial of any concept, "however secularized," of original sin. Her contempt for liberty is straightforward: on pornography she declares, "I would ban the more extreme forms without a second thought, and with precious few worries about the public expressions of healthy sexu-ality that might be banned along with them"; she takes issue with the Supreme Court decision defining flag-burning ("an affront to our collective identity") as free speech; she rejects the idea of an absolute right to abortion, arguing that the question of when life begins must be decided collectively, not left to "individual conscience or convenience."

Despite certain convergences between this brand of illiberalism and that of the anti-pornography movement, the project of assimilating it to feminism is, to say the least, a challenge. Feminism is indeed, as Fox-Genovese puts it (with a disconcerting air of floating a daring new idea), "the daughter of individualism"—not only because of its origins in the demand that the ideals of the enlightenment apply to female as well as male individuals, but because the market opened up alternatives to women's absolute economic dependence on the family. Furthermore, Fox-Genovese and I agree, contemporary feminism has uncovered the profoundly radical implications of the idea that individual rights are innate.

We differ, however, on what this means and how to evaluate it. For Fox-Genovese, the depredations of individualism have been limited by restrictions on who counts as an individual, and the claims of the dispossessed, women especially, are now demolishing those saving limits. As I see it, the problem with liberal individualism in capitalist societies is not its liberating tendencies but its coexistence with, and masking of, systemic domination. Liberal social-contract theory assumes—can make sense only by assuming—an adult, putatively genderless but implicitly male citizen engaging in a public political and economic life, which in turn means taking for granted an apolitical sexual and domestic realm in which patriarchal relations are unquestioned. Capitalist ideology defines the economic rights of the individual not simply as freedom to produce and exchange goods and services or to benefit from the fruits of one's labor but as freedom for some individuals to monopolize economic resources and thereby control the lives of others.

From this perspective, the left-conservative (and right-libertarian) conflation of an unbridled market economy with the expansion of personal freedom comes apart. It is not, for instance, inconsistent— as Fox-Genovese would have it—for feminists to ground their defense of abortion in individual rights while rejecting economic individualism in support of equal pay for jobs of comparable worth; rather, it is contradictory for employers to invoke "individual rights" —their own or those of workers in "male" jobs—to justify the economic and sexist domination involved in systematically devaluing "women's work." To be consistently for freedom and against domination does not, as Fox-Genovese claims, destroy the distinction between freedom and license. Rather, it means making that distinction at the point where my exercise of freedom interferes with yours: the true equivalent of unconstrained capitalism would be unlimited freedom to impose one's will through violence.

A genuinely radical libertarianism is not unconcerned with community. On the contrary, it requires communities committed to negotiating social conflicts and deciding on social priorities in ways that maximize freedom and minimize coercion, that allow people the widest possible latitude in meeting their perceived needs while still respecting the rights of others, including the others in their own households. It also, of course, implies equality of power, including the power of dissident individuals and groups to resist coercion by majorities. In short, such a community is democratic—which means that it gets its validation and its aims, which are always provisional, from the individuals who participate in it.

Critics of social-contract theory have justly argued that social life is a given of human existence: each of us is born embedded in and dependent on social relations. Indeed, the very idea of rights implies a society that recognizes and supports them. Still, we experience ourselves, primally, as individuals with urgent impulses and desires—in relation to others, to be sure, but also apart from and in conflict with them; any parent can attest to how early babies begin to struggle, poignantly, for autonomy. Nor is this struggle synonymous with a destructive will to power: on the contrary, in my view, it is the cumulative suppression of basic human needs for freedom and pleasure that has given rise to the sadistic rage at the root of this century's barbarities, from Nazism and Stalinism to the anomic violence of today's inner cities. For those of us who draw that lesson from history, the idea that human beings have inherent rights and freedoms transcending any given form of social organization is indispensable. This ought to be particularly obvious in the case of women, who have been to varying degrees subordinated in all known cultures, whose sexual and reproductive functions—intimate aspects of their being—have always been collectivized. While men of oppressed classes and races may at least have their subjectivity recognized within their own groups, women are everywhere defined as existing in relation to men and children. How are women's rights to "derive from a collectivity" when the very definition of human society has been so closely linked with the definition of women as a resource?

Fox-Genovese makes passing acknowledgment of this problem, but it doesn't deter her from advocating a society that defines the common good as "the good of the whole, with the whole understood to have an existence in some way independent of, or logically anterior to, the individuals who compose it" and that functions as a collective conscience. In practice that means a society based on the repressive, patriarchal norms of Judeo-Christian morality and enforced by traditional institutions, or some form of authoritarian collectivism based on a secular ideology and enforced by the state, or a combination of the two.

The implications for feminism are perhaps most evident in Fox-Genovese's discussion of abortion. She asserts:

> The vast majority of women who seek abortions are still in their teens, unmarried, and poor. They have scant, if any, prospects of providing bare essentials for a child, and the attempt to do so almost invariably destroys their own prospects. . . . The hard truth is that our society is not prepared to provide adequately for children. . . . The argument for abortion as a woman's individual right, by conflating pregnancy and child rearing, confuses sexual and economic issues. . . . Pregnancy itself does not long interfere with a woman's opportunities to live the life she chooses; child rearing frequently does. A woman can, in principle, afford to share her body—and even to give up drugs, alcohol, and tobacco—for nine months without serious consequences. . . .

This argument accepts the entrenched assumption that a woman's reproductive capacity is not an aspect of her selfhood but a social resource; it ignores the pervasive impact of that assumption on women's alienation from their bodies, their sexuality, and their sense of themselves as agents; and it trivializes women's experience of unwanted pregnancy, which often includes intense feelings of bodily and psychic violation as well as the knowledge that every pregnancy has potentially "serious consequences." For that matter, its economism ridiculously oversimplifies the issues involved in child rearing. Melodrama aside (it is simply untrue that the "vast majority" of women who seek abortions are in economic *extremis*), Fox-Genovese is clearly suggesting that a good enough welfare state could restrict abortion without violating women's rights. If this is the socialist talking, the communitarian surfaces in her endorsement of a collective definition of life, linked to fetal viability: without such a definition, the right to abortion "can logically lead to the right to murder with impunity." Which is to say that the moment women are permitted to determine whether and on what terms they will give birth, Sodom and Gomorrah will ensue.

Fox-Genovese also disapprovingly equates "women's right to liberation from the reproductive consequences of their own sexuality" with "their right to the male model of individualism," suggesting that the desire for sexual freedom is both morally dubious and intrinsically male. (To give her her due, the desire to be out in the world on "honorary male" terms did have a lot to do with the passion of young, childless feminists in the early legal abortion wars—myself included.) In general, one of her more traditionalist objections to individualism is her fear that it leaches out the concreteness of biological difference, defining women as either abstract, genderless atoms or surrogate men. Yet at the same time she rejects sexual difference or female commonality as a basis for feminist politics.

This is not as contradictory as it sounds. Fox-Genovese is positively Gothic in her rendition of "the inescapable conflict between men and women": "As social facts, male strength and female reproductive power pit the sexes against each other in a conflict rendered only more poignant by the attraction that locks mortal adversaries in each other's embrace." It follows that since this conflict cannot be transcended or resolved, either through androgyny or through an unthinkable separatism, there is no point in politicizing it.

I share Fox-Genovese's distaste for notions of solidarity based on women's alleged special qualities or values, as well as her refusal to dismiss the entire corpus of Western culture as monolithically male. (Ironically, this sort of cultural nationalism offers the most plausible framework for a feminism that subordinates individual rights to collective norms.) Her denial that women have a common political interest is another matter. In arguing against the reductive conception of sisterhood as a bond that transcends race, class, and cultural differences, Fox-Genovese is merely echoing what has been feminist conventional wisdom for a decade or more. No feminist on the left would deny that radical feminists' insistence on gender as the primary political division led to a crippling inability to confront the differences among women; nor that an effective feminist politics must take women's complex, multiple identities into account. But Fox-Genovese goes further: in classic left antifeminist fashion, she dismisses the very idea that women's "special oppression" derives from gender as an individualist "temptation," which functions to shore up capitalism by denying class and race. She sees feminist consciousness-raising as a form of middle-class therapy ("The rising self-awareness brought many to confront how much of the early anger, presumably related to the male oppressors, in fact derived from childhood relations with mothers"), political only insofar as it freed women "from the continual replay of familial psychodramas." (For the historical record, rising self-awareness brought at least some of us to confront how much anger, presumably derived from our relations with our mothers, in fact related to our oppression by men.) As for actual feminist successes in opening up new opportunities for women, Fox-Genovese argues that it is mainly middle-class women who are able to take advantage of them, while working-class and poor women have been hurt by the attendant loss of patriarchal protections, especially the male backlash (my word, not hers) against supporting children. (One might ask when poor women, black women in particular, ever enjoyed any patriarchal protections, but never mind.)

At the start of her concluding chapter, the author writes, "However much this book is intended as a feminist critique of individualism, it is bound to strike some—and perhaps many—as a critique of feminism." The implication is that those so struck are stuffy party-liners; feminism is, after all, the most various and contentious of movements. But in truth, little remains of feminism of any stripe by the time Fox-Genovese gets through divesting it of "illusions." While I don't doubt that she believes women ought to get a better deal, she resists any possible means of translating that sentiment into a political challenge to male power and privilege. In a key passage in her introduction, Fox-Genovese makes the familiar economistic argument that feminism is a "symptom" of other social changes, particularly women's increased participation in the labor force—an argument that denies or plays down the role of feminism, as movement or as impulse, in promoting the changes in question. The implicit corollary is that women's equality will also come about as a symptom of economic change. Fox-Genovese never says outright that the woman question will be resolved not by feminism but by socialism; such claims are out of fashion, and for good reason. Yet it seems clear that this is what she means—and that the diffuse quality of her book comes, in part, from the strain of not saying it.

The other major subtext in *Feminism Without Illusions* is perhaps best expressed by the following personal anecdote:

> Early in our marriage we enjoyed playing gin rummy, and, as it happened, I frequently won. Now my husband enjoys winning as much as anyone I know. And one day, when I had not just won, but won big, he turned to me with a wicked gleam in his eye and said, "Yes, but you don't have a penis." We had a good laugh.

Evidently Fox-Genovese means this story as an ironic cautionary tale about the tension between equality and difference, the battle of the sexes and the ways we do and don't transcend it. Myself, I can't help hearing in her husband's joke the intellectual's sublimated equivalent of the truck driver's dick-waving in *Thelma and Louise*. And in Fox-Genovese's appreciative laughter I hear the voice of all social conservatives, saying, in one way or another, settle for sublimation, it's the best you can ever get. If the past decade's defeats tell us anything, it's that no illusion feminism has perpetrated is half so devastating as this one.

Fall 1991

Rebel Girl:

What De Beauvoir Left Us

On May Day, the remnants of my old radical feminist group Redstockings held a memorial for Simone de Beauvoir. I had wanted to go, but couldn't make it, so I heard about it from a friend: Ti-Grace Atkinson talked about going to de Beauvoir's funeral, women spoke about her impact on their lives, someone read a message from Shulamith Firestone. Listening to this account, it occurred to me that in a way my relationship to de Beauvoir had always been secondhand, mediated and refracted by other feminists. When I first got involved in the women's liberation movement, I knew de Beauvoir only through *The Mandarins*, which I'd read, naively, as a novel (a good way to read it, I still maintain). After joining the movement I dutifully began *The Second Sex*, but abandoned it halfway through; it was too detached and distanced, too much the product of a French cultural and philosophical framework, to compete with the overpowering immediacy of all the discussion about *our lives* that permeated those early days of activism. (The woman who recommended it to me had discovered it at a time when America's idea of a feminist was a little old lady brandishing an umbrella.) Not till years later, when I was able to give the book the attention it deserved, did I fully appreciate de Beauvoir's impact on the politics of the feminists I was closest to—as well as those I most bitterly disagreed with.

Nearly four decades after it was first published in France, despite all the commentary the feminist movement has produced in the meantime, dated and parochial as it is in many respects, *The Second Sex* remains the most cogent and thorough book of feminist theory yet written. With its exhaustive portrayal of the ways in which male domination and female subordination penetrate every aspect of everyday life and shape our cultural myths and fantasies, it offers detailed evidence for the basic claims of second wave feminism—that male supremacy is a coherent system of power relations, and that "the personal is political."

If de Beauvoir's existentialist perspective is too innocent (and perhaps too arrogant) for a postmodern, poststructuralist era, it's metaphorically appropriate to her subject. Since the denial of personal autonomy defines women's oppression—and since patriarchal ideology holds that allowing women autonomy would destroy civilization if not the human species itself—a moral defense of freedom is necessarily at the heart of feminism. And for the feminists of my generation, so many of whom were "liberated"—that is, had consciously set out to earn a living, sleep with whom they pleased, and avoid traditional wife-and-motherhood—the collision between our sense of entitlement to freedom and men's stubborn assumption of dominance was not only a political (and personal) struggle but a grand moral drama. De Beauvoir's rendering of woman as the subject seeking transcendence, only to be forced into the position of Other and trapped in immanence, expressed that drama with a clarity that almost made up for her coolness.

De Beauvoir's influence pervades the early radical feminist critiques of Marxism. It was de Beauvoir who first pointed out the reductionism of Engels's attempt to trace women's oppression to the formation of classes, who insisted that sexuality and reproduction had to be primary categories for understanding women's lives; it was also de Beauvoir who argued—even more problematically from a conventional leftist point of view—that social conditions did not *cause* oppression; rather, people responded to those conditions by *choosing* to oppress. "Historical materialism," she wrote, "takes for granted facts that call for explanation: Engels assumes without discussion the bond of *interest* which ties man to property; but where does this interest, the source of social institutions, have its own source?"

Engels and other historical materialists did have an implicit answer to this question: interest had its source in the desire for survival and material comfort. But by de Beauvoir's time it was clear that this common sense approach to the question could not explain the rise of fascism, the failure of revolutionary socialism in western Europe, or the totalitarian perversion of the Russian Revolution. De Beauvoir built her philosophy on the idea that the human subject has an intrinsic impulse toward freedom, but this was if anything less useful than materialism for understanding the dynamics of domination and submission. Her solution to the problem was blaming oppression on "the imperialism of human consciousness," which, she argued, "included the original category of the Other and an original aspiration to dominate the Other." Of all her dubious appeals to a priori truths about human nature, this one seems to me the weakest. And I think it's no coincidence that subsequent feminist thinking about the roots of male supremacy has been muddled at best.

Many radical feminists who considered themselves materialists in the Marxist sense, who saw women as an oppressed class struggling in behalf of their interests (redefined as sexual and emotional in addition to economic), were also deeply influenced by *The Second Sex*. The political formulations that came out of this mix—the dominant tendency in Redstockings—were rich in paradox, like theologians' explanations of how God's divine plan is ineluctable but human beings have free will. Feminist materialists argued that while men's sexual class interests determined their oppression of women, and in fact all men did oppress women, any individual man *could* choose not to oppress women. Therefore, each man bore personal moral responsibility for his acts; determinism could never be an excuse for letting men off the hook. Similarly, women submitted to men so long as they had to avoid punishment, and resisted whenever they felt it was possible: either way, they were acting in their interest. And yet there were always women who (for what mysterious reasons?) chose to take risks, to step out there ahead of everyone else. Sometimes others followed, and then you had a movement.

On the question of "where interest has its source," the feminist materialists suggested that the desire for survival, comfort, freedom, love, sexual pleasure, and emotional support all played a role. On the surface, their understanding of male supremacy wasn't much like de Beauvoir's. In the materialist view, men's stake in their power over women was quite practical—it gained them money, leisure time, and domestic service, not to mention love, sexual pleasure, and emotional support on their own terms. But if you looked more closely at this list of goodies, it wasn't quite so simple. Could you assume, for instance, that sexual dominance was inherently more pleasurable than mutual desire? Or that it made "material" sense to choose love corrupted by the concealed rage of the oppressed over love with an equal partner? Lurking behind the materialist analysis was the de Beauvoirian assumption that oppressors were attached to power for its own sake.

For other factions of radical feminists, this assumption was quite overt. The New York Radical Feminists' manifesto, for example, argued that men exercised power over women to satisfy their egos. As they saw it, men did not value their power because it allowed them to demand women's services, but rather, demanded the services to affirm their power. Ironically, this idea was elaborated in a way that offended de Beauvoir's most basic beliefs about the artificiality of gender: cultural feminists who believed that women's problem was the ascendancy of "male values" attributed the drive for power not to the imperialism of human consciousness but to the imperialism of the phallus.

As a Redstocking, I was basically in the materialist camp, but with a difference; I thought the best tool for understanding sexuality and family life, the keys to patriarchal culture, was psychoanalysis. The radical feminist movement was, of course, resolutely anti-Freudian; here, too, classical Marxist thinking merged with de Beauvoir's. Like that other exemplary female intellectual, Hannah Arendt, whose insistence on evaluating Adolf Eichmann in rational moral terms led her to deny his patent lunacy, de Beauvoir resisted any view of human will that challenged the primacy of deliberate moral choice. Her refusal to admit the potency of unconscious fantasy and conflict not only forced her to assume a primary will to dominate; it also implicitly defined women's response to their oppression in highly moralistic terms. In the universe of *The Second Sex*, the female rebel was the existential heroine. And of course the paradigmatic female rebel was Simone de Beauvoir herself.

For many contemporary feminists, de Beauvoir's life has been an inspiration as well as her work; indeed, her work—not only *The Second Sex* but the novels and the memoirs—is, among other things, a testament to a certain kind of life. It's easy for female rebels to idealize that life, to think of it as liberated without quotation marks. But in fact de Beauvoir was no more able than the most traditional housewife to transcend or circumvent male supremacy; her path involved its own complicated set of sacrifices, tradeoffs, and illusions. Part of the price she paid for being Simone de Beauvoir was to live more in her mind than in her body. De Beauvoir never questioned the patriarchal assumption that human freedom depends on the conquest of nature. Her relationship with Sartre was, judging by her own accounts, far more cerebral than sensual. Like most women who put a high priority on independence she had no children—and while it's a sexist fiction that all women want to be mothers, it's also a fact that so long as motherhood carries drastic social penalties, the decision to avoid it (and relinquish its erotic pleasures) is not exactly free.

Self-reflection on such matters was not de Beauvoir's strong point. Seeing herself as freer than she was, she denied the full import of her struggle—just as many of her radical feminist children, seduced by the politics of moral example, imagined they could make the revolution simply by changing their own lives. But de Beauvoir had to struggle alone; when she stepped out there, few were ready to follow. Partly because of her groundbreaking work, things are different now. In a sense, recognizing the limitations of that work, and of that female rebel's life, is the best way to honor them.

May 1986

2.

Exile on Main Street

Escape from New York

For Americans, long-distance buses are the transportation of last resort. As most people see it, buses combine the comfort of a crowded jail cell with the glamor of a liverwurst sandwich. Though I can't really refute that assessment, I don't really share it, either. As a student with lots of time, little money, and no driver's license, I often traveled by bus. Un-American as it may be, I feel nostalgic about those trips, even about their discomforts. In my no doubt idealized memory, discomfort was the cement that bound together an instant community of outsiders, people who for reasons of age, race, class, occupation (student, soldier), handicap, or bohemian poverty were marginal—at least for the time being—to a car-oriented culture.

It is this idea of community that moves me now. Lately I've been feeling isolated, spending too much time hiding out in my apartment, wrestling with abstract ideas. What better remedy than to take a bus trip, join the transportation-of-last-resort community, come back and write about what I've learned?

I am not immediately struck by the paradox: that in search of community I'm leaving home. Breaking out of my everyday web of connections—to my friends, my women's group, the man I've begun to think about living with—and going on the road.

I

On a long bus trip, the difference between a tolerable ride and a miserable ride is having two seats to yourself. Anyway, there are a limited number of games you can play on a bus, and scoring two seats is one of them. My technique for getting people to sit elsewhere is to take an aisle seat near the back, put something ambiguously proprietary on the window seat (a jacket, say, or a book, not something that's obviously mine like a purse), spread my body out as much as possible, and pretend to be asleep.

As I leave New York on Greyhound's express to Montreal I am self-consciously taking none of these precautions. I throw my backpack on the overhead rack, clasp my trusty Van Morrison tote bag between my knees, sit by the window and try to look inviting. But the bus is half-empty and no one sits with me. Most of the passengers are older women traveling alone, Canadian students, and foreign tourists. A little Hispanic girl skips up the aisle, inspecting faces; she has on a sky-blue skirt and a T-shirt that says DANCE DANCE DANCE. My nearest neighbor sits across the aisle, a plump, dark, curly-haired woman who looks unidentifiably foreign and impenetrably self-contained.

Ten minutes out of the Port Authority terminal, a familiar sensation hits. I recognize it from childhood. Whenever I went to an amusement park I would make a point of going on the roller coaster. Every time, as soon as I was irrevocably trapped in my seat and we had started to move, the idiocy of what I'd done would overwhelm me. But why should I feel that now? I'm not trapped. I can get off the bus at Saratoga Springs and be back in New York by tonight.

Between Montreal and Toronto I watch a teenage couple neck, listen to a bunch of high school girls sing "One Hundred Bottles of Beer on the Wall," and read Doris Lessing's *The Marriages Between Zones Three, Four and Five*. The story is sucking me in despite my revulsion at its basic premise—that the rulers of a certain section of the universe have a benevolent grand design ungraspable by lesser beings, and so their orders must be obeyed however cruel and incomprehensible they seem.

In Toronto I have an hour's wait. Since there are no seats in the crowded waiting room I find a spot on the floor and open my book. A girl who looks about 16 sits down close to me and pretends to be absorbed in a pamphlet. A New Yorker to the core, I make sure I know where my wallet is. The girl has straight blond hair and metal-rimmed glasses; she is wearing a long navy skirt and a gray sweater with a hood. After about 30 seconds she asks me what I'm reading. I pass her the book.

"I've been reading this poem," she says, handing me her pamphlet. It's Kipling's "If." "My name is Joan."

I introduce myself. Joan turns out to be 27.

"Don't you think," she says, "that caring is the most important thing in life? So many people don't care. They sit next to each other the way we were doing and don't talk to each other. What do you think about Christ?" She speaks very fast in a high voice that's hard to hear over the noise of the terminal.

"Well—I don't. I'm Jewish."

"I don't know anyone of the Jewish race," Joan says. "I had a Jewish friend once. You don't believe Christ died for us?"

"Well, no."

"Christ is someone who picks you up when you stumble, you know? Like a little kid. He dries your eyes and helps you go on. I have a lot of bad experiences in my past. Sometimes I backslide, I go out and smoke pot, put Christ on the shelf. But then I call on him again, 'Christ, I'm sorry!' Some Christians can't stand moral flaws in other Christians. Piss on that!"

We cross the border after midnight and stop in Detroit. The atmosphere of the bus has changed completely; it's proletarian, young, funky, and two-thirds black. In the dark several portable radios play disco, though there's a rule against radios without earphones, and the bus begins to smell like marijuana. As it moves onto the highway someone behind me whispers, "*Shift gears*, motherfucker. Come on man, *shift*, man—ah!"

A red-headed college student asks if he can sit with me. "A woman just got on with her child," he apologizes, "and she asked if I'd move so they could sit together." He's a nice kid from a small town in Ontario, but almost immediately he begins encroaching on my rightful space. Men on buses always take up too much space. Sometimes it's hard to tell, when they fall asleep and sprawl all over you, whether they're really asleep.

During the '60s the men I met on buses used to ask if I was a hippie. During the '70s they asked if I was a women's libber. They almost always asked if I had a man in New York. On my first coast-to-coast bus trip in 1963, I was waiting in the Oakland terminal and got into a conversation with a young man. He was 18, he said, and engaged. But now his girlfriend was wanting him to do something he didn't want to do. What did I think, should he do it?

"Well, that depends," I said, with a touch of condescension. "What is it she wants you to do?"

"She wants me to kiss her *there*," he said, jabbing a finger at my crotch. I jumped backward. He smiled innocently. "You got a man in New York?"

But this college student is perfectly okay, it's just that I'm scrunched against the window and resenting it. I consider a friendly confrontation. I'll tap him awake and say, "Excuse me, but this"—indicating the arm rest between our seats—"is really the boundary of your seat, and you're leaning way over on my side, and the seats are narrow enough as it is—" Oh, shit. It's only another six hours to Chicago.

The Greyhound terminal in Chicago is home to a huge, ornate Burger King with white trellises and fake vines. I eat something that passes for an English muffin, then walk a few blocks down deserted Randolph Street, past neon theater marquees flashing incongruously, to the Trailways station, where at 7:30 a.m. I will board the bus to Denver. Trailways stations, this one included, tend to be less crowded, less grungy, and more middle-class than Greyhound stations. It's hard to imagine a rapist lurking in the restroom of a Trailways station. Yet when I think about hitting the restroom to wash and change my clothes, I have a flash attack of urban paranoia. I will wait till the bus stops at some small town in Illinois.

In mid-morning the cooling system quits. The temperature on buses is never right; either the air-conditioning is efficient enough to chill beer, or it doesn't work at all. On this bus at least the windows have vents that can be opened to let in a sliver of air. Farm smells, hay and manure, drift in. The heat and the miles of cornfields, punctuated by gas stations and John Deere Tractor signs, are soporific. For a while the bus is almost empty, but then it begins filling again. It picks up a fat blind woman with hennaed hair and a loud, hearty voice. A young man, blond and bespectacled, wearing a button that reads Humanity Is One, takes her suitcase and heaves it onto the rack.

"Now where has that young man gone with my suitcase?" the blind woman jokes, waving her cane with dangerous exuberance. The young man has been on the bus since Chicago. I've already heard him tell an old lady who got on somewhere in Iowa that he's moving west to work in an organization devoted to persuading intellectuals and technical experts to think about their work in moral terms. Now he notices me looking at him. He asks me where I'm from, what I do. He wants to know how I go about communicating with a particular audience.

"Well, I'm sure my sense of who's reading me influences what I write," I say. "But I don't sit down and consciously think about how to communicate."

"But wouldn't you say," the young man persists, "that a lot of art these days is too obscure for people to relate to?"

For a moment I can't answer because I'm having a peculiar experience. The young man has become an alien creature, a different species. I can't imagine what to say that will communicate across this gap. Finally I get out some words that amount to "Yes and no." The young man becomes an ordinary passenger again, indisputably human. He is smiling; evidently he has noticed nothing strange.

In Omaha I buy some postcards to get change for the toilet. Bus stations are the last great bastion of the pay toilet, though they usually provide a few free cubicles with broken locks, no doors, or clogged bowls. One of my postcards has a picture of the highway, captioned "Driving Beautiful Interstate 80." When we start up again the moon and clouds look like an El Greco painting. I fall asleep, and when I wake up around 3 a.m. the moonscape is gone, leaving nothing but black Nebraska night. The bus is silent; only a couple of reading lights indicate that anyone else is awake. At a rest stop in North Platte I wash down my potato chips with coffee that tastes like Styrofoam and liquid soybean extract.

This afternoon I will be in Colorado Springs, birthplace of my friend and ex-lover Paul, who now makes his home in New York. Paul is about to move in with the woman he's been seeing, and it feels like the end of an era. We lived together through the early '70s, and neither of us has lived with anyone since. Evidently one thing we have in common is ambivalence about creating such bonds. For a long time we couldn't quite let go of each other. For a long time after that I seemed to be attracted only to men who lived in other cities or were otherwise unavailable. For a year I cut myself off from men altogether. Perhaps I had to plunge so deeply into the negative side of my ambivalence in order to say good-bye to it, or try to. When I began to be with someone again it was a bit like moving to a strange country. In the intervening years aloneness had become my norm, my taken-for-granted context. And yet those same years had changed my sense of myself, of men, of the ground rules for relationships, making it impossible simply to pick up where I left off.

In spite of the coffee I fall asleep again. When I open my eyes the first thing that hits them is a store window advertising waterbeds. We've just pulled into Sterling, Colorado, and it's raining. A man in stretch pants and a sweatshirt, with a beard and twinkly eyes, leans across the aisle and offers me an apple.

I I

Lee Ann and her husband Don meet me at the Colorado Springs bus station on Saturday afternoon. In her short shorts and sleeveless top Lee looks slim, brown, and, as always, beautiful. A clergyman's daughter from Michigan, she has an archetypal midwestern beauty with a counterculture overlay—fresh face, candid eyes, freckled nose, long, gleaming, and absolutely straight brown hair. Eleven years ago we converged on the Springs to help run Home Front, an antiwar movement center for soldiers from nearby Fort Carson. At the time Lee was a 20-year-old weaver who traveled light and toked heavily; I was 27 and an activist with ideas about building an alliance between women's liberation and the rest of the left. We shared a lot of history, lived and worked and demonstrated together, met Paul and his family, took LSD, fell in love with the Rockies. I consider our connection unbreakable, though we come from and have gone on (or in my case back) to different worlds, and hardly ever see each other.

I've met Don only once before. He is quietly friendly, but I feel shy with him. We have no history to mediate our different worlds. Then, too, perhaps I'm afraid of getting my loyalties confused. Though Lee and Don have been together for five years, their marriage has not yet shaken down. Lee hasn't been able to get Don to share the housework (though she usually works full-time and keeps the books for his roofing business besides), and she feels that he dominates their sexual relationship. Periodically she blows up and things change temporarily. She feels frustrated and ambivalent: she will have to leave if the situation doesn't change, yet she and Don love each other, "whatever that means," and she thinks he is a genuinely good person, which is more than she can say for certain former lovers.

"I've got to make a phone call," Lee announces as the three of us walk toward her red pickup truck. "We're supposed to pick up some dope."

"So what else is new?" I say, grinning. Whenever I set foot in the Springs I feel as if I've never left.

Lee and Don live several miles out of town; they've bought a roomy house still surrounded by woods, though that won't last long at the rate the city is growing. They are gradually fixing the place up; Don has put in wood paneling in the kitchen and the living room. They have handsome pine furniture, bought on time at Penney's; a fireplace; plants hanging in macrame holders Lee has made; a color TV; a truck and a van; two German shepherds. Lee confesses her yearning for an efficient dishwasher and one of those fancy refrigerators that make ice cubes.

"Lee, you've become an American," I tease. "You used to think it was immoral to own more than one dress." On the other hand, she has always had a taste for toys and gadgets; she kept our commune supplied with slinkies, pinwheels, and other amusements.

"It's this house," Lee says. "For the first time I really want to have nice things."

We take the red pickup over to Lee's friend Carey's place to get the dope. On the way Lee brings me up to date. She's still confused about what she wants—with her marriage, with her life. At the moment she has a temporary job painting, the only woman in the crew, and the men hassle her so much it's driving her insane. The previous winter she went up to Wyoming to take advantage of the construction boom; she got a job, but was fired on the grounds that she was "a distraction."

"I'd like to go back to school. But how would we live? We've got so many bills—for transportation, especially. I can't count on Don to make enough, consistently. And I haven't figured out what I want to do. I want work that's interesting, but I also want to make decent money. I've thought of becoming a fast food manager, but that takes capital, which I don't have." Then there's the question of whether to have a kid. Don wants to; Lee isn't sure. It's so ironic—Carey really wants to settle down and have a family, but her last lover was too unreliable, and this one is too young and uncertain.

Carey and Joe live in a little house with a flower and vegetable garden. I realize after an unsettling minute that I was there years ago, visiting one of Paul's brothers. My sense of deja vu is accentuated by Joe's long hair and embroidered shirt. It's Joe who's selling the dope. When the transaction is done we sit and listen to Emmylou Harris and talk about friends from my Colorado days. An ex-GI, part of the Home Front crowd, agreed to marry his long-suffering girlfriend, then changed his mind at the last minute. A woman I liked, a Vietnam widow who over the years has been hooked on several different drugs, is in terrible shape—still a junkie, and now a prostitute as well.

When we get home Don orders a pepperoni pizza and we smoke. Since I rarely smoke dope anymore, one hit has me floating. I call my man in New York, but he isn't home, so I talk to his answering machine: "Hi. I'm in Colorado Springs, and I'm really stoned." Then we eat and watch *Chinatown* on the color TV.

I spend Sunday night with Paul's parents. Peg and Andrew have five children. They were also surrogate parents to the Home Front staff and, it often seemed, to the entire '60s generation of Colorado Springs. Peg was one of the town's leading peace activists; Andrew, a physician, took care of our bodies. We trooped in and out of their house—a sprawling, modern redwood and glass structure with a spectacular view of the mountains—talking politics, meeting out-of-town visitors, eating holiday dinners, confiding our troubles.

Peg is a vivid woman with a sexual vitality impervious to age. She has long since given up on politics—it all looks so hopeless—and turned her prodigious energy to other pursuits. She makes beautiful, intricate quilts in patterns with evocative names—log cabin, cathedral window, clamshell. She and Andrew are building a passive solar house on the adjoining lot. They will live there and sell their present home.

Peg takes me on a tour of the lot and shows me the plans for the house, which she designed. Then she reports on the marriages, breakups, babies, and other projects of various old acquaintances. She manages to combine a taken-for-granted acceptance of her surrogate children with a complete lack of inhibition about telling them when and how they've gone off the track: "Every time he came over here, he would give me the same rap about Maharaj-ji. Finally I said, 'Bruce, if that's all you have to talk about when you're over here— if you honestly think there's nothing else that's worthwhile—then there's no point in your coming, because you have nothing to say to me.'"

In the morning, after dashing up to the lot for a consultation with the contractor and the surveyor, Peg drives me to the bus. We are almost at the depot when she asks after a mutual friend. I tell her we've drifted apart, partly because of tension over his anti-Zionist politics.

"Well, I don't know, Ellen," Peg says. "I never discuss these things with Jewish people, because they get so defensive."

Oh no. We can't have *this* conversation in five minutes. "We get defensive," I reply, "because we feel threatened, and for good reason— there really is such a thing as anti-Semitism."

"I guess I've never really understood Jewish suffering and Jewish persecution that well, because Jews seem the same as everyone else. Not like blacks."

"If you're 3 per cent of the population, and you get a lot of hostility from the other 97 per cent, it makes you defensive."

Peg frowns, shaking her head. "The Jewish people I know are very aggressive, they're elitist, they look down on people who aren't geared to success, or this society's idea of success—"

"Like me, you mean?"

"Well, you're a little different, you come out of the '60s—"

"You're indulging in a stereotype. What about all the radical Jews? A big portion of the left is Jewish."

"Yes, I know. But the Jewish people I know in Colorado Springs aren't radicals."

I have to get on the bus. I feel schizophrenic, kissing Peg good-bye with the same affection as always, yet thinking oh no, not you too, I can't stand it. What's odd is that I'm not angry. I only wish I could stay and fight this out.

I I I

West of Denver the bus runs through gorgeous canyons and over two mountain passes. I feel nauseated from the altitude; my head aches. The weekend has been a respite, but now I'm running through another session of "What am I doing here?" This trip has not turned out as I expected. I thought I was rejecting my solipsistic impulses and getting out, as they say, among the people. Instead my solipsistic impulses keep flaring up like TB on the Magic Mountain.

The man sitting next to me is stocky, fortyish, rumpled. He was born in a tiny town in Denmark and has been shuttling between there and the San Francisco Bay area for the past 30 years, unable to decide which place he likes better. He owns a farm in Denmark. He is vague about what he does in California. I mention that I'm thinking of stopping off in Reno to play a bit.

"Have you ever played the horses?" he inquires.

"No."

"Good. I know owners and trainers, and it's a crooked business. I once owned a horse myself. Won a harness race. It was a sloppy track and the horse was juiced up. It was what you would call a fixed race."

We move into Utah and the bus begins to fill up with men in wide-brimmed hats. Around 10 at night we stop at a grocery store with a snack bar. A man in a wide-brimmed hat is joking with the woman behind the counter: "I like my coffee the way I like my girls."

"How's that?"

"Fresh."

"Oh, I thought you were gonna say hot and black."

Fun and games! *"I like my coffee the way I like my men." "How's that?" "Sweet." "Oh, I thought you were gonna say strong and full of cream."* I buy some aspirin for my headache. As I walk back to my seat, Horse Race taps me on the shoulder and whispers, "Have you noticed that the old guy in front of you never gets off?" It's true; since Denver the tall, white-haired old man in front of me has stayed in his seat reading a book called *Spiritual Discipline*. I close my eyes and nap. When I wake up my headache is gone and Salt Lake City is emerging from the night, a soft glow on the horizon that turns into glitter and then glare.

By Tuesday morning we're in Nevada. Our driver is talking over his microphone, the one customarily used to warn, "No radios without earphones, no smoking except in the last four rows, no pipes or cigars, none a them *funny* cigarettes." A sign to the left of the driver's seat identifies him as YOUR HOST, JOHN DOE. "The government," he announces, "the U.S. government, that is, owns about 87 per cent of this state. It uses the land for wonderful things, like the atomic bomb and the MX missile." Behind me a middle-aged woman, with dyed blond hair, pink lipstick, and sunglasses is exchanging medical horror stories—unnecessary hysterectomies, incompetent anesthetists— with a teenage girl.

We stop for lunch at Flossie May's Country Cafe in Lovelock. The blond woman wins $10 playing the slot machine. Horse Race sits next to me and says, "The old guy didn't get off, did he?"

"He's reading a book called *Spiritual Discipline*."

Horse Race shakes his head. "He's gonna need it."

As we continue across the desert, John Doe resumes his commentary. "Maybe you'll come back across here sometime during a wild storm. We'll go sideways to Reno, into ditches, it'll be a lot of fun." We pass some electrical installations. "The power company just put in for another raise. They won't use solar power—they use oil, which we have none of, natural gas, it's all imported, so you know whose hands are on it. I get real ticked off thinking of the old people on fixed incomes, who can't pay their bill." We pass Mustang Ranch, the legal whorehouse. "It's like a concentration camp over there," John Doe says cheerily. "All those guards and towers—that's to keep the mafia out." And how do *you* like your coffee?

Serious gamblers may sneer at slot machines, but for amateurs who just want to have a little fun without losing much, they're perfect. They entertain you with noise and colors and lights; they offer continual bits of reinforcement, even if it's only two nickels clattering into the tray; and if you play with nickels and dimes it takes hours to lose any real money. Slots are addictive; once you get into a good rhythm and win a few coins you start to feel rapport with the machine, and you know you can influence what comes up. And in fact I think there's something to the idea that winning streaks, even on nickel slots, are never just luck. In Reno I pass up an opportunity to gamble for krugerrands and stick to the slots. I win 13 bucks, mostly in one orgasmic cascade of dimes. After that I begin to sense that I'm losing rapport with my machine, so I quit and get on the 5:30 bus to San Francisco.

It's a local bus, dilapidated, cramped, and crowded with gamblers returning to Sacramento and the Bay Area. Many are black and Chicano, the first nonwhite passengers I've seen since Colorado. The bus is so small that every time the woman in front of me adjusts her seat back it bangs painfully against my knees; the woman next to me is eating a sandwich in my lap. After Sacramento I spot what I think are two empty seats in the back, but as I'm getting settled my seatmate returns from the john. He is a large black man, expansively drunk. In back of us is a young, fair, funky-hip couple. They've just gotten married in Reno and are expansively newlywed; the groom keeps hugging the bride and announcing, "Mmm, that's my mama!" My seatmate turns to me and says, "Hey, honey dear, my name's Coyle."

"My name's Ellen."

"Hey, how you doin', honey dear?"

"Fine."

"You got a boyfriend?"

"Yes."

"Hey, honey dear. Hey, honey dear. Hey—are you gonna talk to me? Are you mad with me?"

"No, I'd just rather be called by my name, that's all."

The groom leans over and puts his arm around Coyle. "Hey, man, why don't you change seats with my mama? I wanna talk to you."

The transfer is effected. "Hey, man," the groom begins, "you should let that lady alone. She just left her old man, and she hates the whole world. She don't want *nothin'* to do with men."

"What you mean she don't want a man? She *need* a man."

"You ain't lookin' at it from her point of view. She don't want nothin' to do with nobody. Forget it, man."

The newlyweds get off in Vallejo. I get off in Oakland. It's too late to see anything but the lights in the East Bay hills. I tell myself I'm in California. I call my friend Lou, an artist, well known in the lesbian-feminist community. She is stoned and bubbly. She is playing bridge with some women friends. She will come right over and pick me up.

I stand in front of the terminal with my pack. A long coffee-colored sedan cruises by. It slows down as it passes me, and a woman peers out; then it picks up speed and turns the corner. A minute later I see it coming around again. This time it stops and the woman gets out. She's Chicana, with long black hair and large black eyes; she's wearing tight black shorts, a magenta blouse, and bright pink lipstick; she is plump and very young.

"Are you alone?" she says, smiling.

"I'm waiting for a friend," I say, smiling back.

"Do you need a home?"

"No thanks, I'm fine," I say, conveying with my eyes that I know what she's asking and I'm not interested. "My friend is coming to get me."

"Are you sure? I can take you home if you want."

"No, really, thanks."

"Well, okay," she says, still smiling, and goes back to the car. It turns the corner and comes back again. The driver gets out, a tall, thin, light-skinned black man in a neat brown suit and a hat with a snappy brim.

"Look," I say. "I'm waiting for someone. Would you please?"

"Okay," he says politely. "I hope he comes soon."

They leave, and a minute later Lou's car pulls up. Or is it hers? I'm looking at it, trying to see who's inside, when she gets out and waves at me. I wave back.

I V

It's unseasonably cold, and on the bus from Oakland to Los Angeles the heat isn't working. The woman next to me wraps herself in a woolen blanket. I huddle in my jeans jacket, which until this morning belonged to my friend Lou. I love the jacket, but what warms me is my friend's gesture. I hardly ever give my clothes away. I'm not

an impulsive giver. A Marxist might say I've been infected with the
what's-in-it-for-me commodity exchange ethic of capitalism. A feminist might say I've been preoccupied with the unequal struggle to
take care of my own needs. Anyway I'm grateful to Lou for doing
what I find hard to do. It's as if I've received not only a jacket but
a vote of confidence that what I've received I will someday in some
way pass on. I'd like to believe it because at the moment there's a
glass wall between me and the rest of the human race. This wall has
appeared periodically ever since I left New York. I don't know if I'm
on the inside looking out or the outside looking in.

Nearly everyone on the bus is black, including the driver. It's a
cheerful, talkative crowd. The woman in the blanket is going home
for a visit to Bass Drum, Louisiana; the woman across the aisle was
born in Baton Rouge, lives in Fresno, and has nine children; the man
behind me is headed for Galveston. The woman in the blanket asks
him, "You got a wife and kids?"

"I got 11 kids."

"I wouldn't want to be *your* wife."

"Ain't got no wife."

"All those children by the same woman?"

"I've had four wives."

"Buried 'em all, eh?"

We pass a house with a sign out front: FOR SALE $40,000. "In a
few years," our driver remarks, "there ain't gonna be no more middle-
class people like you and me. Everybody's gonna be either beggin'
in the street the way they do in other countries, or they're gonna be
rich. The big companies, the oil and gas companies are makin' it all."

In front of me a woman with a purple scarf calls out, "I don't want
to be rich."

"I do," says the driver. "You gotta make heaven here in this life,
'cause there's nothin' after you die."

"What do you mean?" says Purple Scarf accusingly. "You an
atheist?"

"No, I'm not an atheist. I just think for God to help us we gotta
help ourselves."

The woman in the blanket grins. "He's gettin' himself in trouble.

But I agree with him. We gotta do it ourselves. We're God's instruments. His hands, his feet. He can't do nothin' without us."

She resumes her conversation with the man who's going to Galveston. He tells an elaborate story about lending a woman some money to travel down to Louisiana to buy a home, but when she got there they refused to sell her the home, so she came back to Oakland.

"I don't believe it," says the woman in the blanket. "She ripped you off."

"No, she was okay. You can tell when somebody's honest."

"Well, you didn't tell this one. She was rippin' you off, if you ask me."

My strategy for facing L.A. without a car is to pretend I'm a foreign tourist, complete with street map and the names of cheap hotels copied from guidebooks. My first choice, the Beverly Vista, has a single room without bath. In the terminal parking lot I accost a young man with long blond hair: "Where do I get the number 5 bus?"

He shrugs, grins, stares at my pack and my map; he is drunk. "Where are you going?"

"Beverly Hills."

He bursts out laughing. "You've got a long trip ahead of you. A *long* trip."

The trip takes an hour. For the first part of it I'm the only passenger who is neither Chicano nor over 65. I change buses in a section of downtown L.A. that looks like Times Square. Near the bus stop a preacher out of *Wise Blood* is haranguing a sizable crowd. As the bus turns up Wilshire Boulevard, I'm standing near a Spanish woman in a dancehall costume. Next to her a man with a Hollywood-handsome face and a cheap bright blond wig entertains his fellow passengers by doing some card tricks, then turning an ordinary 50-cent piece into a huge silver coin. An extremely old lady totters onto the bus and falls in a heap. Two men help her up. She's wearing platform shoes with four-inch heels.

The Beverly Vista is plain, clean, and neat, like a European *pension*. Apparently many of the guests are permanent residents. The manager tells me her first name and asks mine. I'm lucky, she says, the hotel is

usually booked months in advance. I feel lucky. In the morning my
friend David picks me up and takes me home for breakfast. He and
his new wife Karin live in a spacious, light apartment on a street with
palm trees, not far from the hotel. The three of us and another friend
of David's talk and eat omelets, chopped liver, whitefish, and bagels.
We are interrupted by a neighbor, Milly, knocking on the back door.

Milly, a middle-aged blond woman who reminds me of Sylvia
Miles, owns an enormous old silver-gray Cadillac, the source of the
problem. She and David and Karin share a large parking space out
in back of the house. By normal standards there is plenty of room
for two cars to drive in and out, but Milly is a lousy driver who has
trouble maneuvering her behemoth. Whenever she wants to leave she
demands that Karin move her own car out of the way. Karin has
begun to feel imposed on, and this time she politely insists that Milly
try driving around her.

The argument does not stay polite. "You little bitch!" Milly shouts.
"I'm a good neighbor—I'm quiet. You should be happy to have me
for a neighbor!"

She leaves, but a few minutes later the phone rings. "All right,
Benny," Karin says. "I'll move it this time, as a favor to you. But
you're the landlord, it's your responsibility to talk to her. She has
to learn how to drive her car. I can't be expected to move my car
every day."

The obstacle removed, Milly eases her Cadillac out. Even with the
whole space to herself she barely misses our back steps. "Am I okay?"
she calls to us. Agitation has clearly not improved her control. "You
shouldn't drive when you're so upset," Karin says. Milly gives her a
Sylvia Miles glare. "*Don't* try to be my friend."

That afternoon I go to a party in Santa Monica, where I've been
invited by Diane, an expatriate journalist friend from New York. The
host is also an old friend. Still I feel uneasy, as I always do at a party
full of strangers. At a New York party it's all too possible to spend
the whole evening standing in a corner, trying to marshal the courage to talk to someone or join one of those little groups that may
as well have signs above their heads saying PRIVATE CONVERSATION.
But this is California, and whenever I look as if I might be at loose

ends, someone makes a point of coming to the rescue. I'm relieved, yet my uneasiness perversely flourishes. I feel I should respond to people's friendliness by being convivial, part of things, *on*, but I'm not up to it. It occurs to me that if this room were a bus I wouldn't have to worry about being conspicuous or invisible, a wallflower or a snob; I would have an automatic legitimacy and purpose.

Later Diane and I have dinner and talk about the usual subjects: work and love. Yes, I'm really involved with someone now, after a long period of being alone. (Of being a loner. The image that comes to mind is a huge NO TRESPASSING sign. I am painting out the letters and will write WELCOME.) Yes, it's certainly a big change. Yes.

v

The eastbound bus is nearly an hour late. I commiserate with the woman behind me on line, an 85-year-old widow. Her husband, a retired physicist, died 17 years ago. "We were very happy," she says. "He worshiped me. I understood how important his studies were to him."

"Do you have children?"

"No. It's just as well. He wouldn't have been able to shut himself up in the den and work."

She is moving from San Diego to Tulsa to be with her sister and help care for her sister's husband, who was recently disabled by a stroke. "People say I should stay in San Diego for the climate. Ridiculous! There's nothing there for me. The people were all unfriendly, except for the old women who were always asking me to do things for them. Drive me here, drive me there, and not one of them ever offered me carfare."

In San Diego she has been living alone. "I like the talk shows— Larry King and Ray Breen. You learn a lot, listening to them. When my husband died I used to listen to Ray Breen—it was like being with other people. He really helped me."

Around 11 p.m. we make our first stop, in Barstow. A bunch of us troop into the coffee shop and sit at the counter. A cute, punky-looking kid in a leather jacket and sunglasses strides in and calls out to the waitress, "Double cheeseburger and an order of fries." The waitress gives him an up yours, buddy, look. "You were the last one to walk through the door, you'll be the last one waited on." Whistles, cheers, laughs from the spectators at the counter. The offender looks abashed, amused; recovering, he attempts a sulk. "Bitch!" he says, unconvincingly.

I sleep and am awakened by a man's voice, somewhere to my rear, yelling and cursing: "Don't touch me, you cocksucker, I'll break your leg and break your head with it." He carries on like this for several minutes; as far as I can make out, someone has brushed against him, and he's construed this as a deliberate insult, an attempted theft, a pass, or all three. People begin yelling at him to shut up and let them sleep. "Hell, I won't shut up! When I have to stop talking, I'll move to Australia!" Finally the driver pulls over, stalks to the back of the bus, and threatens to throw him off at the next stop. He quiets down for a while, then starts in again, in a lower voice: "You're a dope addict! I can tell a dope addict if I hear two words out of his mouth!" By this time it's dawn, and I can see that our foul-mouthed paranoid is an elderly blind man.

In Gallup, New Mexico, in front of the restaurant where we're having lunch, a Navajo man in jeans and a white hat is sitting on a ledge. The blind man starts wandering off in the wrong direction; the Navajo goes after him, takes his arm and turns him around. The driver shouts, in a voice loaded with contempt, "Hey! Don't you bother the people on this bus! Just leave them alone!" As I pass the Navajo on my way into the restaurant, I acknowledge the incident with an uncomfortable, I-know-that-was-racist half-smile. He responds, "Hey, sweetie!" and starts following me; I retreat into the cafe. When I return, he is panhandling. He approaches a teenager who has long, straight hair and a backpack and looks like a granola ad. "You're giving a bad impression of the Navajo people," she says primly. I feel depressed.

In the early '70s, when I lived with my then-lover Paul in a small town in upstate New York, we became close friends with our neighbors, a married couple about our age with a little boy. Jim, the hus-

band, now lives in Albuquerque with his second wife Maya, her son
and their daughter. I haven't seen him in years, but I've had news
of him through Paul; I know that Maya is black, that both of them
have become born-again Christians. In the old days Jim's attitude
toward religion of any sort was actively hostile. Still his conversion
doesn't really surprise me; it seems consistent with his need—which
he also once denied, though less convincingly—for a stable, more or
less traditional family structure.

When we first met, the counterculture was belatedly arriving in
small-town America. Jim and his wife Gail had been straight-arrow
schoolteachers, and she had quit her job when the baby was born.
Jim began letting his hair grow. They both began smoking dope. Our
households were increasingly intertwined; we wandered in and out
of each other's apartments, ate communal dinners, and Paul and I did
a lot of babysitting. Jim hated teaching and Gail hated staying home,
so they switched roles. They had affairs and eventually split up. There
were always tensions between Jim and me—over feminism, over our
uneasy and ambivalent sexual attraction to each other—and there was
always affection. Waiting in the Albuquerque terminal I feel a little
tense, but mostly affectionate.

Jim picks me up in his truck on his way home from work. He looks
pretty much the same—tall, thin, bearded, full of nervous energy.
He has a job managing an employment service and hopes someday
to start his own. "I wouldn't charge fees to people, only businesses. I
can't see anyone having to pay for a job."

I ask him how he likes Albuquerque.

"I hate it. The people are lazy—what I call basic energy, they call
'the New York hype.' I've become a bigot—I'm not into Spanish culture at all, I'm not into adobe houses, I'm not into Indian beads and
jewelry that all looks alike. We have a nice church, but that's about it."
He's thought a lot about moving back east, but Maya, who grew up
in Bedford-Stuyvesant, is worried it wouldn't be good for the kids.
"Maybe we'll go to Colorado," he muses.

Albuquerque is flat, dusty, featureless except for the mountains on
the horizon. The sun glares. Jim and his family live in a complex of
two-story apartment houses next to a highway. Their apartment is

unpretentious and full of children's clutter. Religious homilies hang on the walls, and over the dining room table a tile offers a Recipe for a Happy Home, with instructions like "Combine two hearts. Blend into one."

I meet Maya, a slender woman with light skin and freckles, a mass of black hair, a no-bullshit, this-is-me directness; her son Jeff, who is wearing a green shirt that says "Spirit Power" on the back; and plump toddler Penny. We sit in the living room and Jim asks me what's going on in New York. Automatically I start complaining about the women's movement—so much energy attacking pornography instead of defending abortion rights—then stop in confusion, realizing I can no longer assume agreement, or even sympathy, on such matters.

"I guess you might have a different point of view," I say.

Jim smiles. "Around here the anti-pornography thing comes from the churches—we don't want this in our community, it's immoral. I can get into that."

"Well, I've been curious, needless to say, about how you got into religion."

"I don't call it religion—I can't stand religion. I call it my faith," Jim says, looking nervous. Does he think I'm going to argue with him? We've had some fearsome arguments in the past; we're both capable of dirty fighting. There was a time when I might have tried to argue him out of his faith, but that was before my brother became an Orthodox rabbi. "It comes out of an experience of the holy spirit. It's hard to describe. I haven't intellectualized it, and I don't want to. I can shoot down Christianity logically, just the way I always did, but it's beside the point, because it's an experience of being a new person, looking at things in a different way."

"It sounds like the kind of experience I've had on acid," I say, trying to be helpful. Jim looks nervous again. "Satan is a good counterfeiter," he says gently. "I think that's what the drug movement was about."

I remark on the difference between his attitude toward Christianity and my brother's view of Judaism as above all a reasoned commitment. "You should read what scripture says about the Jews,"

Jim says. "The Christ-killer thing is a lot of crap. That never came from people of faith."

"What does it say?"

"The Jews are the chosen people of the Lord, and they've been repeatedly tolerated and punished for their disobedience. Culminating," Jim says, directing an affectionately exasperated look at me and the stiff-necked people I represent, "with their rejection of His son. Come Armageddon, there are going to be a lot of Jews hailing the arrival of the Messiah."

"You're involved with the women's movement, right?" Maya says. "Why is that crazy person, what's her name, against the ERA? I don't see anything wrong with it." Jim agrees that the argument that the ERA would destroy the family is bullshit. "If I thought it was against the family, I'd be against it."

"Well," I say, "it does challenge the traditional definition of the family. The traditional roles."

"The woman should stay home all the time and have 20 kids," Maya says scornfully. She's about to start work at McDonald's; Penny is in day care.

Maya makes dinner, and as we eat our spaghetti and green beans I tell them about Paul's present love life and my own.

"Do you have any plans for marriage?" Maya asks.

"I don't believe in marriage," I pompously reply, suddenly overtaken with an urge to declare myself, to draw lines. "But we may live together," I add, bracing for anxiety like a bad swimmer in rough surf.

By the time I get up the next morning Jim has left for an early men's fellowship meeting at the church. Maya and I sit and talk about New York, about the Village.

"I love New York, I love the urban atmosphere. But I worry about bringing Jeff up there. I know my kid. On the other hand, I grew up there, and I turned out all right." Racial prejudice is worse out here, she says. But then, she's gotten more prejudiced herself; she can understand where the Indians are coming from, but still she feels resentful having to pay for their publicly supported housing when it costs so much to feed a family.

I ask if Jeff ever sees his father, whom Jim describes as "a hustler and numbers runner." "No, we're not in touch, Jeff hasn't seen him in years. It's just as well—I don't know how I'd handle it if he wanted visitation. I don't know," Maya says, shaking her head. "The last time I saw him, I felt nothing. No love, no hate. I couldn't imagine us making love. It was strange, it was really strange to feel that way."

V I

"Love stinks!" a radio in the back of the bus informs us as we pull out of Albuquerque, late again. I've just spent a few hours with Suzy McKee Charnas, a science-fiction writer and transplanted New Yorker, and she's given me a copy of her latest book, *The Vampire Tapestry*. It absorbs me all the way to Amarillo. Suzy's vampire hero is not the supernatural creature of legend but a predator at the top of the food chain. In order to survive he must mingle with his human prey, pretend to be one of us, yet at the same time maintain total objectivity; he cannot afford either to underestimate human beings or to get involved with them. In the course of the book he commits both sins and barely escapes disaster.

In Amarillo I wait in an almost empty, unnervingly quiet depot from midnight to 3 a.m. On the bus to Dallas I drift into sleep, but wake up as we pull into a station and the driver announces a 30-minute break without announcing the town. I have no idea where we are and can't find out from the timetable because my watch has stopped. This feels intolerable. I turn to an old couple sitting across the aisle and ask, "Where are we?" They look past me. Maybe they haven't heard; maybe they don't like my looks.

Rattled, I get off the bus and walk into the station looking for a sign or some other clue. The bus stations in this part of the country all look alike. They have metal contour chairs in standard colors, Muzak punctuated by arrival and departure announcements, rows of chairs with pay TV, lockers, signs that say "TV Chairs for TV Watchers Only" and "These Lockers are for Use of Trailways Passengers Only," buzzer systems so that a clerk can check your ticket before letting you in.

I stop at the ticket counter. "Excuse me, can you tell me where we are?"

The woman at the counter looks mystified. "Pardon me?"

"What town is this?"

A long pause, a we-get-all-kinds carefully blank expression. "Wichita Falls, Texas."

I sleep again and dream that I'm a vampire who longs to be a human being, like the mermaid in Hans Christian Andersen.

The center of social life on a bus is always the back. People who want quiet and order sit near the driver, the authority figure. This is a rule we all learn around the age of five. On cross-country buses the gap between front and back is accentuated because of the no-smoking-except-in-the-last-four-rows rule. Though I am a nonsmoker, loyal to my tribe, there is no getting around the fact that the goody-goody quotient is higher among abstainers of all sorts. On the overnight bus from Shreveport to Atlanta, I head for the back. Still spooked from my dream, I've decided I need company.

My seatmate, Linda, is almost six feet tall and has long blond hair with dark roots. She's on her way from Oklahoma, where she lives with her fiancé and her three-year-old daughter, to visit her folks in Tuscaloosa. She and her fiancé lived in Colorado for a while, in a condominium in Steamboat Springs, but they couldn't make it economically. What with the construction boom Linda's fiancé was making $13 an hour as a carpenter, but the cost of living was impossible. "The population is mostly single men who raise hell all the time. There are some single women construction workers. The mountains were beautiful, but I couldn't stand it."

Across from us is a chubby kid with a baby face. She looks about 15 and I assume her name is Ann because that's what her T-shirt says. But from her conversation with the guy in back of her I gather that her name is Jeanie—the T-shirt was handed down from a relative—and she has a husband. She's from San Diego and likes country singers and TV. She also likes to talk. She tells a long, detailed story about going to see Johnnie Lee at Disneyland and going backstage and getting her husband to take a picture of her and Johnnie and being rewarded with a kiss from Johnnie.

"Gee, all *I* have is a Johnnie Lee Looking for Love T-shirt," Linda remarks.

"—and this other singer in the show, he was tellin' me about once he was onstage with some musicians? And they were snortin' cocaine and smokin' marijuana? Not realizin' they're onstage! And suddenly the curtain goes up!"

We stop in Jackson for an hour, check out the pinball machines. Linda plays a machine with a Dolly Parton motif. She's a dynamite player and wins four free games.

We're approaching Fayetteville, where I can, if I like, get off the main route and catch a northbound bus to Fort Clare to look up my friend Richard. I haven't called to tell him I'm thinking of coming. Mainly, I tell myself, because I haven't been sure how my schedule would work out, whether I'd have time to make the detour. But also because of ambivalence—I'm not quite sure I ought to do this, I'm worried Richard will feel intruded on. Our friendship began during the same period as my friendship with Jim, when Richard and his lover Coral lived in upstate New York, 10 miles up the road from Paul and me. Richard is black, from a northeastern urban middle-class background; Coral is southern Jewish. The four of us were post-hippies together, enjoying or suffering a moratorium from figuring out what we were doing with our lives. Sometime after we had all moved on, and both couples had split up, Richard went to live in Fort Clare, in his grandmother's house, in a southern small-town world that could not have been more removed from the intellectually sophisticated, predominantly white, countercultural milieu he'd been plugged into even while he was holing up in the Catskills.

It was supposed to be a temporary retreat, but it's lasted about five years. A couple of years ago, when Richard was in New York for a friend's wedding, he told me he was feeling like coming back. I haven't seen or heard from him since. Coral talks to him periodically. Still, whatever it is that keeps him in Fort Clare, soul-searching, identity conflicts, comfort, or plain inertia, it seems to involve a need to cut himself off. So I worry about intruding, but at the same time I figure our bond has been strong enough so that I can presume on it. Better to err on the side of presumption rather than paranoia.

When we get to Fayetteville at nine Saturday morning I finally call, but Richard isn't home. Well, fuck it—the bus for Fort Clare leaves in 20 minutes, and it's only a three-hour ride, which by now seems like no time at all. As it turns out, the ride is a treat; I'm happy to get off the featureless interstate onto a country road that goes through woods, fields, small towns. But when I get to Fort Clare, Richard hasn't come back. I leave a message, explain I can't be reached anywhere, and promise to call back later. In the meantime I'll wander around, maybe find some real food. The bus station is on a highway, surrounded by fast food places, so I ask the ticket-taker where the center of town is.

"The center? What do you mean?"

"Well, the post office, stores—"

"The post office is just four blocks down, but most of the stores are out at the mall."

I walk in the direction of the post office and find the town's main street, or what's left of it in the era of the mall. It's very quiet; there are few people on the street and virtually no women. The only real restaurant is closed; I settle for a snack bar worthy of any bus station. After killing some time in the Christian bookstore, reading about how it's perfectly all right to choose to be single (so long as you also choose to be celibate), I walk down by the river, then back through residential streets to the bus depot, where I try Richard one more time.

Still out. Instantly I have an overwhelming craving to be done with all this. I've had enough. I feel ridiculous hanging around a strange town, three hours out of my way, making futile phone calls. Where is Richard, anyway? Does he want to see me? Do I want to see him? I know that since I've come this far I should be patient and hang around some more. I know if we connect it will be worth the effort. But I'm beyond patience, fed up with effort. Like a child I want to be home *now*.

I want to go straight north, instead of back to Fayetteville, but I'm informed this is impossible within the terms of my special discount ticket from the coast. Disgruntled, resentful, I board the Fayetteville bus. The three hours back feel a lot longer than the trip up. Then there's a long, boring wait till 11:15, when my bus to New York departs. It's the smallest, oldest, dirtiest bus I've been in yet. And crowded—another bus, on its way to Fort Bragg with a load of soldiers, has broken down, and our bus will be making an unscheduled stop there. A large woman with a baby on her lap is sitting next to me. Two soldiers are in the seat behind. One of them, a young guy with a mustache, asks me where I'm going, and we make the usual small talk. He keeps touching me on the shoulder for emphasis, which makes me nervous, and besides I'm in no mood for conversation. As soon as I can politely manage it I turn around and scrunch down in my too-small seat. Undaunted, he taps me on the shoulder.

"How long were you in California?" he inquires when I look up.

"A week." I scrunch down again.

Tap.

"What?" I say, exasperated.

"You know, almost everybody on this bus is gettin' off at Fort Bragg. You won't be crowded after that."

He keeps touching me and I keep trying to back off, impossible in such a small space. Finally I blurt, *"Will you please keep your hands to yourself?"* He immediately shrinks back and looks horribly offended. Though I consider that I am technically in the right, I feel like the blue meanie of all time. I also feel revulsion, for this man, the bus, everyone on it. I am out of place. I want to be home, with people I care about, who care about me. I want to be with my friends and especially my lover. To be welcomed and comforted and told I've been missed. The last time I talked to him I told him I didn't know when I'd be back, I'd call as soon as I knew. But it's after midnight now, and by morning I'll be so close to New York a call will be superfluous.

Somewhere around Richmond I blank out; when I wake up it's early morning and we're in Washington, D.C. Two men, not soldiers, are sitting behind me complaining about inflation. We progress too slowly up the New Jersey Turnpike, the world's ugliest road. Finally the New York skyline looms, and we touch down at Port Authority.

Home. I call the man I've come home to, anticipating pleased surprise. Instead the answering machine clicks on. Somehow, caught up as I've been in my obsession with reconnecting, this obvious possibility had not occurred to me. I feel irrationally betrayed and bereft; isolation clings to me like grime from the road. I reach for the phone again, to call a woman friend, but in the middle of dialing I change my mind. It's after all not so bad to be here alone, with no one know-ing, no one expecting me, no one to take up half my seat or tap me on the shoulder. I start running water for a bath and take my phone off the hook.

July 1981

The People's Picasso

Picasso is an old man who can still get himself young wives.
Picasso is a genius. Picasso is mad. Picasso is the greatest living
artist. Picasso is a multimillionaire. Picasso is a communist.
Picasso's work is nonsense: a child could do better. Picasso is
tricking us. If Picasso can get away with it all, good luck to him!
—JOHN BERGER

Some people try to pick up girls and get called asshole. / This
never happened to Pablo Picasso. —MODERN LOVERS

The Picasso retrospective at the Museum of Modern Art is,
among other things, a reminder of the convoluted relation between so-called high art and mass culture. It's the best attended art
exhibition ever; by the time it ends on September 30 more than a
million people will have seen this definitive collection of works by
the man who, in the popular mind, has become a synonym for modernism. Such an event inevitably raises questions about why people
are going to it and what they're seeing. How does Picasso's status as
a cultural icon affect our perception of his work, and so in a sense
transform the work itself?

In *The Success and Failure of Picasso*, first published in 1965, when
Picasso was still living, and recently reissued, John Berger argues
that as Picasso's fame outstripped that of any previous artist, his
personality—and his myth—came to overshadow his art. If the prerequisite for these developments was the existence of mass media,
the reason for them, in Berger's view, is that Picasso embodied an
idea of genius that appealed to the public imagination. Berger takes
Picasso's assertion that "It's not what the artist does that counts, but
what he is" to be an affirmation of the creative spirit as an end in
itself, a romantic—and, from Berger's Marxist standpoint, ironically
retrogressive—protest by a refugee from feudal Spain against a modern bourgeois world that "was reducing everything, including art,
to a commodity." The bourgeois public, Berger concludes, has been
happy to reward this protest, to identify nostalgically with a form

of rebellion that is "acceptable because it is familiar, because it belongs to the early nineteenth century, to Romanticism, and to the
revolutions which, safely over, are now universally admired."

I think all this is true; I also think it's too simple. If Picasso's myth
is on one level romantic, on another it is quintessentially modern; he
is, after all, the prototype of that contemporary hero (so prominent
in the mythology of the '60s), the rebel who beats the system, who
has it both ways. He may also be the first artist ever to excite that
most modern of suspicions: Is he putting us on? And I don't believe
it's possible to become that sort of figure entirely by accident. In fact,
whatever the overt intention of Picasso's insistence that being counts
more than doing, it stands as a shrewd assessment of the modern artist's actual situation. Far from being a sign of resistance to mass culture, the shift in emphasis from the art work as a self-enclosed formal
entity to the personality of its creator is a characteristic mass cultural
phenomenon. The kind of celebrity a Picasso achieves transforms the
artist's persona into a commodity—or, to put it less pejoratively, an
aesthetic object.

In Picasso's case the shift occurred not only because the details
of his life and his self-conception became available to a mass audience but, paradoxically, because of the immense impact of his work.
Picasso's success no doubt had partly to do with the fact that in some
ways his gifts were those of a great mass artist. He was constantly
absorbing and synthesizing other artists' ideas, and he had the ability
to distill a complex, idiosyncratic visual language into images that
have a vivid, attention-grabbing immediacy. His formal innovations,
in turn absorbed, distilled, and disseminated by the mass media, have
become the culture's visual cliches. His most famous paintings have
been reproduced so often that they are familiar to every halfway educated person, but more to the point, even people who have never
seen *Guernica* or heard of Cubism have experienced them second-
or twelfth-hand and unconsciously assimilated versions of their sen-
sory and emotional messages. By now, since Picasso's art has already
changed our way of seeing, it has largely lost its power to do so.
Under the circumstances it's not surprising that at a certain point his
works began to seem less interesting as objects-in-themselves than as

attributes and extensions of a personality—especially since a personality can be more elusive, fluid, and open-ended than even the most complex painting.

The MOMA retrospective powerfully reinforces this autobiographical (or mythological) bias. For one thing, the need to buy tickets in advance precludes impulsively dropping in for an hour at a time to see a few paintings; I would imagine that most people are doing what I did (twice)—spending the day, trying to take in as much as possible. After a while, inevitably, paintings begin to blend into each other. Furthermore, the exhibit is formidably comprehensive and arranged almost entirely in chronological order. There is no attempt to direct attention to salient aspects of Picasso's aesthetic by juxtaposing formally related paintings from different periods, or different treatments of the same theme, or works that comment on each other in ways that expose the contradictions and ironies of Picasso's development. There is no effort to counteract the familiarity of the work by inviting us to look at it in new ways. It is all merely laid out, without discrimination or editorializing—the sentimental and trivial next to the awesomely brilliant, boring stretches interspersed with electrifying ones. At first I was offended by what seemed an unimaginative approach, but in retrospect I think an aesthetically self-conscious arrangement would have been far less effective. It is impossible to emerge from the show without feeling overloaded, overpowered, and overwhelmed with a sense of Picasso as a larger-than-life presence. Yet it's not really a matter of his personality overshadowing his art. Rather, the distinction begins to break down: you are viewing a man, meeting an art work. The effect is unnerving and compelling.

It is unnerving in part because neither the man nor the art is of a piece; Picasso's sensibility meanders as much as it evolves in any coherent fashion. Since I find his modernity infinitely more interesting than his romanticism, the sections of the exhibit I found most compelling are those in which Picasso most directly confronts modern bourgeois culture, not as an outsider spiritually insulated by his creative genius, but as a participant, for better or worse. There are first and most obviously his pre-World War I cubist paintings and collages, which record the fragmentation of the organic society, breaking down figures and objects into their geometric components, destroying the integrity of the painter's medium by incorporating newsprint, wallpaper, cardboard, and other mass-produced materials. Picasso is not unaware of what stands to be lost through the irresistible momentum of technology and mass culture, nor is he entirely unambivalent. Still, the overriding mood of this work is exuberant. Its radical smashing of conventional visual preconceptions conveys a powerful sense of liberation and expansion, of explosive energy released from confinement.

In an entirely different (yet related) way, Picasso's engagement with his culture defines the work he did during the 1930s, while fascism was on the rise. His paintings and drawings from this period—culminating in *Guernica*—focus obsessively on the themes of sexual hostility, predatory aggression, and suffering, embodied in recurrent symbolic images. There are minotaurs and bulls, typically portrayed as sad, benevolent-looking noble savages, sometimes killing but more often dying or being murdered; mares with long, mannered necks, gaping mouths, and agonized expressions, often being killed by minotaurs (though in one painting the horse has her foot on a wounded minotaur's neck); matadors, often riding horses; ethereal girls in togas and wreaths; weeping, madonnalike women raising their hands in supplication or holding dead children. Anger and violence pervade these images; many of the figures—even some of the benign minotaurs and weeping madonnas—have razor-sharp tongues, fangs, or clawlike fingernails. In one terrifying painting a ferocious cat with huge teeth and talons grips a dead bird. In a 1930 painting very different in its iconography but similar in its basic drift, an amorphous, bloblike Marat lies oozing blood while his assassin, who looks like a dinosaur with a huge mouth full of needle teeth, bends over her prey and stabs him with a stiletto. (So much for the fate of the bourgeois revolution.) At the emotional core of these works are Picasso's conflicting feelings about women: they are victims and victimizers, children and beasts, powerless protectors, the objects of pity, horror, and need.

Whether or not Picasso was aware of Freud, he clearly perceived the connection between sexual and social pathology. In referring to a specific political event, *Guernica* makes explicit the underlying premise of the work that led up to it—that fascism and the nihilistic barbarity of modern warfare are crises of a sadomasochistic culture. Picasso's vision of that culture—*this* culture—is horrific. To look at it with his revolutionary cubist optimism fresh in mind is to come away with a devastating sense of failure: between 1910 and 1937 the energies liberated by modern capitalism have turned obscenely destructive. Yet despite the Rousseauian minotaurs, with whom he obviously identifies, Picasso's attitude is by no means one of romantic protest against modernity. On the contrary, his imagery suggests that the troubles of the present are grounded in the past, that the age-old war between the sexes is a war to the literal death, that psychically we are all its victims and villains, that the religious masochism of feudal Spain and the totalitarian sadism that erupted in bourgeois Europe are symbiotic. In its recognition that the personal is political, this conception of fascism is as radical socially as the cubist aesthetic is formally. Part of the power of *Guernica* is that it is implicitly self-critical, or at least self-questioning.

Perhaps Picasso was too afraid of the implication to pursue it. For whatever reason, after World War II (when he became a Communist and a multimillionaire and the world's greatest living artist and an old man who could still get young wives) he stopped taking risks. Mostly he seems to have been content to cannibalize his past, to imitate and even parody himself. In effect he became a member of his audience, a consumer of his own image—the great occupational hazard of every artist who enters the mass cultural arena. Inevitably the image has come to seem canned, static; finally it, too, is a cliche. The first law of mass culture is novelty: It has little use for an artist who has stopped changing, and even less—after the prurience has subsided—for an artist who is dead.

The paradox of this retrospective is that it makes Picasso come alive, and at the same time kills him off. Picasso is a cultural icon who is nonetheless culturally irrelevant, because his vitality is no longer the sort that can inspire a collective experience or a collective response. He can neither connect nor divide us. The million people—the knowledgeable, the passionate, the curious, the dutiful—who file through MOMA's galleries may make discoveries about Picasso and even about themselves, but they are learning nothing about each other. The most popular part of the exhibit is the first group of galleries, containing Picasso's early work through the blue period. Both times I went, these rooms were so packed I had an attack of claustrophobia and fled. Nor did I feel I missed much. I mention this not to make any claims for my superior taste or to express a horror of crowds. If anything, my point is that the people at the show were less a crowd in any organic sense than a great number of bodies who happened to be in one place at the same time.

For me, Picasso's work is full of contemporary resonances. His cubist and "sexual-political" periods, taken together, suggest with uncanny metaphoric precision the trajectory of the past 20 years—the challenge to received cultural forms; the liberating and exhilarating release of energy; the diversion of too much of that energy to the acting out of destructive fantasies; the cultural crackdown with its increasingly fascistic tone. At least, this is my Picasso and my 20 years. Is it anyone else's? Would I ever think to ask such a question about Cézanne? Would I ask it about rock and roll?

September 1980

Sins of Confession

The confession, as a literary genre, is based on one simple convention: the writer purports to admit to the reader (who may represent society at large, or a particular segment of it) some act or sentiment that the reader can be expected to find immoral, shameful, and/or shocking. The implicit claim of the confession is that the writer is braving condemnation, ridicule, ostracism to tell us something important; its implicit demand is that we suspend our reflex condemnation and hear the writer out. It is not the content of a personal revelation that determines whether it's a confession, but the writer's attitude toward it. Critics who loosely (and almost always pejoratively) label as "confessional" any writing about personal (read emotional, sexual) experience are projecting their own attitude—that the act of publicizing "private" matters is inherently shameful—onto the writer. A confession always makes a moral point or raises a moral issue; the prostitute who reveals all about life in the brothel simply because it's a titillating subject is not confessing, though she may go through the motions for the sake of redeeming social value.

In the classic confession—St. Augustine's is the paradigm—the writer fully concurs in the reader's moral judgment, and accepts a system of moral or religious values that upholds it. The confession, then, becomes at once a depiction of the protagonist's struggle for redemption, an integral part of that struggle, and an argument for the values that make the struggle possible. Turn the argument on its head and you have the anti-confession, in which the writer challenges the values by which he or she expects to be judged, and so recasts the transgressor as a rebel against oppressive norms. The challenge may be political (as with feminists "confessing" to their illegal abortions); or nihilistic, insisting that morality is a sham, that the only law is naked power; or antinomian, taking an aggressive "evil be thou my good" stance. In the soft version of the anti-confession—call it "guilty with an explanation"—the writer's admittedly bad behavior is seen as socially or psychologically determined; the transgressor is recast as victim. Like the traditional confession, the anti-confession is a brief for a particular world view, and it is also concerned with redemption—whether from an unjust social order, or simply from illusion and false guilt.

But there is yet a third confessional mode—pioneered by Rousseau—whose impulse is, on the surface at least, less polemical than documentary: its emphasis is on examining transgressions, rather than condemning or justifying them, and its premise is that the exposure of dirty secrets is in itself a moral act. It's hard for a post-enlightenment person to quarrel with that premise. Who among us does not believe that the truth will make us free? That looking unpleasant realities in the face is the first step to understanding and perhaps changing them? Yet in practice self-exposure does not necessarily lead to understanding, or understanding to change. Often, at the end of a documentary confession, one is left feeling confused and a bit cheated, wondering what, exactly, is the point.

More likely than not the point is a polemic (and with it a bid for redemption) that the writer doesn't want to acknowledge. Bad faith is the great pitfall of all confessional writing. The form offers built-in temptations to justify the unforgivable, abdicate personal responsibility, or demand that the reader's sympathies focus on the confessor's anguished guilt and courageous honesty, rather than on the victims of the acts or attitudes confessed. Many confessions are little more than manipulative pleas for absolution, or covert expressions of anger at victims for provoking guilt ("I've made a clean breast of it, I've said I'm sorry, what more do you want?"). The documentary confession lends itself especially well to such abuses, since it can sneak in all sorts of hidden moral agendas in the guise of pursuing truth for truth's sake.

In her memoir *Ghost Waltz*, Ingeborg Day has written a confession whose method is documentary and whose object is openly redemptive. She resists, succumbs to, wrestles with the temptations of the form, and ends up with a book that is as much about the process of confession as the content of it. The book is also one more piece of evidence—as if any more were needed—that in the post-enlightenment 20th century, redemption is very hard to come by.

Day was born in Austria in 1940. Her father was a National Socialist and a policeman who, along with his fellow officers, had been drafted into the SS when Hitler took over; her mother may or may not have joined the party, but "she loved my father." After the war, Day grew up in a society that, as she recalls it, maintained a thoroughgoing conspiracy of silence about the recent past, the Nazis, and the Jews. Though she knew her father had been a Nazi, she had no real idea of what that meant until, at age 16, she spent a year as an exchange student in the United States, where she learned about the Holocaust from her American hosts, TV war movies, and a high school textbook. Later, while working in New York, she realized she had profound anti-Semitic feelings, which erupted periodically—a sudden flash of hostility toward Yiddish (*"sickening bastardization of my beautiful-beautiful-language"*), a visceral revulsion at a newspaper photograph of Hasidic Jews, a "slight pronunciation problem with the word 'Jew.'" Those feelings, Day says, came unaccompanied by negative ideas about Jews. Nor can she remember her parents conveying any messages, verbal or otherwise, about Jews, though "I have no choice but to assume that my parents made clear, somehow, very early on in my life, that they were anti-Semites."

For Day, redemption means understanding and uprooting her anti-Semitism; it also means finding some way through the emotional impasse of her conviction that she must either repudiate her love for her dead parents and her need to respect their memory or feel forever implicated in their lives. The two tasks are connected, of course. The dramatic climax of the book is Day's conclusion—which emerges one night from her overworked and overtired unconscious—that "It was simple. If I detested anti-Semitism with my brain and my soul, I had to distance myself from my parents to a degree unbearable for me. So I detested anti-Semitism with my brain alone." She protests that she doesn't want to be "free of all that" at the price of losing her parents; it seems that redemption of one sort is damnation of another. Instead she tries to make do with the thought that she has never acted on her anti-Semitism, never let it show: "Had I not observed every decency anyone, myself included, could possibly expect of me?"

It's a bleak, unconvincing resolution, no less for the author than for the reader, and in a sense it's negated by the very existence of the book. Through the act of confession, Day has chosen to bring her anti-Semitism into the public domain. Private anti-Jewish attitudes may or may not have consequences, but a book about them certainly does; if it matters at all it will affect other people's attitudes. Confessions of bigotry are a tricky business; it's easy to fudge the distinction between confessing and expressing, lancing a boil and spreading germs. At one point Day laments, "There are no consciousness-raising groups for bigots." In fact, during the past decade or so there have been many such groups—of men talking about their sexism, white middle-class radicals about their racism and class bias. But the results have not always coincided with the professed intentions. Not only can consciousness-raising about bigotry serve as a socially acceptable way for bigots to reassure each other that they're not alone, and therefore not so bad; made public, it can also become one more assault on the sensibilities of oppressed groups. It is painful and threatening to be subjected to expressions of irrational hostility, whatever their intent. My own feeling as a Jew is that any writer who sees fit to inflict on me the information that she has nasty anti-Semitic emotions had better have a good reason. Still, as a post-enlightenment person convinced that genteel silence is almost always a weapon of repressive authority, I'm not about to suggest that people with nasty emotions (and who among us doesn't have them?) simply shut up. What I do demand of confessed bigots is that they aim for something beyond the cheap pseudo-redemption of catharsis.

Ghost Waltz does aim for something more ambitious; Day is trying to address the difficult problem of emotion versus will. Nonetheless, she often lapses into one or another kind of special pleading. As she explores her parents' past in the context of Austrian history, speculates on what her father did or didn't do and why he might or might not have done it, the book keeps threatening to degenerate into an apologia for ordinary people driven to Nazism by extraordinary social and economic pressures. As she picks at the workings of her mind, unable to fathom or control what she experiences as an alien psychic growth, she indulges in bouts of self-pity: "I was not born like this, it was done to me." Though she recognizes and fights the impulse to see herself and her parents as victims, more sinned against than sinning, it overwhelms her in one chilling passage: "I felt: The legacy of the Holocaust has destroyed my father. . . . I felt: The legacy of the Holocaust has tarnished me beyond all methods of cleansing. I felt: I hate the guts of every Jew alive." Not only have Day and her Nazi father become victims of the Holocaust; the Jews have become their persecutors.

Hard to take, to say the least; nor does it help much that Day is describing her feelings, not endorsing them. If I was (grudgingly) willing to take it, or take it in, and keep reading till the end, it's because *Ghost Waltz* communicates a kind of mulish, defiant integrity that makes you hope Day achieves her redemption and believe that if she fails, it won't be for lack of trying. Day is relentlessly self-conscious and, perhaps more to the point, totally devoid of smugness. She does not enjoy her guilt or feel superior because of it. She never asks for forgiveness except from a self disinclined to grant it. In one of the best passages in the book, she argues with a Jewish friend who tells her she can't possibly be anti-Semitic, not really—an anti-Semite is a *terrible person*. At that moment, Day's concern with showing that her parents were not *terrible people* is thrown back at her, revealed as the irrelevance it is. What matters, Day knows, is not the character of anti-Semites but the existence of anti-Semitism, of, as she puts it, "the necessary seed" that becomes "the jungle, dense and all-consuming."

Yet finally, Day does fail, a failure not of character but of imagination. Her "simple" explanation of her investment in anti-Semitism may be true as far as it goes, but it explains less than it avoids; it makes anti-Semitism into a symbol, without inherent content or meaning. Similarly, her insistence that she has no stereotypical beliefs about Jews evades the question of what her unconscious fantasies might be. Revulsion does not come out of nowhere; it has its source in fear— of invasion? contamination? Surely Day's reaction to Yiddish reflects some notion, however repressed, of Jews as inferior, a threat to her racial purity. And it could be that anti-Semitism links her to her parents in more ways than she knows. Day claims to have "detested and

adored" her father. Given that in the Western psyche the Jew represents (among other things) hated authority, I can't help wondering if
she clings to anti-Semitism not only to preserve her adoration, but to
deflect her hatred. Had Day not blamed her anti-Semitism solely on
her special past—had she been able instead to tap the wishes and fears
that produced anti-Semitism long before Hitler and will produce it
tomorrow—she might have discovered she didn't need it after all.

April 1981

Ministries of Fear

Listening to all the Ramboid crowing that our guys finally got them some terrorists, punctuated here and there by party-pooping moralizing about how we should really be attacking the conditions that lead to terrorism, you would hardly know that the *Achille Lauro* hijacking was a specific act, with its own particular purpose and logic (or lack of it). As far as the government and the media are concerned, it's simply one more example of "terrorism," a label now applied to all sorts of political or quasi-political violence, from the hostage taking in Iran to the assassination of Israeli athletes in Munich to the killing of Aldo Moro to the kidnaping of Patty Hearst and the Nyack Brinks robbery. Well, not quite *all* sorts—it goes without saying that to this administration the crimes of Nicaraguan contras or abortion-clinic bombers are not terrorism. But my point isn't that your murderous lunatic may be my freedom fighter; it's that what passes for public discussion of political violence is simpleminded. Which in part reflects, in part helps to perpetuate the fact that "terrorism"—so much of which is aimed at getting publicity in the first place—is itself increasingly simpleminded and (except, of course, from the victims' perspective) trivial.

Terrorism once had a fairly specific meaning; it was understood to be a kind of warfare, practiced by liberation movements and by governments bent on suppressing them. In its classic form—as immortalized in *The Battle of Algiers*—the point of revolutionary terrorism was to demoralize an occupying army or colonial population by making it feel that a guerrilla lurked around every corner, that any ordinary café could turn into a death trap. Terrorists might attack particular cops or officials in retaliation for specific acts, but in general the targets of terror were defined less by what they as individuals did than by who they were: people who weren't supposed to be there.

The terrorist message was that there was no neutral ground. But most people, even soldiers in occupying armies, even prosperous settlers, didn't relish being held personally responsible for imperialism; they saw themselves as ordinary, decent people trying to live their lives. Through terrorism the revolutionists meant to inspire the question, "Is the empire worth getting my head blown off?" At the same time, back in the metropole, the bloodshed would serve to erode the myth of the happy natives (*French citizens*, in the Algerian case), while the government's counterterrorism would horrify fastidious middle-class intellectuals, again inspiring, on a larger scale, the question of benefits and costs.

Similarly, the point of counterrevolutionary terror (the state, of course, had the advantage of police power, with its apparatus of surveillance, prison, torture, and so on) was not only to punish activists in the movement but to keep the majority of people from joining them. Since the entire subject population was suspect by definition, giving the slightest grounds for suspicion (being in the wrong place at the wrong time, or with the wrong expression on one's face, or simply inflaming some cop's paranoid imagination) could mean death.

What marks political violence as terrorism is that its victims are in a sense incidental. Its purpose is to create a psychology, a climate. To some extent this is true of all war; the purpose of fighting is never just to secure a piece of territory but to intimidate—terrorize—the enemy into giving up. Unlike conventional warfare, terrorism recognizes no clear distinction between combatants and civilians; but in the last 40 years modern bombing technology and the logistics of fighting in the countryside have all but destroyed that distinction. So on one level terrorism is simply an aspect of war that's more or less central depending on the context.

In general, governments turn to open terrorism (secret complicity with terrorists is another story) as a last resort, when normal means of social control have broken down. (Totalitarian states are defined precisely by their institution of permanent, preemptive counterrevolutionary terror; some governments, of course, use totalitarian methods against subordinate races or other "dangerous" elements, while turning a more benign face to the rest of the population.) Terrorism is more likely to be the strategy of choice for insurgents, displaced people, or rebels without organized armies. It's also a prominent feature of the social "wars" fought by groups struggling to maintain their dominance—especially when a putatively democratic government must keep its hands looking clean. Lynching and rape are terrorist tactics. The abortion-clinic bombings are a form of terrorism, aimed at shutting down *all* clinics by burdening them with prohibitive insurance and security costs as well as scaring off medical workers and potential patients.

Terrorism is best adapted to "people's" wars for obvious reasons—anyone who can lay hands on a gun or a grenade or a homemade bomb can be a terrorist. This accounts, in part, for the peculiar self-righteousness with which an American government not known for its nonviolence denounces terrorists, declaring them "common criminals" who are nonetheless uncommonly hateful. Unlike common criminals, terrorists, in claiming political legitimacy, challenge the authorities' *moral* monopoly on force.

That challenge has a decided double edge, and not only because it has come from the right as often as the left (more often, in this country). Only a moral idiot would argue that "people's" terrorism is more of a threat to civilization than the awesome destructiveness and apocalyptic potential of officially sanctioned violence over the past half-century. Yet the fact that anyone can use terrorist methods—and in doing so claim the aura of seriousness that surrounds political crimes, as opposed to "common" ones—poses a threat of another sort. Reliance on such methods tends to take on a momentum of its own, so that they're used more and more casually, with less and less discrimination in the choice of targets or concern for a congruence between means and ends. Finally, warfare is reduced to psychodrama; revolution is equated with the violent acting out of revolutionary fantasy, hatred and *ressentiment*, the impulse to make a spectacular gesture of opposition, or simply the desire to enjoy a hit of illusory power by forcing the world to watch as you hold a gun to someone's head, and listen as you explain why.

Without a mass movement behind them or any chance of being

more than a nuisance to their enemies, groups like the Black Panthers, the Weatherpeople, and their more ambitious European counterparts, not to mention out-and-out crackpots like the Symbionese Liberation Army, could only be caricatures of the revolutionary terrorists they admired—though their guns and bombs were real enough. Worse, in the long run, is the way promiscuous, mindless use of terrorism (or rather its trappings) has corrupted and trivialized national liberation movements. What did the IRA imagine it was saying when it bombed Harrod's at the height of the Christmas shopping season? Bah, humbug? Did the Puerto Rican nationalists who blew up Fraunces Tavern really think they were striking a blow against Wall Street? Did it occur to them that waiters and busboys might get hurt as well as executives?

If the *Achille Lauro* incident has any meaning at all, it's as a metaphor for this sort of solipsism. Like so many "terrorist" incidents, the hijacking was not terrorism in the historical sense of that word, however terrified the captives surely were; it was an obnoxious parody. Four members of a Palestinian sect (perhaps in league with Yasir Arafat, who's been caught before playing good cop in this kind of situation) hijacked an Italian ship full of tourists, mostly West German. Leaving aside the propriety of taking tourists of any nationality as hostages, the Palestinians have nothing against the Italians or the West Germans. But apparently (let's give them the benefit of the doubt) the hijacking was unintended. The original plan was to attack an Israeli port in retaliation for the Tunis bombing; the Palestinians seized the ship only because their weapons were discovered. Well, okay—if the hijackers had used the ship and its passengers simply to bargain for their own safety, I'd be willing to put the whole episode in the war-is-a-dirty-business category. Instead, they threatened to kill the passengers if 50 Palestinian prisoners weren't released—after all, why let good hostages go to waste? Then they gratuitously shot an old man (because he was American, almost as good as Israeli? because he was Jewish? because some hothead lost his temper?). And in the end the only thing they accomplished was to squander a little more of the Palestinians' moral capital.

Am I making a distinction without a difference? War *is* a dirty business, after all, and just wars are full of injustices. I'm not a pacifist, because I think there are times when it's worse, spiritually as well as pragmatically, not to use force than to use it. But I share certain attitudes with pacifists, especially the conviction that moral victories are the only ones that stick, that over the long haul social change happens, and political conflicts are resolved, only through transforming people's consciousness. To the extent that we objectify our enemy and define the terms of our struggle as might makes right, the struggle misses its point. Algeria ended up with the government the FLN deserved. And the "revisionist" strain of Zionism, with its roots in Deir Yassin and its flowers in Lebanon, has propelled Israel toward disaster. So I think it makes sense to look on violence as a tragic last resort, to ask of any violent act that it be necessary to prevent physical destruction or soul-destroying violation, and that it be directed as narrowly as possible to those most responsible for the conflict. I'm glad the French resistance used terror against the Germans—and I think our bombing of Dresden was a war crime. In the Middle East, tragedy may be inevitable, but the capture of the *Achille Lauro* was merely farce.

November 1985

Exile on Main Street: What the Pollard Case Means to Jews

When Jonathan Jay Pollard was sentenced to life in prison, I thought we were in for some national psychodrama, and perhaps some nasty politics. It didn't happen. If you're reading this article because you're angry about (or at) Pollard, you're probably Jewish. If, on the other hand, you're thinking, "Pollard? Oh yeah, one of those spy scandals—was there something special about him?" you're probably not. A *New York Times* poll published in April found that 62 per cent of the Jews sampled, but only 18 per cent of the gentiles, knew that Pollard, an American Jew, had been convicted of spying for Israel.

Pollard, who says that while he was paid for his efforts, he spied out of commitment to Zionism, was sentenced in Washington, D.C., in March. Afterward, the U.S. attorney for the District of Columbia pronounced it "highly unlikely" that he would ever be eligible for parole. If this is true, Pollard, who is only 32, could serve 40 years or more. Such a punishment, for the crime of passing military intelligence to an ally in peacetime, is almost unheard of. In a letter to the *Times*, Robert C. Liebman, an assistant professor of sociology at Princeton, provides some illuminating comparisons: in 1985 an American who, like Pollard, is a former naval intelligence analyst got two years for "stealing secret Navy documents for a British publication"; in 1982 an American who sold "secret electronic-warfare documents" to South Africa was sentenced to eight years (he served two); even a former CIA agent, convicted in 1981 of selling the KGB "information on U.S. intelligence operations and the names of some 30 covert U.S. agents," got only 18 years.

The sentence was also unusual in that it overrode Pollard's plea bargain. He had pleaded guilty, apologized abjectly, cooperated with the authorities, fingered his Israeli contacts; in return the Justice Department had asked for "substantial incarceration" rather than life, the maximum sentence allowed by law. The judge, however, was more impressed by Caspar Weinberger, who presented him with an affidavit—classified, therefore closed to public scrutiny—detailing Pollard's betrayals and charging that "it is difficult for me to conceive of greater harm to national security" than Pollard had committed.

It is difficult for me to conceive of a sillier charge. Reportedly, the information Pollard passed to Israel was mainly about other Middle Eastern states. Even assuming—a large assumption—that the secrets in question are as major as Weinberger implies, Israel's getting hold of them is less a breach of *our* security than a diplomatic embarrassment. To put the least conspiratorial interpretation on Weinberger's overweening outrage, he was furious at the Israeli government's insistence that it had nothing to do with this "rogue operation," closely followed by its nose-thumbing promotion of Pollard's contact, Col. Aviem Sella, just before Sella was indicted for espionage in the U.S. This move was indeed insulting, not to mention incredibly stupid, especially in light of American-Israeli tension over the Iran-contra follies. But it doesn't justify making Pollard a scapegoat. Clearly the combined trauma of a Jew's disloyalty and a Jewish state's arrogance breached the limits of the administration's tolerance: just *who* do these people think they are, anyway?

In the wake of Pollard's sentencing, Jewish organizations worried publicly about anti-Semitism—not the kind implicit in the vindictive sentence (chillingly reminiscent of the Rosenbergs'), but the kind Pollard himself was said to have incited by lending credence to the stereotype of the treacherous Jew. And who knows? Perhaps there would have been a flare-up of bigotry if Jewish spokespeople, with few exceptions, had not hastened to out-goy the goyim by denouncing Pollard and the Israelis in the strongest terms.

As it was, though, the Pollard case ended up revealing little about the current state of Jewish-gentile relations in America except that being a Jewish spy for Israel doesn't mean much in the way of name recognition. Instead, Pollard became an issue among Jews, an occasion for the surfacing of chronic, profound, and painful conflicts over the meaning of Jewish identity and the Jewish condition. Who do we think we are, anyway? Especially when "we" are Americans and Israelis who often think of each other as "they," but rarely say so in public.

The issue was joined when two delegations of Jewish leaders went to Jerusalem to tell the Israeli government that its conduct was offensive to American Jews and had hurt their effectiveness as Israel's advocates in the U.S. In response, Israeli writer and former Labor cabinet minister Shlomo Avineri attacked the Americans as insecure exiles who supported Pollard's sentence out of fear that their own loyalty would be questioned. "Zionism," he wrote in the *Jerusalem Post*, "grew out of the realization that for all of their achievements and successes, when the chips are down, Jews in the Diaspora . . . are seen as aliens—and will see themselves as such. You always told us Israelis that America was different. . . . Your exile is different—comfortable, padded with success and renown. It is exile nonetheless."

This is a familiar Zionist polemic, equal parts truth and bullshit. The truth is that the Jewish organizations' response to the Pollard case was cowardly; worse, it was part of a continuing denial of reality. The American Jewish establishment insists that the mainstream of America's political culture is free of serious, systemic anti-Semitism. To be sure, there is lurking folk anti-Semitism, ready to be provoked by Bad Jews like Pollard, and yes, the Christian right is something of a nuisance, what with its dream of a Christian state—though it does support Israel, which is the bottom line. But the real threat to Jewish interests, so the argument goes, comes from the left—especially from critics of American military power and intervention in the Third World. After all, the Jewish leaders remind those of us on the Jewish left who support Israel's right to exist, it is this very American power that has kept the Jewish state on the map.

What they don't see, or anyway don't talk about, is the inherent fragility of this client-state status. Suppose there's another oil crisis and the U.S. dumps Israel to appease the Arab states? Suppose a severe depression gives rise to a serious anti-Semitic movement and the U.S. dumps Israel to appease American public opinion? Suppose the U.S. and Israel have a major policy dispute and our government tells theirs to shape up or else?

Not to worry, the Jewish leaders tell us. First of all, pluralistic America is different and won't turn against the Jews. And besides, the U.S. and Israel are both bulwarks of anticommunist democracy and sure, all friends have differences, but basically their national interests are one and the same. Well, there's no cruder or more potent metaphor for the profoundly adversarial relationship of nation-states than a juicy spy scandal. The Shamir government, in refusing to put on a halfway credible show of repudiating the Pollard operation, made organized American Jewry look ridiculous by blatantly advertising the unmentionable—that Israel has its own priorities, which don't necessarily coincide with America's, and friendship, shmiendship. Nor does Pollard's fate invite complacency about America's being different.

The irony is that Avineri and likeminded Israeli Zionists are far more sensitive about American Jewish "dual loyalty" than American gentiles seem to be. For them the choice to stay in the Diaspora is incomprehensible unless it's corrupt—a preference for soft living and the illusion of integration over clarity about the Jewish condition and commitment to the struggle for national survival. But the Avineris are trapped in an illusion of their own, which is that Jews in Israel are any less exiles than Jews in New York.

This is the sort of literal-mindedness Orthodox Jewish anti-Zionists must have been thinking of when they condemned as idolatrous the proposal to establish a Jewish state before the coming of the Messiah. For them exile was a religious concept, the Jews' fate in an as yet unredeemed world. For me, a modern, secular Diaspora Jew, it makes sense to think of exile not as a geographical condition but as a political and spiritual one.

In political terms, exile is the distinctive form of Jewish oppression. The basic assumption of anti-Semitism is that Jews are outsiders —powerful, subversive, working toward their own sinister aims, the worm in the apple of society. Avineri is right that when the chips are down, Jews are seen as aliens. And given the right kind of crisis, the aliens can all too quickly become the enemies, the pariahs, the scapegoats, and finally the victims. But Israeli Jews have hardly "returned" from exile in this sense. On the contrary, Israel's position in the world—as the pariah among nations, the alien "Zionist entity" in the Arab Middle East—has recreated the Jewish outsider on a global scale. And Israelis are as dependent on the revocable patronage of the U.S. as Jews have ever been on the evanescent good will of gentile ruling classes everywhere.

Spiritually, exile can be defined as the self-estrangement and identification with the oppressor's values that come of struggling to survive in a hostile environment. Denying or repressing one's Jewishness, siding with anti-Semites against Jews, sucking up to the powerful, compulsive achieving—such are the ingredients of spiritual exile in the Diaspora. But in Israel? What has it meant for Jews to govern (and be governed by) an embattled nation-state whose survival has never been secure?

The irony that Israel, child of the Holocaust, grew up to be a conqueror, an occupier, an invader, the oppressor of its own Arab minority, has often been noted. I want to make another point, one that has more directly to do with what happened to Jonathan Pollard, and with the question of what American and Israeli Jews are to each other: fear has induced most Israelis to support a government that equates survival with military power and no territorial concessions; and this government's policies, along with the right-wing chauvinist ideology that rationalizes them, are undermining Israel's distinctive reason for being—to alleviate the oppression of Jews.

Zionism as a philosophy, even in its leftist versions, doesn't appeal to me. I've never envisioned sovereignty over a piece of land as a solution to anti-Semitism, a negation of the Diaspora, a necessary focus of Jewish identity and culture, or the basis for building a socialist utopia. I see nationalism of all sorts, including national liberation movements, as problematic—an understatement when applied to the Middle East. Yet I support the existence of Israel because Zionism is, among other things, a strategy forced on Jews by a particular historical situation. What it comes down to is that Israel has given Jews something whose lack cost millions of lives: a place where, when you have to go there, they have to take you in.

These days, however, the Israeli government seems to believe that, far from the state's existing to insure the survival of Jews, Jews exist to insure the survival of the state. Its resentment of Jews who choose to live elsewhere took a grotesque form when, around the time the

Pollard case was approaching its denouement, Yitzhak Shamir demanded that the U.S. deny Soviet Jews special refugee status, thereby forcing them to go to Israel. Though Soviet Jews can get exit visas only by claiming they want to join relatives in Israel, most emigrants have chosen to come here. In the interests of "a strong Israel," Shamir wants to change that, and freedom for Jews be damned. Apparently, unsatisfied with maintaining Israeli rule over unwilling Palestinians, he's after a captive population of Jews as well. Let my people go, indeed!

Of course, if Israel is to survive it needs people. But if it can't motivate enough Jews to go because they want to be there, its problem goes much deeper than a lack of bodies. And the fact is that the social and economic consequences of the occupation and the Lebanon war have not only made Israel a place fewer Jews want to go, but a place more and more want to leave.

At the same time, despite the government's professed desire for more immigration from the Soviet Union and the U.S., it is doing its best to make life in Israel unattractive to the educated, secular-minded Jews of those countries by rewarding the militant nationalism of the religious right with increasing deference to its theocratic agenda. For Orthodox fundamentalists intent on getting religious law enforced by the state and imposing traditional religious values on a predominantly secular culture, their secularist opponents are in some sense not really Jews. Rather, they are carriers of alien and subversive modern values. The worm, as it were, in the apple of the Jewish nation.

The right-wing religious parties have instigated the most serious challenge yet to the concept of Israel as a haven for Jews—their campaign to amend the Law of Return, which grants Jewish immigrants automatic citizenship, to include a religious definition of who is a Jew. Though they have succeeded in incorporating some of their criteria into the law (which now stipulates that a Jew is someone born of a Jewish mother or converted to Judaism who has not embraced another religion), they have so far failed to win a provision declaring conversions invalid unless they fulfill Orthodox requirements. The latter demand has been another source of tension between the Israelis and the American Jewish community, which is mostly Conservative and Reform. Hitler, of course, made no such distinctions.

Israel's contempt for, and rage at, American Jews has been evident in its handling of the Pollard affair—particularly the promotion of Col. Sella (who has since resigned because of U.S. government pressure). In one crucial way Israel has never been an ordinary state: the political and moral basis of its existence—and of its claim to international Jewish support, in terms of money, political advocacy, and immigration—is that Jews as a people are connected and responsible for each other. From this standpoint, many American and Israeli Jews cannot accept that what Israel did to Pollard—recruiting a naive ideologue, refusing him asylum as the FBI was closing in, and denying any responsibility for what happened to him—was simply nation-state business as usual, one more confirmation that spying is a dirty business and no game for amateurs. (Predictably, Americans have been more upset by the seduction, Israelis by the abandonment.)

Still, it would be hard to argue that there was any personal animus in the Israelis' treatment of Pollard if they hadn't also gone out of their way to reward Sella—a step that, while disastrous for Pollard, was of no discernible benefit to them. The inescapable public message was that the Pollard operation was a good thing for the country, and the Israeli who "handled" it was a patriot worth honoring, but the American who actually carried it out was an expendable dupe.

Taken metaphorically, this message is a piece of wishful thinking. American Jews are indispensable to Israel's welfare, and it is partly this onerous dependency that makes Israelis so angry. It's hard to admit that you need the money and political support of "exiles" who refuse to give their bodies to the cause. Harder, perhaps, to look at the history of the Jews and realize that dispersion has been crucial to our survival—and still is. The way things are going in the world, it's not unthinkable that one of these days, Israelis may need a haven in America.

Meanwhile, Jonathan Jay Pollard is in prison. The American Jewish establishment has expressed no second thoughts; the Israelis have grudgingly acknowledged pro forma responsibility for the Pollard affair, but decline to blame or punish any individual. None of these respectable Jews dares to recognize how much they and Pollard have in common: they all believe in the nation-state's right to their loyalty, merely differing about which state may claim it. And so they have forfeited the only advantage of exile—the ability to look, with a clear, outsider's eye, at the institutions that oppress us. In that sense, they are all serving a life sentence.

June 1987

The End of Fatherhood:

Family Plots

In *The World According to Garp*—the novel—a good family man crazed by jealousy accidentally crashes his car, killing one of his sons, maiming another, and castrating his wife's lover. *Garp* the movie veers quickly away from that scene, keeping the audience a safe distance from the horror, preferring to concentrate on Garp's eccentric but suitably heartwarming mom. In the climactic scene of *Shoot the Moon*—made in 1982, the same year as the sanitized *Garp*—a man who has left his family deliberately crashes his car into their new tennis court and gets beaten up by his ex-wife's lover. The camera shoves our noses into every detail. The modern era of family movies has begun.

As our cultural myth would have it, the family is not only a haven in a heartless world but a benign Rumpelstiltskin spinning the straw of lust into the gold of love. Sometimes, though, the alchemy goes awry. The most spectacular examples—the Cheryl Piersons, the Lisa Steinbergs—make headlines. The rest make statistics. And these days, it seems, the exceptions are swamping the rule. What has gone wrong? Many argue that the family has been undermined from without—by feminism, sexual freedom, and the decline of religion, or, if you prefer, by poverty, unemployment, and inadequate day-care facilities. Another view, often held in conjunction with the first, is that the fault lies with the viciousness of human nature, the stubborn lust and aggression that resist the family's taming.

Myself, I think it's the myth that's wrong. The oppression of women and children, sexual and emotional repression, and violence are all endemic to the family—which is falling apart because people are increasingly unwilling to put up with it, even as they're terrified to give it up. Yes, women want their freedom, and the destabilizing force of sexual desire has been, as a friend of mine put it, "if not legitimized, at least decriminalized." Men, their authority crumbling, are bereft and enraged. Children are caught in the middle. Instead of Rumpelstiltskin, we have Humpty Dumpty.

In Hollywood, myths die hard and broken eggs are regularly mended; on the other hand, directors and screenwriters are as vulnerable to the workings of the unconscious as everyone else. Which means that their movies sometimes blurt truths they don't intend and often tell lies so half-hearted and unconvincing as to have the same effect.

Consider, for instance, this year's mass culture phenom, *Fatal Attraction*. As the movie ends the camera lingers on an idyllic family portrait of Dad, Mom, and Little Daughter. After 90 minutes of angst, terror, and mayhem, there's no way to take this straight. But the irony comes out of nowhere—unless it's the director's semiconscious comment on his own confusion. On the surface, *Fatal Attraction* seems firmly located in the family-threatened-from-without camp, the threat in this case being that patriarchal bogey, the self-willed, sexual, out-of-control female. By the end the intruder is dead and rightness restored. But if that were all, I wouldn't have sat through a good part of the movie grinning shamelessly. Look a bit closer, and this pro-family parable appears distinctly out of focus.

For one thing, Michael Douglas comes across less as victim than as weakling. Unable to control Glenn Close or protect his family, he mouths patriarchal clichés but has no power to back them up. When Close refuses to accept her status as serendipitous weekend lay, he whines, "Be reasonable. You knew the rules." When she confronts him with her pregnancy he says, "How do I know it's mine?" and then, still not smelling the coffee, "I'll pay for the abortion." And when she asks him that most impudent of questions—if everything is so terrific at home, what has he been doing with her?—he says nothing, as if what he did with her was some vestigial male reflex he can't be expected to account for. His car doesn't crash into anything—it gets trashed by Close instead. His dominant emotion is fear, not only of Close but of his wife, who is Mommy at her warmest and sexiest: he doesn't dare tell her he's been bad.

Close is the inverse of that misogynist staple, the bitch who leads a man to believe she'll have sex on his terms, then tries to say no and gets raped; she leads Douglas on, then won't take no for an answer. "*Whose* rules?" she might have retorted had Adrian Lyne had a better idea of what his film was up to. Sure, she's crazy; you have to be crazy to break the taboos that keep "civilization" going. But her craziness doesn't happen in a vacuum: she sees that the taboos are merely the Emperor's old clothes. In a way her most terrifying move is to pick up Douglas's daughter at school and take her for a roller-coaster ride. On the level of plot this is jarringly implausible—why would the kid go with a woman she'd never met? why would her teachers let her?—but metaphorically it gets to the heart of the matter. Once all the boundaries are blurred, Close could be your wife, the mother of your child. The invasion of the body-snatchers comes home.

After all this unnerving stuff, the retribution at the end seems more a hastily contrived denial than a satisfying catharsis. Indeed, an earlier version of the movie has Close committing suicide in a way that pins her death on Douglas; that ending was changed, according to the producers, because test audiences thought it wasn't exciting (!) enough. Here's my own fantasy climax: as Douglas's wife begins to figure out what's going on, the spectacle of Close's vengefulness ignites her own feminist anger, long smothered under that sweet, nurturing facade. Close then kills Douglas, and his wife provides her with an alibi. Or vice versa. After that, the family portrait shot would make sense.

For the real irony of *Fatal Attraction* is that it has less to do with lust or love or infidelity than with a man's panicky craving for shelter from the storm of female rage. The sex in the movie makes no compelling claims of its own (compare it with, say, the limousine scene in *No Way Out*)—rather it's a double-edged symbol of danger outside the home, cozy security within it. And plausibly enough in this age of real estate as pornography, Douglas's relationship with his wife centers mainly on the suburban house they're buying.

A similar displacement occurs in *Someone to Watch Over Me*, which is also supposed to be about adultery but is really about male role confusion. Far more sentimental (and correspondingly less vivid) than *Fatal Attraction*, *Someone* is positively courtly in its attitude toward women: its set-up is the conventional one of patriarchal law and order—in the person of a cop who is also a good family man—protecting womenfolk from the violence of a male outlaw. But then the confusion starts. The cop is assigned to guard a female murder witness, a rich, beautiful woman whose vulnerability is not just circumstantial—the killer is after her—but existential—she has no husband to protect her, only an arrogant, effete boyfriend. As a result the good family man can't be home to protect his wife and son, who live in a bad neighborhood; worse, his assignment makes them targets of the murderer. What's a poor father figure to do?

In this movie, too, sex is only a signifier; the affair between Mike, the cop, and Claire, the witness, is a metaphor for huddling against disaster, safety eroticized. The real issue is, who gets the protection when there's not enough to go around? Who needs it most? Existentially, there's no contest—it's lonely Claire, whose wealth only underscores her need (since the Victorian sexual iconography operative in this film equates upper-class women with the feminine essence, working-class men with the masculine). Ellie, the feisty working-class housewife (a cop's daughter, yet) can take care of herself; she throws her errant husband out and learns how to shoot. Banished from home, the protector becomes the unprotected, drifting with Claire in that poignant limbo the family myth assigns to outsiders. After his wife saves his life by shooting the killer, he goes back to her and the kid not because they need him but because he needs them.

The ghost of patriarchy past, who haunts both these movies, emerges as the bloodthirsty main character of *The Stepfather*. No messy stew of obfuscation and idspeak here; what you see is what you get—a gruesome, comic, and totally uncompromising demolition of the myth. Which may have something to do with why, despite the boosting of a number of critics, it was barely noticed, while *Fatal Attraction* is breaking box office records. On the other hand, it seems to be doing well in video—in, as they say, the privacy of people's homes.

The Stepfather is the fantasy of the wicked stepmother turned inside out: its protagonist marries women with kids, and when they don't live up to the standard of his beloved old TV sitcoms, he murders them all and moves on. A year after hacking one bunch to death, he has settled in an all-American town (which he discovered through a magazine feature on the best places to raise a family), become a real-estate agent ("I really believe I'm selling the American dream"), and married a widow with a teenage daughter.

"Jerry Blake" is an affable homebody who putters around in the basement, building a birdhouse—a replica of the family's house, which he mounts on a conspicuously long pole. But there are signs of strain, hints of a repressive, perhaps abusive upbringing that has made him "old-fashioned" about his stepdaughter's blossoming sexuality. Whenever reality intrudes on his Father Knows Best program, he retreats to the basement and freaks out, banging his hammer around, cursing, and muttering, "What we need is a little order around here! A little order!"

Stephanie, the daughter, is on to him. She sees his phoniness— "It's like having Ward Cleaver for a dad," she complains to a friend— and senses the violence underneath. At first her only ally is that professional subverter of family loyalties, the psychiatrist she sees because she's having trouble in school. Her mother loves her, but—in one of the movie's more brilliant touches—is blinded by the joys of marital sex. "I never thought I'd love anyone that much again," she tells her daughter, and the code soon becomes clear: a romantic marriage is her license to fuck, and she's going to hold on to it as long as possible. Still, when Jerry explodes at Stephanie for letting a boy kiss her goodnight, Mom takes her side. A cursing session in the basement ensues, after which Jerry secretly quits the real-estate office and begins spending his days in a nearby town, building a new identity; he gets a job there selling insurance (another way, as he points out to his new boss, to protect the family), rents a house, and starts cultivating his future neighbor, a woman living alone with her children.

In *Fatal Attraction* and *Someone to Watch Over Me* the patriarchs manqué come in from the cold (or the heat), in *The Stepfather* and *Shoot the Moon* they run amok, but they're all responding to the same thing: a loss of power that has left them without a sense of themselves. "Who am I here?" asks the stepfather, when he inadvertently uses his new name in front of his wife. "Jerry—" she begins, alarmed. "Thanks, honey," he says—and smashes her in the face.

Ironically mirroring the marginality of women in the world, the men in these movies are, when not actively endangering their families, at best peripheral to the islands of domesticity they're supposed to head. Except in *Someone to Watch Over Me*, they are lone males in all-female households, mother-daughter sororities portrayed as self-contained, vital, full of sensual juices. The stepfather is constantly intruding—on a mother-daughter romp in a pile of leaves, a mother-daughter heart-to-heart. "If it weren't for him, Mom and I would be *fine*," Stephanie complains to her shrink.

In *Shoot the Moon*, Diane Keaton is the ever-competent heart of the haven, the sun around which four daughters revolve, and that centrality is the nub of Albert Finney's resentment. Feeling like an outsider, he is unfaithful and then leaves, only to realize that he has merely made his status literal. Furious at Keaton's seeming equanimity and frustrated because his oldest daughter, still angry that he left, won't see him, he breaks into his former house and spanks the daughter with a clothes hanger. He spends time with the other kids and, overwhelmed by the logistics of managing them, mutters, "How does she do it?"—not in sympathy for Keaton but in bitterness at what he experiences as her intolerable power. ("I was in awe of you," he later tells her, to her evident puzzlement; the way she sees it, he's a famous writer, while she was unappreciated, unloved, and subject to his nasty temper.) The essence of that power is simply that in some fundamental way Keaton doesn't need him. It's all downhill from there: even his new lover, chosen because she doesn't awe him, puts him on notice that he's expendable. "If you don't come through," she says cheerfully, "I'll find somebody else."

The wages of male irrelevance are—shades of George Gilder!—impotent violence or just plain impotence: by Freudian coincidence, the wives in *Fatal Attraction*, *Someone to Watch Over Me*, and *The Stepfather* all shoot the villain after men have failed to do the job. In *The Stepfather*, two strong candidates for the role of male rescuer—Stephanie's psychiatrist and the brother of the most recently murdered wife—get killed in the attempt. Mom shoots Dad with the brother's gun; Stephanie finishes him off with a shard of glass; she then proceeds to mow down his birdhouse pole with a chain saw.

Amid all this imagery of self-sufficient matriarchy and women with metal penises, it strikes an odd note that none of the wives have jobs. After all, power relations in the family would hardly be in such upheaval, nor families without men so numerous, were it not that women in the workforce are now the norm. The unlikelihood kept niggling at me as I watched these movies: surely a woman whose working-class husband has moved out would stop at the employment office before the shooting gallery; surely a middle-class lawyer's wife would be bored out of her mind living in the suburbs with one school-age child. For that matter, surely a rich writer who is something of a bully would use his financial clout to humble his economically dependent wife. (The only time this issue arises in *Shoot the Moon*, Finney objects to Keaton's contracting to build the tennis court and warns her that he won't pay for it. She swats him away: "Who's asking you to?" But if he won't, who will? Maybe the contractor, who becomes her lover, will do it for free? Apparently not, since Keaton later tells Finney that it cost $12,000. Where the money came from remains unclear.) It seems that men still want to believe in prefeminist paradise, even without them; the hardest thing of all is to admit that home, as they used to know it, is becoming a thing of the past.

The classic family movie, *It's a Wonderful Life*, celebrates the good family man as foundation of the social order. Jimmy Stewart has always dreamed of breaking away from the conventional small-town life to which he seems destined. As a young man he plans to go to college, to Europe; not wanting to tie himself down, he resists the lure of the hometown girl who loves him. But in response to urgent familial and community demands—and also because he falls in love in spite of himself—he gives up his dreams, stays in town, marries, and takes over the family business, building and financing houses. While his kid brother goes off to college, then joins the Navy and comes home a hero, Stewart can't even fight in the war because of complications of an ear infection he got saving his brother's life in a childhood accident. Outwardly resigned, he is a deeply frustrated and eventually desperate man.

What finally reconciles him to his life is realizing how absolutely he is needed: when, through supernatural intervention, he gets a glimpse of the world untouched by his presence, what he sees is a wasteland of moral disintegration and chaos. His brother dies, his uncle goes crazy, the druggist mistakenly poisons a child, the town party girl becomes a whore—all because he isn't around to help.

Capitalist greed triumphs (this is a liberal, or at least populist, version of the myth) because his building and loan company isn't there competing with the local (wifeless, childless) Scrooge; working people can't buy their own homes or start their own businesses, and their all-American town turns into a honky-tonk strip. Worst of all, Stewart's wife (the luminously sexy Donna Reed) ends up a timid, old-maid librarian.

In a pivotal scene Stewart, driven to the brink by the prospect of undeserved bankruptcy and prison, actually lashes out—verbally— at his loving wife and children. They are shocked into silence, and the scene itself is shocking, the rent in the social fabric palpable and painful. Stewart walks out contemplating suicide, but we already know he will be saved, the fabric mended, chaos averted.

A similar silence falls in *Shoot the Moon* as the family gathers around its patriarch, who is lying on the ground, beaten and bloody, after his tennis-court rampage. But this time the chaos that's been conquered is embodied in the family man himself, and the silence is that of a funeral. *The Stepfather* takes the dialectic one step further: the distinction between order and chaos, love and violence, disappears. After Stephanie has stabbed him in the chest, just before he dies, the man who has tried to murder his stepdaughter looks at her with longing, hurt, forgiveness. "I love you," he whispers. You can tell from his face that he means it.

December 1987

Andy Warhol, ?–1987

When Andy Warhol was shot in 1968, I went to the hospital along with my then-lover, also a journalist, who had gotten me interested in Pop Art a couple of years earlier. We didn't know Warhol personally and weren't trying to visit him. We just went and hung around waiting for news. I don't remember the details, only the conviction that we had to be there and the feelings of love and alarm that had only partly to do with an artist we cared about.

At the time, it was a commonplace among those of us who wrote about pop culture that artists whose mass-mediated personas were at the core of their art were ripe targets for assassination (Bob Dylan was the main focus of my own ruminations on this subject). Celebrity as an art form collapsed the distinction between artists and their work at the same time that other boundaries were dissolving—the sort that kept the soup can in the supermarket, the performer onstage, the spectators in their seats, the hipster in the ghetto, the murderous fantasy safely encapsulated in the unconscious.

Warhol—for whom Jackie Kennedy or Marilyn Monroe was as much an art object as any consumable artifact, and who was himself the celebrity-artist par excellence—was arguably more responsible than anyone else for obliterating the line between the avant-garde (which was supposed to appeal to an elite and be disturbing and subversive) and mass art (which was supposed to reach millions and reinforce the American dream). And as everything became an object of mass consumption, as art shaded into politics, image into action, the televised Vietnam War into the Abbie and Jerry show, it made sense that someone somewhere would cast some star in his or her own violent movie. The convolution I didn't foresee was that the star would be a film-maker and the would-be assassin one of his actresses.

Or, of course, that the next day Warhol's injury would be eclipsed by Bobby Kennedy's murder.

As it happened, the shooting of Andy Warhol had a political dimension, at least in Valerie Solanas's mind. A couple of Warhol's obituaries solemnly refer to Solanas as a member of a group called S.C.U.M. (Society for Cutting Up Men). Actually, so far as I know, the sole member of this "group" was Solanas herself. Whether she envisioned killing Warhol as a S.C.U.M. project I have no idea; she did, however, write *The S.C.U.M. Manifesto*, a supremely tasteless and wonderfully zany parody of male supremacist thought, which argued that biologically men were not only inferior but superfluous. I never read it as anything but satire, but later I noticed that there were feminists who took it seriously and either loved it or were indignant. I can't believe Solanas meant it seriously, but then again how would I know?

This is the kind of question Warhol would never ask. "Seriousness" was another of those categories that became useless in the '60s. The Beatles were on AM radio and therefore could not be "serious." "Art" was "serious" and Brillo boxes and comic strips and "consumerism" were "not serious" and so Pop Art had to be a "put-on." It's all the most banal ancient history now that the pop sensibility has been institutionalized as postmodernism, but in those days where you came out on this stuff defined identities and changed lives. Warhol's vision— that of the wide-eyed child or anthropologist in an exotic land that just happened to be ours—helped to free me from rules about what to take seriously that I didn't even know I was obeying. All through my teenage years, for instance, rock and roll had been my emotional center, yet I'd assumed it wasn't "serious," accepted without question that it was marginal to my "real life." Which meant that I couldn't draw (except secretly, behind my own back) on what it taught me about sex, love, and other kinds of transcendence.

It's been a long time since I've thought much about Warhol. I never read *Interview*, and I haven't really paid attention to his recent work. That's partly because his influence is so pervasive, the aesthetic assumptions he pioneered so taken for granted in my own cultural milieu. But it's also because the context is different. In a reactionary time mass culture is no longer a fount of subversive energy. Sure, there are battles being fought over culture as over everything else, but they aren't the kinds of battles that lend themselves to the wide-eyed anthropologist treatment. To the end, Warhol remained fascinated by the rich and famous. But in the '80s money isn't about poor Liverpudlian kids beating the system; it's about making millions on insider trading. And as for fame, I don't read *Interview*—or *People* for that matter—because I find celebrities boring. They no longer reflect back to me what I'm terrified of being or long to become—or secretly believe I am.

So when I heard that Andy Warhol was dead I had no impulse to go to the hospital or call my old lover and reminisce. And yet I wish I could think of something to do that would fit the occasion. Because I feel bereft, and again my feelings have to do with something more than the man himself. Andy, who once said "I like my paintings because anyone can do them," would understand.

March 1987

In Defense of Offense:

Salman Rushdie's Religious Problem

A novelist transgresses the taboos of one of the world's most politically powerful organized religions: he treats what for devout Moslems are absolute truths and sacred writings as if they were simply the stuff of myth, a narrative like any other, fair game for his irreverent imagination. Islamic governments ban the book; in other countries political pressure and threats of violence lead to its suppression; Moslem demonstrators hold book burnings. Finally, in a dramatic denouement, the dictator of an Islamic theocracy calls on the faithful around the world to execute the author for blasphemy.

You'd think it could hardly be clearer who is the oppressor and who the victim in this scenario. Yet a lot of people have got it turned around. As they see it, the Moslems who want Salman Rushdie's book or even his life stamped out are not religious zealots bent on imposing their world view on the rest of us—they are people who have been cruelly insulted and are lashing out in self-defense. Rushdie, on the other hand, is not being subjected to intolerable persecution for being an exponent and a symbol of secular modernism—he is guilty of moral insensitivity for offending the religious sensibilities of a billion Moslems (this dubious statistic is always invoked as if it somehow proves the magnitude of Rushdie's sin, rather than the intimidating character of the ayatollah's decree).

Thus Cardinal "Catholics would be foolish to read the book" O'Connor condemns Rushdie's work and the threat to his life with unctuous evenhandedness. President Bush begins his slap on Khomeini's wrist with, "However offensive that book may be . . ." The British government assures Iran that in protecting Rushdie's life it is not defending his "offensive" book. Pat Buchanan has no sympathy for a man who not only doesn't respect religion, but is a leftist ("Let Ortega give Rushdie shelter"). Juan Gonzalez of the *Daily News* defines the issue as the power of publishers and "upscale white Americans" to ignore the voices of "a billion Moslems," and points out that not only foreigners but "*American* Moslems, of which there are at least 8 million, declared the book profanity against Islam." S. Nomanul Haq, a tutor at Harvard, writes Rushdie an open letter in the *Times* that says the death sentence is too bad, but he asked for it: "You have elicited the rage of entire nations. This is a pity. But, Mr. Rushdie, you have cut them and they are bleeding: Do something quickly to heal the wound." Liberal Christian theologian Harvey Cox criticizes the writers who demonstrated in support of Rushdie: "They don't seem to engage the actual hurt and rage of the people." Jimmy Carter lectures: "A direct insult." Ironically, Rushdie's own apology for offending, made under the worst kind of duress, did not move his enemies for a moment (Haq accurately dismisses it as "glaringly perfunctory"), yet it has helped to give credence to the notion that he has something to answer for.

It's not exactly news that in the modern world one group's absolute religious truths are another's inspirational myths, historical-cultural narratives, utopian displacements, absurd fairy tales, or pernicious dogmas. If absolutists are offended, hurt, outraged to an unbearable degree by the simple public expression of opposing versions of reality, their quarrel is not just with Rushdie but with the history of the last two centuries. Their passion attests less to the depth of their faith than to a panicked recognition of its fragility: Rushdie was, after all, born a Moslem; if he could be seduced by these alien ideas, why not they? That recognition lurks behind the double standard implicit in the argument that people have a right to have their religious beliefs "respected," i.e., not challenged in any way: in practice this right is claimed only for the absolutists, who are presumed to be incapable of tolerating, let alone respecting, heretical views. The champions of authoritarian, patriarchal religions offend my most cherished beliefs every time they open their mouths, yet I don't hear anyone agonizing about my hurt feelings (granted, I can't claim to represent a billion radical libertarian feminists).

When this spinach comes from the right, it's easy to spit out. More troubling are the left-sounding arguments, stated or implied, that Rushdie's offending Islamic sensibilities and white Westerners' supporting his right to offend amount to racism, religious bigotry, and/or cultural imperialism. Why, some commentators have asked, is Moslem outrage at *The Satanic Verses* any less legitimate than Jewish outrage at Louis Farrakhan, or at the Holocaust-never-happened school of history? There is a confusion of issues here. As a secular Jew, I was appalled by Farrakhan not because he offended Jews' religious beliefs, but because he was a demagogue arousing his political constituency against "Jewish power." Similarly, the Holocaust is not some article of faith that revisionist historians have offended, but a well-documented actual event whose existence they've denied, on the basis of no evidence but their conviction that Jews have pulled off a gigantic conspiracy to fool the world. In short, the issue raised by these examples is not offenses to Jewish orthodoxy but hostility toward Jewish people, in the context of Jews' history of oppression by dominant non-Jewish cultures.

Since Moslems, as mostly Third World people, have surely been oppressed by the West, I don't assume it's beyond possibility that *The Satanic Verses* might contribute to Moslems' oppression as well as offending their orthodoxy. Nor, for obvious reasons, can my opinion be authoritative. But if Rushdie's detractors are going to make that argument (Juan Gonzalez even claims that according to unnamed Moslem leaders, "the book is racist and anti-Semitic, as well as anti-Moslem"), they ought to offer some evidence. Is Rushdie's treatment of Islamic themes designed to harass, intimidate, or silence Moslems? Does it obstruct Moslems' freedom to practice their religion or make them more vulnerable to religious discrimination? Stigmatize them as racially or otherwise inferior? Perpetuate stereotypes or lies about them? Incite hatred or violence against them? Defend Western colonialism? Where's the pork?

There's some truth in the idea that the outrage at Rushdie expresses Moslems' resentment at the historic domination of their countries by the West; it's also, I believe, a classic displacement of people's anger at their political and economic powerlessness in general. But this only points up one of the more destructive functions of authoritarian religions—diverting people's "hurt and rage," in Cox's words, from their real problems and real enemies onto scapegoats.

Similarly, there's some substance to the claim that the fervor in support of Rushdie contains an element of Western chauvinism, raising the specter of a monolithic mass of Oriental barbarians beleaguering us enlightened folks. But the remedy is not to apologize for Rushdie's book, or qualify the protests. It's to keep emphasizing that the struggle against our own brand of fundamentalism is far from won—ask any American librarian, science teacher, or abortion clinic head—and that the virulence of Khomeini's attack on Rushdie reflects, among other things, conflict between fundamentalists and modernists within the Moslem world.

It seems to me that the deference of some liberals and leftists to "the people's" outrage actually has little to do with the possible political implications of Rushdie's largely unread words. Rather, it reflects the same kind of knee-jerk populism that led most of the left to celebrate the Iranian revolution in the first place. To a lot of people it was simple: the Shah was an unpopular, despotic ruler propped up by the West, the revolution an indigenous, popular movement. To me, it was nothing to cheer about that the majority of Iranians were rejecting one despot in favor of another—especially one who made no secret of his intention to purge the country of "Satanic" liberal ideas, wipe out the meager gains Iranian women had made toward achieving some semblance of human rights, and reinstitute the most medieval, tyrannical form of religious authority.

I rejected then, and still reject, the argument that a taste for democratic freedoms is a cultural peculiarity of the West, and that to judge a Third World country by the presence or absence of those freedoms is an imperialist offense to their right of self-determination. To begin with, the argument is contradictory: without the democratic principles of freedom and equality, there would be no concept of the right to national self-determination, let alone anti-imperialist movements based on that idea. There were secularists, democrats, liberals, and feminists in Iran before Khomeini killed or exiled them; there are secularists, democrats, liberals, and feminists in other Islamic countries; and there are immigrants like Salman Rushdie, who have voted with their feet for a freer life. Are they all tools of Western imperialism, poisoned by Satan, as the ayatollah would say?

The idea that only Westerners are authentically interested in freedom, with its inevitable implication that Third World democrats are irrelevant, a species of imitation Westerner, is deeply racist—another version, in fact, of the unwashed barbarian stereotype. It is also sexist. Of the thousands of Moslems demonstrating against Rushdie in the streets of New York, not a woman was to be seen; of all the voices raised publicly against the book, not one that I've heard has been female. This, too, is part of fundamentalist Moslem culture. To claim that it's imperialist to criticize a culture that subjects women to the authority of their husbands, keeps them cloistered at home, denies them the right to go to school, work, travel, or own property—a culture in which girls must endure clitoridectomies and wives can be put to death for adultery—is to deny women's humanity.

Freedom is a radical idea—in the end, perhaps, the only truly radical idea. West or East, relatively few people are willing to carry democracy to its logical conclusions. Last summer I spent a weekend in the country at a conference of former '60s radicals, Americans all. It was hot, it was green, and my four-year-old daughter decided to run around naked. One of the conference participants, a Southerner, was offended. She should be covered up, he said, out of respect for his culture. In my culture, however, children shouldn't have to be embarrassed about their bodies. Or adults, for that matter. My daughter's clothes stayed off, mine stayed on, and the conference went back to discussing the future of the left.

March 1989

Beyond Pluralism

There is more than a little continuity between the intellectual turmoil on the fractured Western left and the past decade's cultural and political ferment in Eastern Europe. Jeffrey C. Goldfarb's thoughtful exploration of the latter, *Beyond Glasnost: The Post-Totalitarian Mind*, is also something else: an argument—in a deceptively unassuming, anti-ideological voice—about how to conceive of and move toward freedom; an argument that could hardly be more relevant to the debates among American radicals. Which is why I found myself scribbling notes in the margins, arguing back, and in general doing the sorts of things I do when a writer prods me to check out familiar territory from a new angle.

Like Hannah Arendt, whose imprint (along with Orwell's) is all over this book, Goldfarb believes that totalitarianism is a distinctive social order that transcends its rightist or putatively leftist content; it is, as he puts it, "best understood as the cultural form necessary for modern tyranny." A totalitarian culture proceeds from an ideological "truth" held to explain all of history and human experience; it attempts to reconstruct every aspect of social life in conformity with this truth; contradictions, however blatant, must be denied and recognition of them forbidden. The official truth is expressed in an official Orwellian language that penetrates the entire culture and functions to make the truth of actual experience inexpressible. While this totalizing project is never fully realized—there is always some resistance, even in concentration camps, and behind the Newspeak that governs the routine public transactions of daily life, private reality with its ordinary language goes on—it constructs an alienated, pervasively censored public world, thus isolating and impoverishing the private world as well.

In the Nazi and Stalinist eras this monopoly on public discourse was enforced by terror. The abatement of that terror led to a crisis among theorists of totalitarianism, some of whom abandoned the concept altogether, while others refused to believe de-Stalinization was real. Goldfarb takes a different tack. He insists on the cultural continuity between Stalinist and post-Stalinist regimes; official truth and Newspeak still reign. But in the absence of terror, the cultural status quo is enforced by means of a process he calls "legitimation through disbelief." Though everyone knows the official truth embodied in Newspeak is a lie, the normal business of living—working, studying, traveling, getting apartments, and so on—requires everyone to act and speak otherwise. The result, Goldfarb suggests, is that people come to doubt the possibility of living truthfully, and this cynicism reinforces the system.

As Goldfarb sees it, the subversive achievement of the Soviet bloc's democratic opposition—best exemplified by Solidarity—has been to create a "post-totalitarian" sensibility and culture, a zone of free public expression that, by eschewing Newspeak and maintaining its independence from official truth, undermines the authority of the whole totalitarian structure. Focusing mostly on Poland, Goldfarb analyzes the work of oppositional writers like Adam Michnik, Vaclav Havel, and Milan Kundera and traces the development of oppositional culture, from its appearance "within the interstices of command, as officially accepted critical expression," where differing viewpoints could be expressed so long as "speech [was] channelled through some version of the official syntax," to the emergence of genuinely autonomous art, literature, and theater, to an explosion of free, contentious political speech, and ultimately to the confrontation at Gdansk.

Though from a conventional political standpoint Solidarity lost that showdown, in fact the crumbling of official truth accelerated, and post-totalitarian culture has continued to gain ground everywhere in Eastern Europe. From this perspective, *glasnost* is Gorbachev's attempt to preserve the existing system by accommodating the post-totalitarian impulse with reforms; of course, as with all such strategies, there remains the question of who is coopting whom.

The greatest strength of *Beyond Glasnost* (shouldn't it really be *Before*—or *Beneath*?) is its vivid and convincing account of the interpenetration of culture and politics. As the continuing backlash against '60s cultural radicalism increasingly takes the form of denial that it accomplished anything, this book is an implicit refutation. Not that Goldfarb makes analogies to Western countercultures—on the contrary, he argues that it's precisely the totalitarian situation that makes an alternative culture so crucial. Yet the very starkness of the clash between totalitarian culture and its opposition clarifies the issues in a way that sheds light on our more murky reality: I think, for instance, of how a generation's rejection of the Newspeak of official sexual morality, or a bunch of Berkeley students' exercise of free public speech on campus, has influenced our political life.

When Goldfarb does extrapolate from the totalitarian context, it's to make an argument that inspired my more truculent marginal notes. Insisting that "the fundamental problem is the idea of totality," he rejects all systemic analysis of the human condition—indeed, any theory that claims a disjunction between appearance and reality—as inimical to truth and freedom. Systemic theories, in Goldfarb's view, are inherently ideological, which is to say reductionist, and therefore tyrannical; they assimilate personal and cultural life to politics, denying the autonomy of family, religion, art, science; they discount people's lived reality as mere appearance, and do violence to human diversity. He opts instead for a radically pluralist vision of autonomous social spheres that aligns him (ambivalently—he doesn't like their theoretical abstruseness) with the poststructuralist/postmodernist wing of the contemporary cultural left.

I'm still a modernist at heart, at least on this question. Theory arises from the perception that there are, in fact, gaps between appearance and reality and connections among seemingly disparate phenomena that need to be explained. It's not the idea of totality but the will to power that perverts theory into dogma. Nor is totalitarian ideology necessarily systematic—Nazism was a contradictory mélange of scientism and myth, held together by an emotional rather than a rational logic.

A systemic explanation can never be complete. So long as it is a genuine attempt to understand the world it will be open to challenge and to revision in light of new information; to the extent that it hardens into orthodoxy it becomes its opposite, a form of systemic ignorance. But denying the gaps and connections and the need to understand them merely imposes another kind of official truth: it silences and isolates those whose lived reality does not conform to the socially validated appearance.

If, for example, one accepts—as Goldfarb does—the conventional distinction between public and private, and defines politics as properly belonging to the public sphere, the family and religion appear to be private realms, which totalitarian culture politicizes. It follows that the aim of post-totalitarian culture is simply to leave them alone. But the reality is that both the family and the church are (among other things, of course) systems of political authority that have historically functioned, separately and together, to subordinate women and children. To speak of these institutions—from the men's point of view—as purely private is to make that subordination a nonissue.

Goldfarb thinks the queasiness of many Western secular leftists about the role of the Catholic Church and the strain of militant traditionalism in the Solidarity movement (a queasiness I've shared) misses the point. In the context of totalitarian culture, he argues, the simple existence of honest public speech has an impact that transcends its content: it opens up space for everyone. And the Church's main significance has been as an independent base of support for oppositionists—secular as well as religious—and their journals, theaters, and other cultural projects. His argument convinces me, as far as it goes. (As if to underscore the point, a couple of weeks ago a thousand young people marched in Warsaw to protest the Church's attempt to repeal legal abortion. "We've Had Enough of Red and Black [Catholic] Dictatorship," one of their banners read.) But if cultural pluralism in Eastern Europe spawns a women's liberation movement—as it surely will—that movement will of necessity draw on, and contribute to, a systemic analysis of "private" life.

On a very different level, Western advocates of postmodern politics are also reacting to a hegemonic Marxism turned instrument of domination. Insisting on a variety of voices, a multiplicity of movements, and the decentralized guerrilla tactics of deconstructive critique is a logical and healthy response. Yet it's not enough: to tackle such systemic problems as ecological breakdown, the crisis in the family, the brutality in our cities, we need to make connections, and to disentangle appearance (the appearance, for example, that there's no money for public purposes) from reality. Ideally, there should be a creative tension between building models of the totality and tearing them down. Or, as two of our great systemic thinkers called it, a dialectic.

May 1989

Now, Voyager

When I was a kid, I loved the Hayden Planetarium. I don't know what it's like now, but the show used to begin with a simulated sunset. Gradually the sky would darken and the stars come out, till I was sitting engulfed in a night more absolute, dusted with lights infinitely more numerous and brilliant, than the ordinary city nightscape could ever be. It was thrilling no matter how many times I saw it. I read to death a booklet the planetarium put out called *The Sky Above Us*, which, along with some basic information about the solar system and the galaxy, retold the myths about various constellations—Pegasus, Orion, the Great and Little Bears. Space was, for me, the home of the imagined and the imaginary: on one level those points of light were the rings of Saturn, the red planet Mars; on another they were bears and horses and hunters; on still another, memorials to the mythic heroes and heroines and their tragic fates.

Later, I read a lot of science fiction and began to understand space as a metaphor for liberation and loneliness: there were all those images of men (sic) watching from their spaceships as the earth receded, tumbled through the expanding universe like a rolling stone. The origin of the universe worried me. Isn't it a contradiction in terms for the universe to begin? How can the boundless have a boundary? Aren't we really talking about the shattering of the universe—the eternal All One—by change, therefore time, therefore history? But then, how can a true unity be shattered? And if there never was a unity, don't we have to envision an infinite series of beginnings? Since I'd never heard of Lacan or Derrida, I didn't know these were naive questions.

My response to the Challenger explosion was horror, depression, and a sense of some missing connection I couldn't define. Finally I

realized that this was the first time something about the space program had really moved me. Even the first man on the moon had not
excited me as much as the planetarium shows of my youth. In fact,
I somehow missed watching the moonwalk on TV. I don't remember the circumstances—did I purposely decide not to watch it? did
I forget? did I have a deadline?—but the deeper reason is clear: I
felt alienated from the American version of space flight. I wanted to
go to the moon myself—what science fiction fan doesn't? I at least
wanted to imagine going to the moon myself. But NASA's iconography left no room for such fantasies. Not only was the space program
in those days as masculine as a cowboy in a foxhole, not to mention
relentlessly WASP and middle-American, it was sealed off, owned by
a separate, secret society—the military. Surprise, surprise: space had
been packaged and sold to Congress as a metaphor for conquest.

The Right Stuff, a book that gets better and better on rereading,
is not about space but about the psychology of fighter pilots. My
thumbnail review used to be that Tom Wolfe had used the space program to explore his personal obsessions about the nature of heroism,
which was a perfectly legitimate thing to do, but gave the book a
kind of tail-wagging-dog quality. Now it seems to me that Wolfe's
perspective is right to the point—that the story of the astronauts is
not about space, not about the experience of space, at any rate, and
that this is a central irony in the book. How could I have missed it?
(How could I have missed the moonwalk?) I even thought, at the
time, that The Right Stuff was a little boring. I know about that kind
of boredom—it's the product of repression. I was angry about . . .
losing space, and I didn't want to think about it.

On the other hand, I've never shared the antispace bias nice progressive people often express. Yes, the effort to "conquer" space may
be a piece of cold war public relations, a conspicuous form of phallic
display, an assault on the limits of "man's" control over his environment, and now, most ominously, an arena for extending the arms
race. But it's also an expression, however distorted, of human inven-
tiveness and curiosity and mysticism and aesthetic passion. I have
no patience with the argument that before spending all this money
and energy to send people into space we ought to abolish poverty,
cure cancer, and more or less solve all earthly problems. It's one more

version of the bread-before-roses, keep-our-noses-to-the-grindstone mentality: we shouldn't go to rock and roll concerts while a war is going on; we shouldn't worry about sexual happiness till we've gotten rid of capitalism; so what if (insert name of favorite socialist dictatorship) is repressive—it has free medical care; and so on.

There's something laughable in the grim notion that we should work through our global dilemmas in some predetermined, common-sense order, as if nothing we might learn from going into space (or listening to rock and roll, or thinking about sex) could make hash of our ideas about poverty and how to abolish it. For both proponents and detractors, the military model of space flight coats the strange-ness and terror of the enterprise with a deceptive familiarity. However NASA may define the conditions and the symbolism of space travel, it is ultimately dealing with the unpredictable and unknown. However space flight may be pressed into the service of nationalism and mili-tarism, the nature of the journey is anything but parochial: it allows us, for the first time, the possibility of literally seeing the world from another perspective. The potential effect on human life and culture is equally limitless; at this point we can't begin to know what there is to find out. I suspect there's going to be a lot of fighting over who controls space—and I'm talking about metaphors as well as weapons.

In the months before the shuttle flight, I followed the Christa McAuliffe saga fairly closely. I identified with her, as I was meant to. A civilian, a woman, a teacher—who could resist? This was still pub-lic relations, after all. Would they have chosen someone who was less wholesomely attractive, less of an all-American mother? Had they weeded out candidates with a history of, say, abortion rights activ-ism? It didn't matter (much); she, as they say, was us. I wondered what she would say afterward, if she would be excited by what she saw in a way no professional astronaut had admitted being—at least in *The Right Stuff*. I never wondered whether she thought about facing death. The shuttle flights were too routine, the only astronaut deaths too far in the past and on the ground at that.

Yet the disturbing truth is that McAuliffe's death humanized NASA as her participation in a routine success would not have done. Death is, among other things, a reminder of the uncontrollable, the unpredictable, and the unknown. I find myself imagining (as I would not, under better circumstances, have done) the moment of liftoff: this ordinary person (us), the thrill, apprehension, perhaps disbelief in being about to go where none of *us* has gone before. The rest is silence.

Some of my more cynical friends are saying, and they are not entirely or even mostly wrong, that despite immediate troubles for NASA the disaster will be a boost for the space program, for Reagan, and for star wars. Certainly the explosion, replayed hundreds of times, made a spectacular media event. The awful mental image of McAuliffe's children and parents watching her blow up on TV merges all too easily with that of Marilyn Klinghoffer watching as her husband is led away to be shot. The postmortem homage to courage and risk-taking fits comfortably into the rhetoric of an administration that equates venturing to the stars with venture capital. Sooner or later, maybe it's already happened, some asshole is bound to opine that Christa McAuliffe *went for it.*

But there's another side to being reminded that space flight is not just an impersonal exercise in American technological virtuosity but a human enterprise, with tragic failures, lost gambles, and irremediable suffering. For it is abstraction from that human specificity that allows patriotic—or antipatriotic—platitudes to crowd out our imagination and stunt our vision. Imagining the fateful moment, the moment time stopped, I'm surprised to find that I recover my old visions of what it would be like to be out there. I imagine the experience as erotic, playful; I imagine it as entering a secret world I'll be able to describe only in clichés: "What a beautiful view," as Alan Shepard put it in *The Right Stuff.* I imagine it as being at once totally exotic and somehow familiar, like giving birth. "So this is it," I thought as my daughter was being born. I imagine myself looking back at earth and thinking something like this.

March 1986

The Drug War: From
Vision to Vice

Wandering through the Brooklyn Botanical Gardens on the first expansively warm day of the year, snatching some time out from my work-ridden, pressured, scheduled dailiness, my daughter asleep in her stroller, I found myself thinking, "This would be a beautiful place to trip." A weirdly anachronistic thought—I haven't taken any psychedelic drugs in 15 years and have no serious desire to do so now. Even if I could negotiate the unencumbered 24 hours or so I always needed to go up, stay up, and come down again, it's the wrong time. The vibes, as we used to say, are not to be trusted—there's too much tension, anxiety, hostility in the air. Besides, right now I lack the requisite innocent optimism. Bogged down in material concerns I once managed to ignore, in thrall to New York's Great God Real Estate, I feel somewhat estranged from the Tao. "But what if something bad happened?" was my next unbidden thought that day in the park. "I have a child—can I afford that kind of risk?" Which of course answers its own question; a first principle of tripping as I remember it is that the main thing you have to fear is fear itself.

Whether or not I ever feel free to take psychedelics again, they remain, for me, a potent emblem of freedom. Somehow they disarranged the grids I'd imposed on the world, untied the Laingian knots I'd imposed on myself. They allowed me, for the moment, to see things freshly—the splendor in the grass, the glory in the flower, the ridiculous self-inflation in my self-hatred—and feel saner than I'd ever thought possible. This was an experience of intense pleasure, emotional catharsis, and enlightenment in its most playful, least solemn sense. My fellow trippers and I were always breaking out into what seemed to straight onlookers like maniacal laughter: sometimes we laughed because the people around us had turned into elegant giraffes and scared birds and angry terriers; sometimes because we realized how silly our most serious obsessions were; sometimes just because, like Lou Reed, we saw that *everything was all right*. If the vision and the feeling always faded, leaving glimpses, fragments, intimations behind, still they were real—or as real as anything else. They suggested what human beings might be if we grew up differently, if certain kinds of damage were not inflicted.

But that was in another country, or another language. If people still take drugs in search of transcendence, they don't talk about it in public. The one counterculture drug that's made it into the mainstream is marijuana, and its gestalt has changed radically in the process—where once it was valued as a mild psychedelic, now it's mostly used, like alcohol, to smooth out the rough edges. These days drugs are a metaphor not for freedom or ecstasy but for slavery and horror. It's the "hard" drugs—especially heroin and cocaine—that obsess the American imagination; rarely do we see the word "drug" without "abuse" or "menace" next to it.

On this issue the ideological right's triumph over '60s liberationism has been nothing short of a rout: it is now an unquestioned axiom of public discourse that drugs and drug taking of any but the purely medicinal sort are simply, monolithically, evil. Dope is the enemy that unites Ronald Reagan and Jesse Jackson, that gets blamed for everything from the plight of the black community to teenage alienation to America's problems competing in the world market. (Even Lyndon LaRouche features drug pushers in his paranoid cosmology, right up there with international bankers and Zionists.) In this climate, anyone who suggests that the question of drugs has real complexities, that some kinds of drugs and some kinds of drug taking are not a terrible thing and may even, under certain circumstances, actually be, well, a good thing, can expect to be as popular as Paul Krassner at a Women Against Pornography convention.

And yet the use of illegal drugs has never been more pervasive, visible, and socially accepted, especially among young people. As I write this, I'm looking at recent issues of *Time* and *Newsweek*: in the same week *Time*'s cover story was "Drugs on the Job," *Newsweek*'s "Kids and Cocaine: An Epidemic Strikes Middle America." How do you run a War Against Drug Abuse when Rambo is smoking crack?

The gap between ideology and behavior is increasingly filled with hysteria; while the cultural left has been busy combating various forms of sex panic, drug panic has come into its own. Frustrated by its inability to choke off the supply of drugs, the government has begun looking for ways to stifle the demand. The notorious campaign to spray paraquat on Mexican marijuana was a primitive version of this "demand side" strategy; the idea was not really to ruin the crop but to make people afraid to buy the stuff. Now efforts to deter and punish users have gone into high gear. The logic of such a mania to control the behavior of millions of individuals is totalitarian. And totalitarian is not too strong a word for the proposal of the President's Commission on Organized Crime that all companies test their employees for drug use, beginning with the federal government. Edwin Meese, true to form, commented that such a measure would not violate the Fourth Amendment, since testees would be consenting to a search in return for the "privilege" of applying for a job. (Listen, if you don't like it, my coke dealer has an opening.)

It's scary living in a time when a president's commission and a U.S. attorney general dare to talk this way so openly; scarier when you realize that many corporations—*Time* lists Exxon, IBM, Lockheed, Shearson Lehman, Federal Express, United Airlines, TWA, Hoffman-La Roche, Du Pont, and (!) *The New York Times*—are already requiring urinalysis for job applicants, without legal impediment or significant public opposition. Many other companies "merely" test suspected users; all branches of the armed forces now conduct random testing of servicepeople. And anything seems to go when checking on the purity of athletes, charged with the thankless burden of being wholesome "role models" for our nation's youth.

Yet this isn't simply a civil liberties issue; it's a question of cultural schizophrenia. I don't know of any polls on the subject, but sheer probability suggests that most of the miscreants insidiously wrecking our economic fiber by getting stoned on the job must have voted for Reagan. Perhaps the definition of an authoritarian society is one in which people won't stand up for or stand behind what they do, and prefer to think about the contradictions as little as possible.

Yes, the counterculture indulged in a lot of mindless romanticism about drugs, exaggerating their world-changing, soul-saving potential and minimizing their dangers. But there was also a thoughtful side to psychedelic culture, a salutary self-consciousness about the process of drug taking and what it meant. It was widely understood, for instance, that drugs were more the occasion or catalyst of "psychedelic experience" than the cause of it; that what shaped people's trips was their state of mind and their surroundings—"set and setting," as the then still professorial Alpert and Leary put it in their early LSD lectures. After all, for thousands of years people had been attaining similar states of mind through meditation and other non-pharmacological practices.

We took seriously the idea that drugs were good or bad depending on how you used them and whether they enhanced or restricted your freedom. It was probably best to take psychedelics in a spirit of curiosity and acceptance, leavened with an appreciation of the absurd, though on the other hand it was probably best not to make any rules about it. Drug abuse, in psychedelic terms, meant fetishizing the drug—looking to it as a solution rather than a pathway, or trying to repeat a particular good trip rather than following the serendipitous wanderings of one's mind. This fetishism could become the equivalent of addiction: it was a not insignificant risk along with the possibility that our minds would wander into hell rather than heaven, or that a drug powerful enough to knock our consciousness off its usual tracks might be powerful enough to do terrible things to our brain cells. We were willing to take these risks in the interest of seeing things differently—and this, ultimately, was the "menace" our cultural guardians were so determined to stamp out.

Of course, psychedelics were not the only '60s drug scene: speed, heroin, downers, and, to a lesser extent, cocaine also flourished. The ideological assault on drugs has conflated them all, making for a predictable irony: psychedelics and the idealism surrounding them have gone underground, while the hard drugs, which no one, including their users, ever defended in the first place, become more and more entrenched. In the '80s drugs are merely a vice, which is to say a covert and private rebellion that affirms the system, an expression of and hedge against boredom, impotence, and despair. They are also a mirror—coke embodies the compulsive nervous energy of the "opportunity society," smack the isolation of the excluded poor. Like Victorian pornography, dope in the Age of Meese shows us that every era gets the menace it deserves.

April 1986

The Drug War: Hell No,

I Won't Go

At last the government has achieved something it hasn't managed since the height of '50s anti-Communist hysteria—enlisted public sentiment in a popular war. The president's invocation of an America united in a holy war against drugs is no piece of empty rhetoric; the bounds of mainstream debate on this issue are implicit in the response of the Democratic so-called opposition, which attacked Bush's program as not tough or expensive enough. (As Senator Biden—fresh from his defense of the flag; the guy is really on a roll—put it, "What we need is another D-Day, not another Vietnam.") To be sure, there is controversy over the drug warriors' methods. Civil libertarians object to drug testing and dubious police practices; many commentators express doubts about the wisdom of going after millions of casual drug users; and some hardy souls still argue that drugs should be decriminalized and redefined as a medical and social problem. But where are the voices questioning the basic assumptions of the drug war: that drugs are our most urgent national problem; that a drug-free society is a valid social goal; that drug use is by definition abuse? If there's a war on, are drugs the real enemy? Or is mobilizing the nation's energies on behalf of a war against drugs far more dangerous than the drugs themselves?

By now some of you are wondering if I've been away—perhaps on an extended LSD trip—and missed the havoc crack has wrought in inner-city neighborhoods. One of the drug warriors' more effective weapons is the argument that any crank who won't sign on to the antidrug crusade must be indifferent to, if not actively in favor of, the decimation of black and Latino communities by rampant addiction, AIDS, crack babies, the recruitment of kids into the drug trade, and control of the streets by Uzi-toting gangsters. To many people, especially people of color, making war on drugs means not taking it anymore, defending their lives and their children against social rot. It's a seductive idea: focusing one's rage on a vivid, immediate symptom of a complex social crisis makes an awful situation seem more manageable. Yet in reality the drug war has nothing to do with making communities livable or creating a decent future for black kids. On the contrary, prohibition is directly responsible for the power of crack dealers to terrorize whole neighborhoods. And every cent spent on the cops, investigators, bureaucrats, courts, jails, weapons, and tests required to feed the drug-war machine is a cent not spent on reversing the social policies that have destroyed the cities, nourished racism, and laid the groundwork for crack culture.

While they're happy to use the desperate conditions of the poor as a club to intimidate potential opposition, the drug warriors have another agenda altogether. Forget those obscene pictures of Bush kissing crack babies (and read his budget director's lips: money for the drug war is to come not from the military budget but from other domestic programs). Take it from William Bennett, who, whatever his political faults, is honest about what he's up to: "We identify the chief and seminal wrong here as drug use. . . . There are lots of other things that are wrong, such as money laundering and crime and violence in the inner city, but drug use itself is wrong. And that means the strategy is aimed at reducing drug use." Aimed, that is, not at solving social problems but at curbing personal freedom.

Of course, it's not all drugs Bennett has in mind, but illegal drugs. And as even some drug warriors will admit, whether a drug is legal or not has little to do with rational considerations such as how addictive it may be, or how harmful to health, or how implicated in crime. Bill Bennett drinks without apology while denouncing marijuana and crack with equal passion; heroin is denied to terminal cancer patients while methadone, which is at least as addictive, is given away at government-sponsored clinics. What illegal drugs do have in common is that in one way or another they are perceived as threatening social control. Either (like heroin and crack) they're associated with all the social disorder and scary otherness of the so-called underclass, or (like marijuana and the psychedelics) they become emblems of social dissidence, "escape from"—i.e., unorthodox views of—reality, and loss of productivity and discipline. Equally important, illicit drugs offer pleasure—and perhaps even worse, feelings of freedom and power—for the taking; the more intense the euphoria, the more iniquitous the drug. Easily available chemical highs are the moral equivalent of welfare—they undercut the official culture's control of who gets rewarded for what. And they invite subversive comparisons to the meager ration of pleasure, freedom, and power available in people's daily lives.

Illegal drugs, furthermore, are offenses to authority by definition. Users are likely to define themselves as rebels—or become users in the first place as a means of rebelling—and band together in an outlaw culture. The drugs are then blamed for the rebellion, the social alienation that gave rise to it, and the crime and corruption that actually stem from prohibition and its inevitable concomitant, an immensely profitable illegal industry.

From this perspective, it makes perfect sense to lump marijuana with crack—while different in every other respect, both are outlaw, countercultural drugs. From this perspective, mounting a jihad against otherwise law-abiding citizens whose recreational drug of choice happens to be illegal is not a hugely expensive, futile, punitive diversion from addressing the real problems of our urban wasteland; it goes straight to the point. After all, hard-core addicts presumably can't help themselves, while casual users are choosing to ignore two decades of pervasive antidrug moralizing. The point is that the cultural changes of the '60s and '70s eroded traditional forms of authority, loosening governmental and corporate control over people's lives. And the drug war is about getting it back.

One means of achieving this is legitimizing repressive police and military tactics. Drugs, say the warriors, are such an overriding national emergency that civil liberties must give way; of course, laws and policies aimed at curbing dealers' and users' constitutional rights will then be available for use in other "emergency" situations. Another evolving strategy is to bypass the criminal justice system altogether (thereby avoiding some of those irritating constitutional obstacles as well as the public's reluctance to put middle-class pot-smokers in jail) in favor of civil sanctions like large fines and the withholding of government benefits and such "privileges" as drivers' licenses.

But so far, the centerpiece of the cultural counterrevolution is the snowballing campaign for a "drug-free workplace"—a euphemism for "drug-free workforce," since urine testing also picks up off-duty indulgence. The purpose of this '80s version of the loyalty oath is less to deter drug use than to make people undergo a humiliating ritual of subordination: "When I say pee, you pee." The idea is to reinforce the principle that one must forfeit one's dignity and privacy to earn a living, and bring back the good old days when employers had the unquestioned right to demand that their workers' appearance and behavior, on or off the job, meet management's standards. After all, before the '60s, employers were free to reject you not only because you were the wrong race, sex, or age, but because of your marital status, your sex life, your political opinions, or anything else they didn't like; there were none of those pesky discrimination or wrongful firing suits.

The argument that drug use hurts productivity only supports my point: if it's okay to forbid workers to get stoned on their days off because it might affect their health, efficiency, or "motivation," why not forbid them to stay out late, eat fatty foods, fall in love, or have children? As for jobs that affect the public safety, if tests are needed, they should be performance tests—an air controller or railroad worker whose skills are impaired by fatigue is as dangerous as one who's drugged. Better yet, anyone truly concerned about safety should support the demands of workers in these jobs for shorter hours and less stressful working conditions.

In the great tradition of demagogic saber-rattling, Bush's appeal seeks to distract from the fissures of race, class, and sex and unite us against a common enemy: the demon drug. The truth is, however, that this terrifying demon is a myth. Drug addiction and its associated miseries are not caused by evil, irresistible substances. People get hooked on drugs because they crave relief from intolerable frustration; because they're starved for pleasure and power. Addiction is a social and psychological, not a chemical, disease.

Every generation has its arch-demon drug: alcohol, reefer madness, heroin, and now crack. Recently *The New York Times* ran a front-page story reporting that drug experts have revised their earlier belief that crack is a uniquely, irresistibly addictive drug; crack addiction, they assert, has more to do with social conditions than with the drug's chemistry. Two cheers for the experts; surely it shouldn't have taken them so long to ask why crack is irresistible to the black poor but not to the white middle class. Perhaps they will take the next step and recognize that so long as crack is the only thriving industry in the inner city—and integral to its emotional economy as well—there's only one way to win a war on drugs. That's to adopt the method the Chinese used to solve their opium problem: line every dealer and user up against the wall and shoot. And try not to notice the color of the bodies.

If the logic of the drug war for blacks and Latinos leads to a literal police state, for the rest of us it means silence and conformity. In recent years, much of the drug warriors' ideological firepower has been aimed at the '60s. Members of my generation who took any part in the passions and pleasures of those times—that is, most of us now between, say, 35 and 50—are under enormous pressure to agree that we made a terrible mistake (and even that won't help if you aspire to be a Supreme Court justice). Which makes me feel irresistibly compelled to reiterate at every opportunity that I have taken illegal drugs, am not ashamed of it, and still smoke the occasional joint (an offense for which Bush and Bennett want to fine me $10,000, lift my driver's license, and throw me in boot camp). I believe that taking drugs is not intrinsically immoral or destructive, that the state has no right to prevent me from exploring different states of consciousness, and that drug prohibition causes many of the evils it purports to cure.

According to the drug warriors, I and my ilk are personally responsible not only for the deaths of Janis Joplin and Jimi Hendrix but for the crack crisis. Taken literally, this is scurrilous nonsense: the counterculture never looked kindly on hard drugs, and the age of crack is a product not of the '60s but of Reaganism. Yet there's a sense in which I do feel responsible. Cultural radicals are committed to extending freedom, and that commitment, by its nature, is dangerous. It encourages people to take risks, some of them foolish or worse.

It arouses deep longings that, if disappointed, may plunge people into despair (surely one aspect of the current demoralization of black youth is the peculiar agony of thwarted revolution). If I support the struggle for freedom, I can't disclaim responsibility for its costs; I can only argue that the costs of suppressing freedom are, in the end, far higher. All wars are hell. The question remains which ones are worth fighting.

September 1989

Coming Down Again

This essay is dedicated to the memory of Vic Dyer.

T hat Blake line," said my friend—for the purposes of this article I'll call her Faith, a semi-ironic name, since she is a devout ex-Catholic—"It's always quoted as 'The road of excess leads to the palace of wisdom.'"

"That's not right?" I said.

"It's 'The roads of excess *sometimes* lead to the palace of wisdom.' Very different!"

I looked it up. There it was in "The Marriage of Heaven and Hell," the "Proverbs From Hell" section, directly following "Drive your cart and your plow over the bones of the dead": "The road of excess leads to . . ." etc. No matter, I realize the poet is playing devil's advocate; anyway I'm willing to concede that Faith is more of an expert on the subject than I (or, possibly, Blake). Not that I haven't had my moments, but Faith's are somehow more—metaphoric. I think, for instance, of the time that, drunk and in the middle of her period, she engaged in a highly baroque night of passion and woke up in the morning to find herself, the man, and the bed covered with gore, a bloody handprint on her wall.

Two years ago Faith joined Alcoholics Anonymous. When she told me, I was doubly surprised. First, because I had never thought of my friend as having "a drinking problem"—a condition I associated with nasty personality traits and inability to function in daily life, certainly not with the all-night pleasure-and-truth-seeking marathons that had seemed to define Faith's drinking style. The other surprise was that AA was evidently not the simpleminded, Salvation Army-type outfit I had imagined; somewhere along the line it had become the latest outlet for the thwarted utopian energies of the '60s counterculture.

Faith's AA group, which included cocaine and heroin junkies as well as alcoholics, functioned (or so I inferred) as a kind of beloved community. Within that community one's alcohol or drug problem was a metaphor for human imperfection, isolation, confusion, despair. True sobriety—not to be confused with compulsive abstinence or puritanical moralism, which were merely the flip side of indulgence—was freedom, transcendence. The point was not self-denial but struggle: confronting the anxiety and pain indulgence had deadened. AA, in short, was a spiritual discipline that, in its post-'60s incarnation, had much in common with that most secular of spiritual disciplines, psychotherapy.

Among the welter of feelings I had about Faith's new project was envy: I was frustrated by the lack of community in my own life. Having first begun living with a man and then decided to have a baby, I had plunged into the pit of urban middle-class Nuclear Familydom and its seemingly inexorable logic—an oppressively expensive apartment, an editing job (more lucrative than writing, less psychically demanding), a daily life overwhelmed with domestic detail ("moving sand," the therapist I was complaining to, a fan of *Woman in the Dunes*, called it), a Sisyphean struggle to keep a love affair from dissolving into a mom-and-pop sandmovers' combine, and a disquieting erosion of other human relationships. Those of my friends who did not have young children lived in another country, of which I was an expatriate, while other NFs of my acquaintance seemed either content to stay on their own islands or, like us, too exhausted from sandmoving to have much time for bridge-building.

My life as a mother did have a dimension of transcendence, marked by intense passion and sensual delight; yet while I'd always insisted that real passion was inherently subversive, my love for my daughter bound me more and more tightly to the social order. Her father and I had remained unmarried, as a tribute to our belief in free love, in the old-fashioned literal sense, and our rejection of a patriarchal contract. But the structural constraints of parenthood married us more surely than a contract would have done. If there was spiritual discipline involved, it had nothing to do with changing diapers or getting up at night—that was just putting one foot in front of the other, doing what one had to do—but rather with the attempt to maintain an ironic ("Zenlike," as I thought of it) detachment from our situation, to think of Nuclear Familydom as an educational experience, an ordeal, like Outward Bound.

It didn't help that I was going through all this during the worst orgy of cultural sentimentality about babies and family since the '50s. On the other hand, it seemed unlikely that the flowering of my own procreative urge—along with that of so many of my '60s-generation/ feminist peers—had been a simple matter of beating the clock. The pursuit of ecstasy—in freedom of the imagination and a sense of communal possibility as much as in sex, drugs, or rock and roll— was no longer our inalienable right. Babies, however, were a socially acceptable source of joy.

At a time when anti-drug hysteria was competing with pro-family mania for the status of chief '80s obsession, the same logic could be applied to sobriety. So another of my reactions to Faith's detoxifying was uneasiness. Abstinence might not be the point, but it was the means (unless one somehow achieved the satori of genuinely being able to take a drink or drug or leave it alone). As a metaphor it was troublesome. And it was catching on: Faith pointed out with no little glee that the new aura of AA had lent cleaning up an unprecedented glamor. (As a rule it's still true that whatever my generation decides to do, whether it's cleaning up or having babies, becomes a cultural phenomenon. Ecstasy by association, as it were. Neoconservatives hate us more for this than for anything else.) I was less pleased than she to read Elizabeth Taylor's announcement that she had joined the ranks of the sober. Liz Taylor, whom I'd always cherished as one of the few famous women to barrel down the road of excess with a vengeance—eating, drinking, swearing, fucking, marrying, acquiring diamonds as big as the Ritz. . . . Faith had little sympathy for my discomfort, noting that Liz had scarcely been a happy boozer these last years, burying herself in all that weight: now she was, judging from the press accounts and especially the pictures, in better shape physically and emotionally than she'd been in a long time.

If I find sobriety as a pop ideal threatening, it's not for the obvious reason. I've never been a drinker, and except for a brief period when I took a lot of psychedelics and smoked marijuana more or less regularly, my forays into drugs have been sporadic and experimental—for the past decade or so virtually nonexistent. The point of drugs, for me, was always the eternal moment when you felt like Jesus's son (and gender be damned); when you found your center, which is another word for sanity or, I assume, sobriety as Faith understands it. But I never found a drug that would guarantee me that moment, or even a more vulgar euphoria: acid, grass, speed, coke, even Quaaludes (I've never tried heroin), all were unpredictable, potentially treacherous, as likely to concentrate anxiety as to blow it away. Context was all-important—set and setting, as they called it in those days. My emotional state, amplified or undercut by the collective emotional atmosphere, made the difference between a good trip, a bad trip, or no trip at all.

For me, the ability to get high (I don't mean only on drugs) flourished in the atmosphere of abandon that defined the '60s—that pervasive cultural invitation to leap boundaries, challenge limits, try anything, want everything, overload the senses, let go. Unlike the iconic figures of the era and their many anonymous disciples, I never embraced excess as a fundamental principle of being, an imperative to keep gathering speed until exhaustion or disaster ensued. (My experience of the '60s did have its—"dark side" is a bit too melodramatic; "rough edges" is closer. But more about that later.) Rather, since my own characteristic defense against the terror of living was not counterphobic indulgence but good old inhibition and control, the valorization of *too much* allowed me, for the first time in my life, to have something like *enough*.

Transcendence through discipline—as in meditation, or macrobiotics, or voluntary poverty, or living off the land—was always the antithesis in the '60s dialectic: in context it added another flavor to a rich stew of choices and made for some interesting, to say the least, syntheses. But its contemporary variants are the only game in town, emblems of scarcity. Another metaphor: runners by the thousand, urging on their bodies until the endorphins kick in. The runners' high, an extra reward for the work-well-done of tuning up one's cardiovascular system. What's scarce in the current scheme of things is not (for the shrinking middle class, anyway) rewards but grace, the unearned, the serendipitous. The space to lie down or wander off the map.

Of course, there's a moral question in all this: the Elizabeth Taylor question, or, to put it more starkly, the Janis Joplin question. If ever anyone needed some concept of sobriety as transcendence—not to mention a beloved community offering the acceptance and empathy of fellow imperfect human beings for whom her celebrity was beside the point—it was Janis. The embrace of excess strangled her: would I drive my cart and my plow over her bones? I think of Bob Dylan, avatar of excess cum puritanical moralist, laying into the antiheroine of "Like a Rolling Stone" for letting other people get her kicks for her. And I think of Faith again, of an incident that, unlike the Night of the Red Hand, doesn't make an amusing or colorful story: expansive on wine, wanting to be open to the unearned and serendipitous, she let a pretty boy she met in a club come home with her. Inside her door the pretty boy turned into a rapist, crazy, menacing; lust gave way to violence.

But I don't want to oversimplify in the other direction. It was not the '60s, after all, that caused Janis Joplin's misery; what we know about her years as odd-girl-out in Port Arthur, Texas, makes that plain. The '60s did allow her to break out of Port Arthur, to find, for a painfully short but no less real time, her voice, her beauty, her powers—her version of redemption. Had rock and roll, Haight-Ashbury, the whole thing never happened, I can't imagine that her life would have been better; it might not even have been longer. Nor does Faith regret her time on the road. Among '60s veterans in AA there is the shared recognition of a paradox, one that separates the "new sobriety" from its fundamentalist heritage: taking drugs enriched their vision, was in fact a powerful catalyst for the very experience of transcendence, and yearning for it, that now defines their abstinence. It's crucial not to forget that the limits we challenged—of mechanistic rationalism, patriarchal authority, high culture, a morality deeply suspicious of pleasure, a "realism" defined as resignation—were prisons. Still are.

The image of excess that bedevils the conservative mind even more than reefer madness is that of the orgy—anonymous, indiscriminate, unrestrained, guiltless sex. As contemporary mythology has it (and as the right continually repeats with fear and gloating) the sexual revolution of the '60s was an exercise in "promiscuity"; because of

AIDS, promiscuity is now fatal; therefore the sexual revolution was a disastrous mistake. This syllogism, which takes the now-devastated gay sex-bar-and-bathhouse world as the paradigm for '60s sexual culture, says less about the actual habits of that culture than about the envious prurience of this one. But then, myths generally have more to do with imaginative reality than with the practical sort, and if the idea of AIDS as retribution (God's or nature's) wields power far beyond the constituencies of Pat Robertson and Norman Podhoretz, if the white, non-needle-using heterosexual population's fears of contagion have far outstripped the present danger, it's in part because the traditionalist's sexual nightmares are the underside of the counterculture's dreams. There was the dream of recovering innocence, dumping our Oedipal baggage, getting back to the polymorphous perversity of childhood and starting over; the dream of a beneficent sexual energy flowing freely, without defenses, suspicion, guilt, shame; the dream of transcending possessiveness and jealousy; the dream, at its most apocalyptic, of universal love: it was one thing to have sex with strangers, quite another if the strangers were your brothers and sisters, if you need not fear games, or contempt, or violence.

Few people tried seriously to live this vision, even in circles where LSD and hippie rhetoric flowed as freely as libido was supposed to; the New York writers and artists I hung out with were positively snarky about it all. Yet the dreams put their stamp on us. Context, again, was crucial, and in these skittish days it bears repeating that the context of sexual utopianism was, in the first place, the near-universal revolt of young people against what are now nostalgically referred to as "traditional values": That is, women's chastity policed by the dubious promise of male "respect" and lifetime monogamy; by the withholding of birth control and the criminalizing of abortion; by the threat of social ostracism, sexual violence and exploitation, forced marriage and motherhood. Men's schizophrenia, expressed in hypocritical "respect" for the frustrating good girl and irrational contempt for the willing bad one, pride in their lust as the emblem of their maleness and disgust with it as the evidence of their "animal natures." Homosexuality unspeakable and invisible. By the end of the '50s the sexual revolution had begun, but the first version to gain ascendancy was a conservative one—it defined sex as a commodity, or a form of healthy exercise, that merely needed to be made more available. Furious at the moral code we'd grown up with—I knew no one of either sex who didn't feel in some way crushed by it—yet uninspired by the curiously antierotic liberalism proposed as an alternative, we were ripe for ways of imagining sex that might begin to heal our wounds.

Imagination was the key (as John Lennon was to claim, in a song too often misjudged as simpleminded). My own sexual behavior remained relatively conventional; during most of the years when the '60s sexual imagination was at its height, I was living with lovers— for the most part monogamously. While I rejected monogamy as a moral obligation, it was mostly the sense of freedom I wanted, the right (after the years of not enough) to feel open to the world's possibilities, without prior censorship. I disliked the idea of the on-principle Exclusive Couple; it was smug, claustrophobic. On acid trips I perceived that there was indeed another kind of sexual love, better than romantic love as we knew it, more profoundly accepting and trusting, free of the insecurity that demands ownership. I even left one man for another in pursuit, or so I thought, of that version of the dream. Of course, to be capable of translating such transient flashes of perception into my real, daily life, I (and he) would have had to be born again, into a different world, and my new relationship was soon as mired in coupledom as the other one had been.

Still . . . a couple of years later, this same man and I were sharing a two-family house with a married couple and their baby. I decided, for once, to act on my fantasies of extending sexual intimacy beyond the sacred dyad, and my initiative was enthusiastically received by all concerned. From the conventional point of view I got my come-uppance. It turned out that while the husband and I were pursuing an enjoyable experiment, expanding our friendship, transcending the nuclear family, and so on, our mates were doing something rather different—were infatuated with each other, in fact. It hurt, it was disruptive, it made me for a time feel like killing two people. Yet I could never honestly say I was sorry I'd started the whole thing. The power of that urge to stretch the limits could not cancel out jealousy and possessiveness, but it could compete. And, in a sense, win. Though a respect for history compels me to add that my friend, the family man who also wanted more, later divorced his wife, remarried, and became a born-again Christian.

History and its convolutions. . . . The affirmation of love's body against the life-denying brutality of "traditional values" was at the heart of what made me a feminist. As a popular Emma Goldman T-shirt implied, if I couldn't fuck it wasn't my revolution. For me, for thousands of women, the explosion of radical feminism was a supremely sexy moment; we had the courage of our desires as we'd never had before. It was not only that we could make new demands of our male lovers or seek out female ones; not only that we were reject-ing the sexual shame and self-hatred endemic to our condition. We were making history, defining our fate, for once taking center stage and telling men how it was going to be. Sisterhood was powerful—therefore erotic.

And yet it was feminism—not the new right, certainly not the as-yet-unknown AIDS virus—that first displaced the counterculture's vision of sex with a considerably harsher view. I don't mean only, or even primarily, the brand of feminism that has attacked sex as a form of male power, the sex drive as an ideological construct, and "sexual liberation" as a euphemism for rape. In the early radical feminist movement such polemics were regarded as eccentric (though I was not the only one who, with overt relish and unconscious condescen-sion, admired them as rhetorical excess, a dadaist provocation, part of the exhilarating racket of newly discovered voices transgressing the first law of femaleness: be nice). Most of us felt about the sexual revolution what Gandhi reputedly thought of Western civilization—that it would be a good idea. There was, however, the little matter of abortion rights; there was the continuing legal and social toler-ance of rape; there were all those "brothers" who spoke of ecstasy but fucked with their egos, looked down on women who were "too" free, and thought the most damning name they could call a femi-nist was "lesbian." And then—our new sense of ourselves might be aphrodisiac, but the rage that went along with it wasn't. Nor were men's reactions—ridicule, fake solicitude, guilt, defensiveness, hys-teria, and, when none of that shut us up, what-do-you-bitches-want fury—much of a turn-on for either sex.

It was the best, the worst, the most enlightening, the most bewil-dering of times. Feminism intensified my utopian sexual imagination, made me desperate to get what I really wanted, not "after the revolu-tion" but *now*—even as it intensified my skepticism, chilling me with awareness of how deeply relations between the sexes were corrupted and, ultimately, calling into question the very nature of my images of desire. For my sexual fantasies were permeated with the iconography of masculine-feminine, seduction-surrender, were above all centered on the union of male and female genitals as the transcendent aim of sex (not, surely not, one form of joining among others). Why did I want "what I really wanted," and did I really want it? And—oh, shit, forget about utopia—what were the chances of steering some sort of livable path between schizophrenia (or amnesia) and kill-joy self-consciousness in bed?

But there was one more convolution to come: feminism inspired gay liberation and with it a renewed vision of untrammeled sex as the key to freedom, power, and community. Ironically (at least from my point of view), it was a vision of sex among men. The lesbian movement of the '70s was not primarily about liberating desire (though there were, of course, plenty of individual and subcultural exceptions) but about extending female solidarity; for the gay male community solidarity was, at its core, about desire. To this version of the sexual revolution I was, of course, doubly an outsider. That aspect of the gay male imagination that most repelled and fascinated the straight world, the culture of anonymous, ritualistic sex and sensation for pure sensation's sake, repelled and fascinated me. It seemed the epitome of distance and difference—except when an evocative piece of fiction or theater, or more rarely a conversation about sex with a gay man, would awake in me some ghost of a forgotten fantasy, reminding me that otherness is at bottom a defensive illusion.

AIDS, paradoxically, has impressed this on me in a deeper and more lasting way. That's partly because the issues AIDS raises transcend sex, per se. The eruption of a massive plaguelike epidemic, of a sort we were supposed to have "conquered" long ago, not only threatens to test our economic resources and social conscience in unprecedented ways, but attacks the fundamental faith of our scientific-technological culture—that we can dominate nature. And for this very reason, the sexual significance of AIDS transcends the demographics of high and low risk groups. On one level the sexual liberation movements embody the revolt of "the natural" against social domination, yet they are unthinkable without technology. Modern

contraception, safe childbirth and abortion, antibiotics drastically reduced the risks of sex, and in doing so encouraged the heady fantasy
of sex with no risk at all. AIDS is hardly the first challenge to that fantasy: women found out a while ago that the only truly zipless contraceptives, the pill and IUD, were dangerous—sometimes deadly—
and in some parts of the world, resistant strains of gonorrhea are
already out of control. I suspect that as we learn how to "manage"
AIDS—with imperfect but workable vaccines, treatments that keep
people alive and functioning, condoms and other precautions—our
sense of it as a dramatic watershed, a radical break with the past, will
diminish (even, eventually, for gay men), just as condoms themselves
will become an ordinary part of sexual culture instead of an emotionally charged symbol of (take your pick) all hated barriers to delight
or rampant permissiveness. Still, our sexual imagination is bound to
change. The idea of achieving safe sex through chemistry will come
to seem a quaint piece of Americana, akin to the notion of abolishing
scarcity through unlimited economic growth.

So does this mean the conservatives are right, the dream is over?
A lot of erstwhile dreamers, gay men especially, are feeling a kind of
rebellious despair as they contemplate the shadow of death between
desire and act. What can sexual freedom possibly mean if not pleasure
unconstricted by fear or calculation? Yet—and I speak as a woman
who is passionately pro-abortion, who remembers nostalgically the
ease and security of the pill—there is something muddled about a
logic that equates freedom with safety. Freedom is inherently risky,
which is the reason for rules and limits in the first place; the paradox
of the '60s generation is that we felt secure enough, economically
and sexually, to reject security. The risks people took were real and
so were the losses: the deaths, breakdowns, burnouts, addictions, the
paranoia and nihilism, "revolutionary" crimes and totalitarian religious cults, poverty and prison terms. Though the casualties of drugs
and politics have been more conspicuous, sex has never been safe—
certainly not for women and gay men: in a misogynist, homophobic
culture suffused with sexual rage, to be a "whore" or a "pervert" is to
"ask for" punishment.

In many post-AIDS elegies to sexual liberation lurks a sentimental idea of gay male culture as paradise lost, a haven of pure pleasure

invaded by the serpent of disease. Yet the appeal of the gay fast lane on the road of excess surely had something to do with being outlaws, defying taboos, confronting and ritualizing danger, assimilating it to the marrow of a pleasure that was, in part, a triumph over fear. It could not be a coincidence that the sexual anonymity invested with so much excitement had historically been a survival strategy for gay men in the closet. At the same time, gay men's pursuit of sex without attachment reflected a widespread male fantasy—one that men who want sex with women must usually conceal or play down. For many men, freedom to separate sex from relationship without guilt or hypocrisy has always been what sexual liberation is about. But the conventionally masculine dream of pure lust is, I'm convinced, as conservative in its way as the conventionally feminine romanticism that converts lust to pure emotion—or, for that matter, as the patriarchal values that subordinate passion to marriage and procreation. All are attempts to tame sex, to make it safe by holding something back. For the objective risks of sex would not terrify us half so much if they did not reinforce a more primal inner threat. To abandon ourselves utterly to sensation *and* emotion—to give up the boundaries and limits that keep us in control—would be, for most of us, like cutting loose from gravity and watching the earth spin. Dissolution of the ego is the death we fear; the real sexual revolution, the one no virus can keep us from imagining, is the struggle to face that fear, transcend it, and let go.

My favorite statement about risk and excess is also my favorite '60s joke. It's a Fabulous Furry Freak Brothers comic strip in which one of the skanky protagonists gets busted for dope. At the police station he is granted his one phone call. The last panel shows him burbling euphorically into the phone, ordering one large with pepperoni, mushrooms, green peppers.

The road of excess is a roller coaster, the palace of wisdom a funhouse. Liberation is playful, useless, unproductive, for itself—*too much*. Like Little Richard's screams, Phil Spector's wall of sound, Dylan's leopard-skin pillbox hat, Janis's feather boa, the foxhunt on *Sgt. Pepper*. Or, to stick with our main metaphor, the custom cars Tom Wolfe immortalized, Ken Kesey's Pranksters' Day-Glo bus, the

Byrds' magic carpet, Jefferson Airplane. The trouble is, the trip always ends up heading for somewhere, loaded down with all the tragic baggage of human deprivation and yearning. And when that happens, the vehicles start going off the track, over the edge, down the slippery slope from yes she said yes she said yes to just say no. Which is where irony comes in.

I'm a political person, a political radical. I believe that the struggle for freedom, pleasure, transcendence, is not just an individual matter. The social system that organizes our lives, and as far as possible channels our desire, is antagonistic to that struggle; to change this requires collective effort. The moment a movement coalesces can be, should be, itself an occasion of freedom, pleasure, and transcendence, but it is never only that. Radical movements by definition focus attention on the gap between present and future, and cast their participants, for the present, in the negative role of opposition. Fighting entrenched power means drawing battle lines, defining the enemy. In the '60s and after, the strains of radicalism I identify with have defined the enemy as all forms of domination and hierarchy—beginning but not ending with sex, race, and class—and from this point of view, as a French leftist slogan from the May '68 upheavals put it, "We are all Jews and Germans." Which doesn't mean that we're all equally victims and oppressors, or that the differences don't matter, just that there are few of us who haven't abused power in some contexts, suffered powerlessness in others. And that all of us, oppressors and victims alike, have had to make our bargains with the system— bargains often secret even from ourselves—for the sake of survival and, yes, for those moments of freedom, pleasure, and transcendence that give survival meaning.

So to be a radical as I've defined it implies self-consciousness and self-criticism, a commitment to (in the language of that segment of the '60s and '70s left most heavily influenced by feminist consciousness-raising) confronting not only our own oppression but the ways we oppress others. And since it's politics we're talking about, not therapy, this confrontation is of necessity a collective process . . . and already we're in very deep waters indeed.

In 1970 I was living with a group of people running a movement hangout for antiwar GIs. It was my first venture into the mixed left since becoming a radical feminist, and my sense of embattlement was acute. Predictably, I was angriest at the men I felt closest to, the ones I knew really did care—about me, about having good politics; so often they simply *didn't get it*, a solid, dumb lump of resistance masquerading as incomprehension of the simplest, clearest demands for reciprocity. At the same time, another woman in the project, a feminist from a working-class background, was confronting me and the rest of our group of predominantly middle-class lefties about the myriad of crude and subtle ways we were oppressing her and the mostly working-class soldiers we worked with. And I began to see it all from the other side: my good intentions; my struggle to see my-self as my friend saw me, to change; my continual falling short; my friend's anger and hurt when I just *didn't get it*; my own dumb lump that, to me, often felt indistinguishable from the core of my identity. Male guilt made me furious ("Don't sit there feeling guilty, just get your fucking foot off my neck"), but now I was mired in guilt, re-sentful about having to feel guilty, guilty about being resentful, and so on.

In "Salt of the Earth," an ostensible ode to the "hard-working people," Mick Jagger suddenly blurts that they don't look real to him, they look so strange. On one awful acid trip I saw with excruciating clarity just how deeply and pervasively I experienced poor people as alien, how the very word "poor" embodied that implacable distance called pity. And of course I saw that from the other side too. I don't remember if this glimpse into hell-as-other-people made me any less angry at men, but it certainly made me more despairing: I didn't look real to them; the rest was commentary.

More and more it seemed that everything that gave me pleasure, kept me sane, soothed (or distracted from) the wound of female otherness was a function of my privileges—education, leisure, cer-tain kinds of self-esteem, work I enjoyed that let me live like a bohe-mian, and most crucially the luxury of distance, therefore insulation, from certain kinds of human misery. I might agree, as an intellectual proposition, that only a violent revolution could break the power of the corporate state, but imagining what that meant filled me with re-vulsion and terror; I was glad there was no practical prospect of it. What my friend really wanted (I knew, because I wanted the same thing from men) was that I give up my blinders and live, no exit, with relentless awareness of her pain, as she had to do: only then would I be truly committed to revolution, whatever it entailed. To my shame I couldn't do this, couldn't bring myself to what I saw as a self-immolation at once necessary and intolerable.

Something was wrong, I realized dimly, something was out of whack. Political virtue equated with sacrifice, pleasure with corruption—how had I gotten back *there*? Yet seeing how class distorted my vision had shaken my faith in my judgment. Part of being oppressed was having one's perceptions negated; part of being an oppressor was doing the negating. I reminded myself of this when a soldier I didn't like or trust became my friend's lover and moved into our house. My friend thought I was cold to him for class reasons—he was uneducated, inarticulate, with a kind of bumpkin style. I accepted her analysis, suppressed my qualms, and tried to welcome the man as housemate and brother. Then it turned out that everything he had told us, even his birthday, was a lie.

I felt ambushed, but I'd done it to myself, pursuing revolutionary purity by handing someone else responsibility for my choices (yet another form of exploitation, she would have said if she'd known). Yes, there was something wrong, something sinister, even: I didn't have the words for it, didn't yet have Jonestown and Cambodia as reference points, but I smelled death. This was where excess led when fed by desperation and hubris instead of exuberance and hope. I was depressed for a long time. Many years and shrink sessions later it occurred to me that I was addicted to being right.

In an earlier, more innocent time I am sitting with friends in a coffeeshop in Toronto. We are New York rock critics in town for some festival or press junket. Our hair is very long, our dress ranges from East Village Indian to neo-pop. We have smoked some hash and are giggling with abandon. We order hamburgers and sundaes, then spaghetti, then, as I recall, more ice cream. The waitress smiles at us, inspiring a frisson of mock-paranoia around the table: *does she know?* Suddenly it strikes me very funny that the dope is illegal and the food is not.

Segue to the present, one of those days when conversation with my daughter, Nona, age four, goes something like this: "I want gum. I want a lollipop. I want ices. I want a cookie. I want another cookie, a *different* cookie. I want a Coke. I want candy. *That* candy. I want . . . ."

"You had ices today. No sweets till after dinner. No candy. No more cookies. You'll rot your teeth. You'll upset your stomach. You won't eat real food. NO!"

"I want—"

Once I answered by singing, "You can't always get what you want." That silenced her for a minute. I finished the verse. She looked at me thoughtfully. "But I *want* candy," she said.

This is no doubt the kind of exchange detractors of the '60s have in mind when they dismiss the counterculture as "infantile." I feel them looking over my shoulder as I play the part of repressive civilization frustrating limitless desire. I think they miss the point.

I love sugar. Controlling my craving for sweets is always a struggle, giving in to it an ambivalent, illicit pleasure. Sugar is my quick fix for anxiety or depression, an effortless and reliable consolation in a demanding, insecure world: the only problem is, a minute later you're hungry again. Determined to spare Nona this compulsion, I decided on a strategy even before she was born. I got her father to agree that we would treat sweets as casually as any other food, neither forbid them nor limit them nor insist that she finish her "real food" first. If we didn't give her the idea that sweets were evil/special/scarce, they would hold no fascination for her, and we could trust her to set her own limits. In short, we would put to the empirical test our cultural-radical faith in the self-regulating child.

Our strategy didn't fail; it never got a fair trial. Neither of us could stick to it. After a while I grasped the obvious: if I were capable of treating sweets as casually as any other food, I wouldn't have had to make an issue of it in the first place. And the anxious double messages I was transmitting were more likely to encourage an obsession with the stuff than if I'd followed the conventional advice, set limits I was comfortable with, and enforced them.

I do that now, but it's a matter of damage control. For Nona sweets are the object and the symbol of desire. Often the litany of Iwant-candygumcookies is code for wanting more from us. More time and patience and acceptance. More babying and reassurance. More freedom and power. We try to listen to what she's really saying, to give her what she wants when it's also what she needs. But we are parents in an age of scarcity and constraint, in the grip of family life, which is structured to insure that no one gets enough time, patience, acceptance, babying and reassurance, or freedom and power. In protest, Nona demands too much; we deny her for her own good; and so it begins again.

Winter 1989

Epilogue: The Neo-Guilt Trip

Americans are tired of greed and ready to embrace decency and compassion." By now I've heard some version of this sentiment too often to dismiss it as new-decadespeak; a real collective attack of conscience seems to be coming on. And I have to say that even as I stand on line to order my Donald Trump dart board, this nouveau guilt makes me nervous. The image it brings inexorably to mind is that of a compulsive eater about to enter the vomiting phase of a binge-purge cycle.

The thing is, I haven't yet recovered from America's last bout of purgatory. During the era of the energy crisis and Jimmy "Moral Malaise" Carter, we suffered through a nonstop lecture to the effect that the days of wine and roses were over, and that everything we liked, from sex and drugs to driving, shopping, feminism and psychotherapy was immoral, narcissistic, unaffordable or all three. Reagan won the 1980 election on a not-so-subliminal platform of freedom from guilt. True, sex and drugs were still taboo, but we were to be allowed, indeed actively encouraged, to channel our thwarted desire for some sort of joy in life into "opportunity," that is, making and spending money, vicariously identifying with people who make and spend money, and getting sadistic thrills from stomping all over the poor, blacks, women and gays. Then Reagan, with his awesome power over our fantasy life, was gone and Americans began to gag on the mountain of nacho-cheese tortilla chips that the decade's frantic orgy of acquisition represented.

Of course, the nation's repressed guilt has been lurking around all along, in the form of workaholism and our fabled obsession with health and fitness. But now people are noticing homelessness, the fragility of our health-care system, the fact that our supposed civilization will soon be buried under the residue of all those nachos. So it looks like we're about to go from greed straight back to guilt—without ever going through genuine pleasure.

Pleasure. Does it sound like a dirty word to you? No wonder, given how relentlessly it's been attacked not only by puritanical conservatives but by liberals who uncritically accept the Reaganite equation of pleasure with greed and callousness. (I think, for instance, of a recent newspaper article that described our society as a snake pit of "crime, violence, poverty and hedonism.") Yet life without pleasure—without spontaneity and playfulness, sexuality and sensuality, esthetic experience, surprise, excitement, ecstasy—is a kind of death. People deprived of pleasure don't get kinder and gentler but meaner and nastier. Indeed, it's not an excess of pleasure but pleasure-starvation on a mass scale that we have to thank for the rampant piggishness and urban violence that plague us.

Guilt always backfires because it only aggravates the pleasure shortage. Which is why I'm so nervous at the prospect that in the name of compassion and decency Americans will make themselves miserable with recrimination, self-loathing and appeals to idealism and self-sacrifice. And that at some point they'll abruptly decide they've had enough, and start stuffing themselves again with whatever's handy—another version of Reaganism, or (given a deteriorating economy) worse.

There's gotta be another way. Suppose we were to demand an end to the awful condition of our cities—the homelessness, the Third World infant-mortality rates, the breakdown of services—not out of moral obligation, but because life in surroundings that are dangerous, devoid of public amenities and poisoned by class and racial hostility just isn't much fun? Suppose that instead of packing the jails and forcing workers to pee on command in a futile attempt to stamp out illegal drugs, we were to ask why, for so many of us, drugs—legal or otherwise—seem to be the only pleasure game in town? Instead of beating our breasts, we might take our cue from pleasure-loving radicals like Emma Goldman, certainly no enemy of the poor, whose sentiments were paraphrased on a famous T-shirt as, "If I can't dance it's not my revolution." Or from Eastern Europe and its atmosphere of exuberant celebration as its people throw off decades of grim authoritarian rule. But then, there's no need to go so far from home: our own Declaration of Independence pronounces the pursuit of happiness an inalienable right. What if we really started taking this seriously—for everyone? Do I hear music?

May 1990

Permissions

Most of these essays first appeared in *The Village Voice*, © Village Voice Publishing, Inc. Used by permission. "Nature's Revenge" originally appeared in *The New York Times Book Review*; "Toward a Feminist Revolution" (in somewhat different form) in *Social Text*; "Radical Feminism and Feminist Radicalism" (in a slightly longer version) in *The '60s Without Apology*, ed. Sayres, et al., University of Minnesota Press; "Feminism Without Freedom" in *Dissent*; "Coming Down Again" in *Salmagundi*; and "The Neo-Guilt Trip" in *Mirabella*. "Peace in Our Time? The Greening of Betty Friedan" and "Sisters Under the Skin? Confronting Race and Sex" first appeared in the *Voice Literary Supplement*. "Marriage on the Rocks" combines two articles from *The Village Voice*, "California Split" and "Don't Marry, Be Happy"; several sentences have been added to "Lust Horizons: Is the Women's Movement Pro-Sex?" also from the *Voice*. A few passages in "Identity Crisis" are taken from "Multiple Identities," published in *Tikkun*. Dates of publication appear at the end of each piece.

Index

UNIVERSITY PRESS OF NEW ENGLAND publishes books under its own imprint and is the publisher for Brandeis University Press, Brown University Press, University of Connecticut, Dartmouth College, Middlebury College Press, University of New Hampshire, University of Rhode Island, Tufts University, University of Vermont, and Wesleyan University Press.

Library of Congress Cataloging-in-Publication Data

Willis, Ellen.

No more nice girls : countercultural essays / Ellen Willis.

    p.   cm.

Includes index.

    ISBN 0–8195–5250–X (cl)   ISBN 0–8195–6284–X (pa)

    1. Feminisim.   2. Radicalism.   3. Democracy.   I. Title.

HQ1154.W54   1992

305.42—dc20   92–53868